Y0-BDO-772

3 2355 00384390 1

DATE DUE

The Paradox of Gender Equality:
How American Women's Groups
Gained and Lost Their Public Voice

Drawing on original research, Kristin A. Goss examines how women's civic place has changed over the span of more than 120 years, how public policy has driven these changes, and why these changes matter for women and American democracy. The right to vote and democratic participation provided a dual platform for the expansion of women's policy agendas. As measured by women's groups' appearances before the U.S. Congress, women's collective political engagement grew between 1920 and 1960, when many conventional accounts claim it declined, and declined after 1980, when it might have been expected to grow. This waxing and waning was accompanied by major shifts in issue agendas from broad public interests to narrow feminist interests.

Goss suggests that ascriptive differences are not necessarily barriers to disadvantaged groups' capacity to be heard, that enhanced political inclusion does not necessarily lead to greater collective engagement, and that rights movements do not necessarily constitute the best way to understand the political participation of marginalized groups. She asks what women have gained—and perhaps lost—through expanded incorporation as well as whether single-sex organizations continue to matter in 21st-century America.

KRISTIN A. GOSS is Associate Professor of Public Policy and Political Science at Duke University.

CAWP Series in Gender and American Politics

SERIES EDITORS:
Susan J. Carroll, Rutgers University
Kira Sanbonmatsu, Rutgers University

TITLES IN THE SERIES:
When Protest Makes Policy: How Social Movements
Represent Disadvantaged Groups
by S. Laurel Weldon

The Paradox of Gender Equality:
How American Women's Groups Gained
and Lost Their Public Voice
by Kristin A. Goss

Center for American Women and Politics
Eagleton Institute of Politics
Rutgers University
www.cawp.rutgers.edu

THE PARADOX OF GENDER EQUALITY

*How American Women's Groups
Gained and Lost Their Public Voice*

Kristin A. Goss

The University of Michigan Press
Ann Arbor

Published in the United States of America by
The University of Michigan Press
Manufactured in the United States of America
⊗ Printed on acid-free paper

2016   2015   2014   2013   4   3   2   1

A CIP catalog record for this book is available from the British Library.

Library of Congress Cataloging-in-Publication Data

Goss, Kristin A., 1965–
    The paradox of gender equality : how American women's groups gained and lost their public voice / Kristin A. Goss.
        p.   cm. — (CAWP series in gender and American politics)
    Includes bibliographical references and index.
    ISBN 978-0-472-11851-9 (cloth : alk. paper) — ISBN 978-0-472-02873-3 (e-book)
    1. Women—Political activity—United States.   2. Women's rights—United States.
3. Women—Suffrage—United States.   4. Political participation—United States.
5. Democracy—United States.   I. Title.

    HQ1236.5.U6G673   2012
    323.3'40973—dc23

                                                        2012025918

For Grant

Contents

Acknowledgments

This book started as a simple, straightforward undertaking. It ended up becoming an all-encompassing, sometimes frustrating, but always exhilarating labor of love that consumed more years than I'd care to divulge. As the project grew and morphed, I accrued incredible debts to many kind, patient, and generous people.

First, I am grateful to the following institutions for providing the funds that made this book possible: the Ford Foundation; the Duke Center for the Study of Philanthropy and Voluntarism; the Duke Center for Strategic Philanthropy and Civil Society; the Aspen Institute's Nonprofit Sector Research Fund; the William and Flora Hewlett Foundation; the David and Lucile Packard Foundation; and the Center for Nonprofit Management, Philanthropy, and Policy at George Mason University. I thank Professors Alan Abramson, Charles Clotfelter, Joel Fleishman, and Theda Skocpol for providing or connecting me with these invaluable resources.

Many people contributed comments to the public presentations, book chapters, journal articles, manuscript drafts, and brainstorming sessions that eventually came together as this book. For their valuable insights I thank Maryann Barakso, Frank Baumgartner, Jeff Berry, Tony Brown, Brian Brox, Pam Constable, Donna Dees, Larry Dodd, Elizabeth Frankenberg, Joe Galaskiewicz, Elisabeth Gidengil, Cheryl Graeve, Jay Hamilton, Hahrie Han, Katie Herrold, Marie Hojnacki, Josh Horwitz, Bruce Jentleson, Cathy Jervey, Betsy Lawson, Brenda O'Neill, Rachel Seidman, Shauna Shames, Steven Rathgeb Smith, Elizabeth Stanley, Nancy Tate, Jacob Thomsen, Sue Tolleson Rinehart, and Jacob Vigdor.

Nearly a dozen leaders of national women's organizations sat down with me, sometimes for hours, to help me interpret my findings and to offer their perspectives on the evolution of women's civic place. I thank these women for spending so much time with me: Justine Andronici, Anne Bryant, Martha Burk, Alice Cohan, Kim Gandy, Marcia Greenberger, Heidi Hartmann, Pat Reuss, Eleanor Smeal, Nancy Tate, and Leslie Wolfe.

I am grateful to have had the opportunity to present early findings at invited talks before the University of Florida Political Science Department, the Georgetown University Library, and the Georgetown University Conference on Nonprofit Advocacy as well as at meetings of the International Political Science Association, the American Political Science Association, the Midwest Political Science Association, and the Southern Political Science Association. I thank everyone who showed up at these sessions to listen and ask thought-provoking questions that illuminated holes in my data and arguments. Portions of the book have appeared in Kristin A. Goss and Theda Skocpol, "Changing Agendas: The Impact of Feminism on American Politics," in *Gender and Social Capital*, ed. Brenda O'Neill and Elisabeth Gidengil (New York: Routledge, 2006), 323–56; in Kristin A. Goss, "Never Surrender? How Women's Groups Abandoned Their Policy Niche in U.S. Foreign Policy Debates, 1916–2000," *Politics and Gender* 5, no. 4 (2009): 453–89; and in Kristin A. Goss, "Foundations of Feminism: How Philanthropic Patrons Shaped Gender Politics," *Social Science Quarterly* 88, no. 5 (2007): 1174–91. I thank anonymous reviewers from three journals— *Perspectives on Politics, Women and Politics,* and *Politics and Gender*—who helped me refine my thoughts. I also thank the anonymous reviewers who read the full manuscript and made it infinitely better for their thoughts.

For excellent research assistance, I thank Cariza Dolores Arnedo, Kate Guthrie, Gina Ireland, and Ann McClenahan, who slogged through mounds of hearing testimony, articles, and other documents that provided the raw fodder for the story told here.

I am deeply indebted to several scholars who shared data with me. Debra Minkoff compiled information on women's organizations from a 1963 directory; her work contributed to the analysis of changes in women's organizations' orientations published as Goss and Skocpol (2006) and discussed in chapter 4. Robert Putnam provided me with his longitudinal data on membership in various women's organizations. Debby Leff supplied her unpublished senior thesis, which provided unparalleled insights into how female elites defined "women's issues" in the early 1970s. Michael Heaney and Fabio Rojas provided an analysis of the gender composition of the antiwar movement. Matt Grossman compiled figures for me on the presence of women's groups, relative to other organizations, in various policy-making venues from the mid-1990s through the mid-2000s. It is difficult enough to find time to do one's own work, let alone the work of colleagues. I am extremely grateful to these generous scholars.

At Duke, I have been surrounded by wonderful people who make the Sanford School a great place to work, including Susan Alexander, David Arrington, Butch Bailey, Rob DiPatri, David Gastwirth, Astrid Gatling, Charity Greene, Jadrien Hill, Rita Keating, Belinda Keith, Karen Kemp, Bruce Kuniholm, Pam Ladd, Fernande Legros, Mary Lindsley, Anita Lyon, Andrea Marston, Helene McAdams, Doug McClary, Patrick Morris, Ed Ocampo, Beth Osteen, Seema Parkash, Stan Paskoff, Nancy Shaw, Melissa Squires, Kate Walker, and Janet Williams. My fellow members of the League of Women Voters of Arlington—especially Mary Finger, Dorothy Nieweg, Ann Ross, Sue Swisher, and Nancy Tate—offered many helpful insights about changes in women's engagement. The librarians at the Foundation Center (especially Janice Rosenberg and Caroline Herbert) and at Georgetown University provided exceptional assistance when I was collecting the data. In many ways, this is a book about people who show up when it counts. I am grateful to the late Bill Bradley, Kim Porter, and Rob Thomas for doing so when it really mattered.

I owe special debts of gratitude to several colleagues and collaborators. Michael Heaney identified hybridity as the concept to employ when thinking about the emergence of new women's organizations. Our collaboration on a 2010 article, together with superb insights from Jeff Isaac and Dara Strolovitch on that work, sharpened my thinking about how to capture the ideas underlying women's mobilization and its evolution.

My Duke colleagues Anirudh Krishna and Fritz Mayer reviewed early chapters and delivered incisive comments and moral support at our regular get-togethers. Two other colleagues, Phil Cook and Charlie Clotfelter, later helped me to reframe the introduction and offered valuable insights to make the book accessible to people who don't study politics or gender.

Seven exceedingly generous women took many, many hours not only to read the entire manuscript in its overly long initial incarnation but also to offer pages and pages of comments that opened my eyes to new ways of looking at the evidence, to say nothing of sparing me much embarrassment. I can't begin to thank Anne Costain, Nancy MacLean, Eileen McDonagh, Marie Morris, Kira Sanbonmatsu, Theda Skocpol, and Dara Strolovitch for their contributions.

I have been immeasurably lucky to have spectacular mentors. Phil Cook of Duke University has served as my statistics teacher, adviser on two graduate theses, coauthor, and senior colleague. In ways too numerous to count, he has taken care of my intellectual development. Eileen McDonagh of Northeastern University and Theda Skocpol of Harvard University have blazed a trail for women in political science and have spent their professional lives looking out for younger colleagues, including me. Their big hearts and moral example are wondrous, and their national awards for mentoring are richly deserved. Duke's Dalene Stangl has showed the way for women in the field of statistics. She has been my mentor, social safety net, midweek dinner companion, and dear friend for nearly two decades. I hope I embarrass her a lot by saying how much her example and presence mean to me.

I thank the editors at the University of Michigan Press for being so patient when I needed it and so efficient when the time came to shepherd this project through. I am deeply indebted to Melody Herr as well as to the editors of the CAWP Series in Gender and American Politics, Sue Carroll and Kira Sanbonmatsu.

I am lucky to have a circle of smart, funny, compassionate, accomplished, and all-around fabulous female friends and relatives who have sustained me and reinforced my conviction that sisterhood still matters. My life would not be the same without Nili Abrahamsson, Kristin Amerling, Barbara Asnes, Alma Blount, Sally Caraganis, Betty Chen, Frannie Allen Clifford, Audrey Cowgill, Laura Cratin, Jessica Dorman, Carol Drayton, the late Charlotte Ellertson, the late Gabriele Ellertson, Natalie Ellertson, Maya Foo, Brenna Goss, Heather Goss, Kaela Goss, Shirley Goss, Wanda Goss, Zeta Graham, Rebecca Kramnick, Kitty DeLio LaForte, Marsha Mardock, Kathy Matusiak, Kiki McGrath, the late Ann McLaughlin, Judy Minier, Marie Morris, Becky Peters-Combs, Karen Price, Lisa Price, Shelley Price, Betty Shearer, Karen Springer, Dalene Stangl, Liz Stanley, Gretchen Tripp, Beth Watkins, Peggy White, and Betsey Wildhack. I also thank the significant others in their lives, including my brother, Dave; my uncles, Jim Bulman, Doug Caraganis, Bill Goss, Richie Goss, and Jack Shearer; and my honorary dad, Walter "Buzzy" Morris.

I offer my deepest thanks to my parents-in-law, Bill and Imy Williams, who have always treated me like a beloved daughter and who enriched this book by offering their first-person insights into what it means to be an engaged citizen.

This book was written with unending gratitude to my parents, Doug and Georgia Goss, who gave me everything and died too soon.

Finally, I thank Grant Williams, the gentle soul who entered my life more than two decades ago and never left. I am proud to have him as a husband, best friend, and father to our three "kids," Harry, Bess, and Teddy. Grant has good-naturedly supported me in ways too numerous to count, including enduring a commuter marriage. I dedicate this work to him, with great appreciation and abiding love.

ONE

Women's Citizenship and American Democracy

In 1947, the Truman administration announced an ambitious plan to rebuild Europe after World War II. The $13 billion European Recovery Program, better known as the Marshall Plan, laid the moral and strategic foundation for U.S. foreign aid in the postwar era. It was and remains one of the most important and far-reaching public policies in American history.

When the Senate Foreign Relations Committee held hearings on the controversial plan in early 1948, American women formed one of the most prominent constituencies testifying for the bold proposal. Seven women's organizations, each claiming between 20,000 and 8,000,000 members, marched to Capitol Hill to urge Congress to grant President Truman's full request for aid to hasten European reconstruction, stabilize the global economy, and normalize trade relations across the Atlantic.[1] The groups represented a diverse cross section of the population: middle-class clubwomen, elite women, labor union women, peace activists, and Jewish women.

The groups' words before Congress mixed lofty themes of international cooperation with hardheaded policy analysis. A witness for the 98,000-member American Association of University Women declared that "the United States is on trial and what we do now will be the final test of our sincerity and leadership." She urged Congress to allocate the full amount the president had requested on the grounds that it reflected the best judgment of technical experts and signaled that the United States was sincere about reconstructing Europe: "The entire world is sitting in judgment and the future of every citizen depends on whether we delay."[2]

Although composed of women, these groups purported to represent the national interest and humanity generally. The representative of the 70,000-member National Council of Jewish Women, for example, assured Congress that her group was "united for common action" for "the improvement of the lot of their fellow men."[3] These groups grounded their moral authority as a public interest lobby in their practices of careful study, dispassionate analysis, and lengthy consensus building—democratic processes that were similar to but in some ways purer than those utilized by the partisan Congress. The 83,000-strong League of Women Voters, for example, recounted its 28 years of work in the field of government, buttressed by conferences on the Marshall Plan held in eight cities and hundreds of local communities.[4] The Marshall Plan passed, of course, and foreign policy—both internationalist and isolationist—continued to top organized women's agenda into the 1950s and 1960s.

In the 1990s, Congress considered another landmark foreign aid bill, the Foreign Affairs Reform and Reconstruction Act. The act abolished several key arms control and international development agencies and moved their functions to the Department of State. These agencies embodied the internationalist foreign policy that women's groups in earlier decades had fought mightily to defend and expand. Congress held hearings on this bill as well, but women's organizations were nowhere to be seen.

Around the same time, however, women's groups did show up to lobby for foreign policies to combat discrimination and human rights abuses against women, including the landmark Trafficking Victims Protection Act of 2000, which increased penalties for selling human beings into servitude and created special visas to provide safe quarter to trafficking victims. However, the nature of women's groups' foreign policy advocacy in the late 20th century differed in crucial ways from their foreign policy work at midcentury. For one, the general-purpose mass-membership groups of old had been replaced by staff-led, professional organizations that had developed expertise in emerging policy niches. Such groups included the Women's Rights Project of Human Rights Watch and the Women's Commission for Refugee Women and Children. Second, women's groups were advocating almost exclusively on behalf of women's rights, status, and well-being. They spoke out against discrimination in the foreign service and for equal treatment in the distribution of development assistance. Third, and perhaps most important, even though congressional engagement in international affairs was on the rise, women's groups simply did not appear very often at foreign policy hearings. The decline was both curious and a stark shift from midcentury.

The story of women's groups and foreign policy is interesting in and of itself, but it also presents a host of larger, tantalizing questions. How has the role of women in public policy debates evolved over the past century? Might the case of foreign policy, in which active and broad-minded engagement gave way to a smaller and narrower role, be emblematic of larger changes in women's place in Washington? What issues constitute "women's issues," and how have those definitions evolved over time? How have women organized themselves to be heard in the halls of power? What moral claims have grounded their organizations and policy advocacy? What forces have shaped the various dimensions of women's collective engagement? Do these patterns matter for women's voice or even for the performance of American government? Should we be concerned about or reassured by shifts in American women's policy advocacy? Using a fresh historical approach and a trove of original data, this book addresses these questions.

This is a book about American women's citizenship from the late 19th century to the dawn of the 21st. We often think of citizenship as the rights that the state confers on us. In contrast to this top-down perspective, I focus on citizenship from the ground up: as a process by which everyday citizens organize to affect the laws that govern them. I examine how women have come together *as women* to move America toward its promise of a more perfect union and how the victories they have achieved have both enabled and inhibited their capacity to organize going forward. Women's citizenship is not merely about the laws that formally structure their rights but also about how women themselves have defined and acted out their public roles in the halls of power.

This is also a book about America's political development more generally. Over the past decade, scholars and civic leaders have raised alarms about the sad state of civic participation in America—particularly those forms of participation that involve face-to-face engagement (Putnam 2000; Skocpol 2003). These observers have offered many theories, sometimes in tension with one another, to explain the decline (see, e.g., Macedo et al. 2005; Putnam 2000; Skocpol 2003). Women—a large, historically well-organized, and politically consequential segment of the polity—offer an illuminating window on the patterns and drivers of democratic participation. Tracing women's development as collective political actors allows us to evaluate many common assumptions about the relationships among inclusion, participation, and voice. In exploring these themes, the book brings into focus the critical role that public policy has played, not only as a goal of political groups' collective action but also as a force shaping the nature and scope of their public engagement.

American women have undergone profound changes since the late 19th century. Some of these changes women themselves have brought about through individual and collective policy work; other changes have come courtesy of larger social, economic, and political forces that have affected the polity generally. These changes, in turn, have affected the role of women in public life. I consider both what women have gained through their advocacy and what they may have lost.

Women's Groups as Instigators of Inclusion

Visiting the United States in the 1830s, the French aristocrat and chronicler of democracy Alexis de Tocqueville famously remarked on Americans' tendency to form associations to accomplish collective goals (Tocqueville 1994, Part 2, 106). A century later, an eminent historian characterized America as "a nation of organizers" (Schlesinger 1944). American women have played an underappreciated role in defining America as a pluralist democracy in which social innovation and political pressure work their way from the outside in. Over the centuries, women have organized charitable relief societies, mutual-aid associations, social reform groups, political party groups, legislative lobbies, and political action committees. As Nancy F. Cott (1987) has correctly noted, women laid the groundwork for the participatory, interest group politics that for good or ill define America today.

Working on behalf of females and other constituencies, women's groups have been important forces in the development of the American state.[5] The array of transformational and in many cases enduring policy reforms that women's groups have spearheaded is breathtaking: abolition, temperance, the organization of charitable services, suffrage, the development of kindergartens and playgrounds, an end to lynching, pure food and drug laws, maternal and child health, free trade, peace, multilateral engagement, juvenile justice, environmental conservation, workplace protections, a federal role in education, black civil rights, women's rights, universal health care—the list goes on. In short, women's charitable, advocacy, and electoral work over more than a century helped lay the groundwork for the regulatory and social programs that structure modern life.

Women's groups have often advocated on behalf of proposals that would most directly affect women: suffrage, citizenship rights, spousal military benefits, equal pay legislation, funds for breast cancer research, gender-based development aid, and so forth. But women's groups have also spoken on behalf of others—children, victims of crime, senior citizens, racial minorities—who have difficulty speaking for themselves and who were often neglected by male politicians and male-dominated associations. Before America had public interest lobbies, women's organizations took it upon themselves to advocate universal concerns, such as clean air, good government, and national security. Women's groups played an important agenda-setting role by bringing to elites' attention issues that affected everyone but that women encountered first as they went about their domestic tasks (Jeffreys-Jones 1995). Thus, women's groups were key players in advancing polices that fulfill the Constitution's promises of justice, tranquillity, liberty, and general welfare.

From the Gilded Age through much of the 20th century, women's organizations were the primary vehicle through which females participated in public life. These groups constructed and interpreted women's interests, voiced women's perspectives, developed women's policy agendas, and articulated the narratives that lent women authority in the political sphere. When women were disenfranchised and otherwise marginalized, women's groups provided safety and power in numbers, allowing women to advocate in favor of controversial issues such as female suffrage as well as policies benefiting all measure of humankind. Indeed, women's organizations historically have managed to turn women's marginalization into a source of moral authority. Compared to other types of associations, women's groups "have exceptionally activist populations with strong roots in their organizations' cultures" and are "unique among American associations for their high levels of activism" (Knoke 1992, 403).

Women's organizations have offered unique advantages over mixed-gender groups and other outlets for civic and political participation. Female organizers have been able to use solidary and purposive incentives rooted in women's shared experiences as wives, people of color, mothers, senior citizens, lesbians, homemakers, professionals, laborers, and combinations of these politically relevant categories to overcome the problem of free riding that is endemic to voluntary associations (James Q. Wilson 1995). Women's organizations also have allowed females to exercise political voice and leadership and develop civic skills and networks that are useful in mixed-gender settings, including legislative arenas. In an era before large numbers of women worked outside the home, women's organizations provided an alternative path to work of public significance (A. Scott 1991). Virginia Sapiro (1984, 135) concludes that "women's impact has, in many senses, been greatest when they worked through women's organizations."

Waves of Women's Engagement?

The period examined by this study—roughly 1880 through 2000—witnessed enormous political, economic, and social transformations for both women and the United States. In heretofore underappreciated ways, women's collective political engagement shaped and was shaped by these eras and events: industrialization; the Progressive Era reform movements; the Great War; the Great Depression and the New Deal; World War II; the Cold War; the Great Society; the civil rights, consumer, and environmental movements; the Reagan Revolution and devolution of government; the advent of computers and the Internet; the proliferation of media outlets and forms; and the expansion of global capitalism and governance. To this long list, of course, we must add the transformation in women's lives, both public and private. Women's fates and fortunes have been profoundly influenced by the arrival of birth control and legalized abortion, the movement of large numbers of married women and mothers into full-time careers, declining fertility, changing patterns of marriage and divorce, and the liberalization of public beliefs about gender roles and responsibilities. The book documents the myriad ways that women's organizations have sought to advance, halt, adjust to, or otherwise cope with these developments through policy advocacy on Capitol Hill.

In conventional parlance, it is common to speak of women's engagement as unfolding in "waves" of agitation for women's rights. In the first wave, which had its origins in the mid-19th century but was most active in the 1880–1920 period, voluntary organizations advocated on behalf of both state suffrage laws and a constitutional amendment, ratified in 1920, that guaranteed women the right to vote. In the second wave, which arose in the mid-1960s and reached its heyday in the 1970s, "women's liberation" and women's rights groups sought to dismantle discriminatory laws and social norms that hindered women's personal and professional development. The third wave refers to loosely organized efforts by younger women to articulate a new feminism that combines cultural and often "feminine" or sexual expression with an agenda oriented around intersectional oppression and social justice (Baumgardner and Richards 2000; Dicker 2008; Henry 2004). The wave metaphor, which has been traced to a 1968 *New York Times Magazine* article (Dicker 2008), is straightforward: Women's collective mobilization follows a pattern similar to ocean water. It gathers, grows, crests, and then crashes, before receding to begin the pattern again. Thus, women's history is said to have been marked by activist wave periods and postwave periods characterized by political quiescence.

Scholars have long recognized that political women's activity continued between waves, and they recently have begun to challenge the utility of the wave metaphor itself (see, e.g., Andersen 1996; Cott 1992; Hewitt 2010; Kaledin 1984; Meyerowitz 1994). While these revisionist studies typically are based on case studies, I bring to bear evidence that documents systematically over more than a century the contours of women's collective action. In the process, I illuminate shortcomings in the wave perspective and the assumptions underlying it.

One assumption is that waves of agitation for expanded rights constitute the most interesting and fulsome periods of women's collective action. This study shows that although women's collective action clearly surges during waves, it does not necessarily recede—and may in fact continue to grow—after the wave has supposedly crested. Thus, privileging the great rights movements, important as they have been for the lives and fortunes of millions of women, threatens to neglect the very important work that women's organizations, including minority women's organizations, have done after visible policy victories (see, e.g., Cott 1992; Hewitt 2010). Second, wave accounts, constructed from cases of movements for women's rights, tend to downplay the wide array of issues—often having little or nothing to do with feminist concerns—that women's groups have advocated for and against during both nonwave and wave periods. Finally, with its focus on feminist organizations, the wave narrative neglects the consequential activities of other types of women's organizations that operate in the charitable and political realms.

I provide evidence that nonwave periods were not only of great interest, but they were also some of the most active decades in women's history. In light of these patterns, Eileen McDonagh (2011) has suggested that the proper metaphor for women's collective activism may be rivers rather than waves. Thus, I consider the alternative that rivers of women's activism flowed across a broad policy terrain, branching into different streams, some of which dried up and others of which gained force.

Documenting Women's Participation

To document women's collective participation, I use four sets of original data developed from a seldom-used but rich and systematic source of information on democratic participation in policymaking: groups' testimony before Congress. The testimony data, hand-assembled from more than 30 linear feet of bound volumes and cross-checked with newly available online records, provides an unparalleled window into women's groups' policy advocacy from the late 1870s, when they first began testifying, through 2000, when this study ends. The main dataset contains all appearances by women's groups before Congress in that period—more than 10,400 appearances by some 2,100 local, state, and national organizations. These appearances are coded along a number of dimensions, including the substantive issue on which the organization was testifying. I utilize the coding scheme for issue interests developed by the Policy Agendas Project (www .policyagendas.org). The project has assigned every postwar congressional hearing to one of 21 policy domains (e.g., agriculture) and one of 228 subdomains (e.g., food inspection and safety).

The three other datasets allow us to evaluate alternative aspects of women's groups' participation: the level of their engagement with regard to more than 700 particularly important laws (Stathis 2003); the rhetorical strategies they used to ply their influence in two prominent policy domains (foreign policy and health care); and the presence of women's organizations relative to other types of interest groups and witnesses appearing before Congress at 10-year intervals. These datasets, along with my interviews of national women's group leaders and organizational ecologies, allow me to place women's advocacy into a broader context and to understand the dynamics on the ground.

The data, described in greater detail in appendix A, measure key constructs of women's groups' policy role: which groups testified and how often; how prominent the "women's lobbies" were in any given period; what issues and interests drew the attention of women's groups; how broad their issue agendas were; whether they participated in particularly important legislative debates; and what kinds of narratives they used to command authority before Congress. Furthermore, the data show how these various dimensions of participatory citizenship evolved over a long and transformative period: from four decades before passage of the 19th Amendment, which guaranteed universal suffrage to women, through the next big women's rights movement of the 1960s and 1970s, until the dawn of the 21st century. Thus, I look not only at periods of surging women's activism but also at periods where women are conventionally portrayed as shying away from public life. Likewise, I examine how women's groups advocated breakthroughs in women's rights and what these groups did to protect those policies once enacted. In most studies, women's participation is measured in terms of aggregate rates of individual acts, such as voting or joining organizations. Examining collective participation before Congress provides a more comprehensive view not only of how much women participate but also on what grounds and to which ends.

To be sure, congressional testimony does not capture the full range or effect of women's organizational activities. These data are likely to privilege certain groups: larger Washington-based organizations that have connections and professional advocacy staffs; those representing more resourceful women; and, most of all, those concerned with national policy issues. The data are likely to underrepresent local and state-focused groups, groups of particularly disadvantaged women, charitable and self-help groups, and organizations focused on institution building as opposed to policy change. It is critical to emphasize, too, that these data do not tell us whether women's groups were influential or successful in their advocacy efforts. Because measuring interest group influence is difficult (Baumgartner et al. 2009; R. L. Hall and Wayman 1990), we might consider congressional testimony simply as a signal of groups' preexisting credibility with and importance to political elites. (See appendix A for a fuller discussion of the limitations of the data.)

These caveats aside, congressional hearings provide a good barometer of what ultimately concerns this study: women's groups' participation in national policy debates. Congress began routinely holding hearings at the dawn of the 20th century (Truman 1951, 216), and they have evolved into a way for Congress to gather political and policy information from issue publics and political constituencies as well as to demonstrate respect for participatory democracy. For their part, interest groups have used hearings as a "propaganda channel" to expose their issues to a wider public and air their grievances (Truman 1951, 372). Testifying before Congress is one of the most common activities for women's organizations, with 84 percent reporting in a 1985 survey that they testified, far more than reported other popular forms of participation such as drafting regulations, filing lawsuits, or running media campaigns (Schlozman 1992, 364).

Participation in hearings sheds light on women's place in the political order. Testifying tells us what policies on the national agenda women want to influence. Testifying also illuminates the issues on which Congress considers women's voice to be authoritative. Equally important, presence in congressional hearing rooms provides a glimpse of the resources that women can offer Congress—such as policy knowledge, political information, and influence on voters—and how valuable legislators view those resources to be. Although testimony may not be directly influential, it is often a signal of a group's visibility and expertise within a policy realm (Grossman 2012, 90–91). In interviews with congressional staff members in 2006, one scholar of interest groups found that "the most prominent and involved advocacy organizations in testimony were also the most involved in policymaking behind the scenes" (Grossman 2012, 91).

While some women's organizations have more to offer Congress than do others, one of this study's surprising findings is that a great diversity of groups have been given a voice on Capitol Hill. They include not only resourceful advocates, such as associations of female professionals and Washington-based lobbying groups, but also small local service and civic organizations; groups representing poor, minority, elderly, and other dis-advantaged women; college sororities; wives' groups and auxiliaries; and patriotic organizations. The range of groups testifying suggests that Congress has been far more welcoming of the diversity of women's experiences and perspectives than many observers would imagine.

Creating an Empowered "Civic Place" for Women

The changing patterns of women's organizations' public engagement—its volume, scope, policy priorities, and rhetorical grounding—provide a window into the changing understandings of what I term women's civic place. Civic place encompasses the civic identity on which groups draw to construct their interests and justify their political authority, the modes of collective action that groups deploy to press those interests, and the policy niche that groups legitimately occupy. A civic identity is a political construction that signifies collective beliefs about citizens' claims against and duties toward their fellow citizens. Civic identities might include laborer, pauper, veteran, and mother. Each is rooted in some facet of individual experience that helps to establish one's role in the political order. Drawing on the civic identities of the individuals they represent, organizations develop modes of collective action, such as internal procedures and governance structures, to reflect and represent those understandings. These organizations then use civic identities and organizational modes to assemble and speak out on policy agendas of concern to their constituents. Groups marshal their resources and rhetoric to occupy niches within the broader policy terrain. In these ways, groups of citizens acquire their civic place.

In adopting the term *place*, I am cognizant of its historically pejorative usage signifying the oppression of less-advantaged groups, as in "keeping women in their place."[6] I wish to reclaim the term to signify group empowerment through political engagement. The notion of civic place is akin to the notion of place more generally—a metaphorical location that connotes rightful inclusion. Civic place embraces a broad construction of citizenship in its various dimensions.

Gender Identity and Women's Civic Place

What does it mean to be a woman? In terms of biology, we have a good sense of the answer. On average, women look and sound different from men, and women alone have the capacity to conceive and bear children. In the realm of politics and public policy, however, the question of gender difference is less clear-cut. Indeed, for more than 150 years, women's activists have been divided over many questions, including: Do women bring distinctive experiences and perspectives to bear on policy discussions? Do women have different policy positions from men? Do women care more deeply about certain issues? Should women organize separately to express their voice, or are their interests better served by assimilation? How might women express both their egalitarian yearnings and their different perspectives without compromising either?

These questions—the topic of much scholarly study—have important implications for women's role in democratic decision making. This book tackles the conundrum of women's political identity, which has typically been formulated as whether women are best understood as "the same as" men, or as "different from" them. Roughly speaking, sameness understandings envision women as full, rights-bearing citizens with claims to equal status in the competitive "male" worlds of politics and the market. This formulation roughly tracks the dominant Lockean liberal strand in American political culture, with its focus on individualism, antistatism, and liberty. Women traditionally used sameness arguments to advocate the expansion of their right to equal treatment under law—what I term the "equal-claimant" framework.

By contrast, "difference" accounts emphasize women's roles as responsibility-bearing citizens who can bring a distinctive ethic of maternal care to society and public policy (Dietz 1985; DiQuinzio 2005; Elshtain 1981; Ruddick 1989). This formulation roughly maps onto the less dominant yet nonetheless powerful civic republican strand in American political culture, with its emphasis on citizen virtue, duty to the commonweal, and mutually supportive collective action. Women traditionally used difference arguments to advocate other-regarding policies, such as children's welfare and world peace, as well as certain social protections for women themselves. Difference-rooted arguments suffused a second framework for women's collective action, the maternal framework.

Notions of sameness and difference have animated the visions, strategies, and dilemmas of women's organizations since at least the mid-19th century. Advocacy groups have used these understandings to promulgate their vision of women's issues and interests, to convey women's authority as a political force, and to validate their knowledge of sound public policy. Although equality and care need not be at odds (Lister 2003), they often have come into conflict in women's policy advocacy, with the pursuit of one value threatening to diminish the other. Martha Minow (1990, 19) has identified "the dilemma of difference" as a fundamental feature of women's history. Indeed, many of the great policy battles within organized womanhood—over the Equal Rights Amendment (ERA) or national child-care proposals or abortion, for example—have revolved around women's groups' different perspectives on women's essential sameness or difference (Luker 1984; Mansbridge 1986; Michel 1999).

Yet over time, women's organizations also have sought to manage or avoid the seemingly inevitable collision between sameness and difference perspectives. In the early 20th century, women's organizations drew on sameness at some times and difference at others (Kraditor 1971; Sarvasy 1992). At midcentury, female advocates found a way to fuse these two understandings into a third, politically useful, hybrid identity—what I term the "good-citizen" framework. Like the equal-claimant framework, the good-citizen framework portrays women as formally undifferentiated from men; at the same time, like the maternal framework, it takes advantage of implicit understandings of women's difference. More recently, women of the "postfeminist" era have found ways to combine sameness (equality) and difference (maternalism) in new and creative ways that take advantage of the enduring aspects of both while discarding the aspects that feel outdated to many women (Goss and Heaney 2010).

In sum, working from different shared experiences, women have come together in organizations large and small to showcase different interpretations of their citizenship. One interpretation focused on civic responsibility: what women owed and could bring to the polity. The other interpretation focused on civic, political, and social rights: what the state owed to women. The balance of rights and responsibilities shifted over time, often in ways that are counterintuitive, and influenced the direction of women's groups' policy advocacy.

Sameness and Difference among Women

Thus far, I have discussed women's sameness and difference in relation to men. However, feminists have argued that this dyadic construction implies the existence of a politically distinct group of "women." In fact, women are divided along lines of race, class, sexual orientation, age, political ideology, and family status, among other characteristics. Given the diversity of women's ascriptive traits and the diversity of lived experiences that often go hand in hand with those traits, one might ask whether it even makes sense to ask big questions about the evolution of American women's policy interests and agendas.

Not surprisingly, women's organizations and movements have grappled with and even foundered on such questions. Early women's clubs and organizations—even the suffrage movement—were often segregated by class and race and internally divided about women's proper roles in the public sphere. After suffrage, progressive female activists battled among themselves and with their conservative counterparts about whether equality policies such as the ERA would help or harm women. During the second wave movement, poor women and their more advantaged sisters clashed about whether paid employment constituted women's liberation or women's oppression (Taylor 2010) or whether to support affirmative action in higher education (Strolovitch 2007, 40). Meanwhile, lesbians challenged their straight sisters' assumptions about gender and family roles. The heterogeneity of women's perspectives, which played out in countless battles over organizational strategy and policy agendas, were rooted in the heterogeneity of women's lived experience. Indeed, as Nancy A. Hewitt (2000, 3) notes, "Sisterhood or a common set of values can constrain as well as liberate women."

Thus, when this book speaks of women, it is with recognition that women are a diverse, splintered, internally fractious group with certain commonalities that have emerged as politically relevant throughout American history. A work that examines patterns of women's collective engagement from the proverbial 30,000 feet necessarily will miss the very real and important differences and divisions playing out on the ground. To the extent possible, I supply vignettes illustrating the broad range of identities and perspectives that the women's interest group universe embodies.

The Dilemma of Citizenship: Does Incorporation Enhance Participation?

The case of American women allows us to explore the complex and often counterintuitive relationship between two understandings of American citizenship: legal citizenship and participatory citizenship. Legal citizenship connotes formal inclusion as embedded in public policy—the civil, political, and social rights of belonging (T. H. Marshall and Bottomore 1992). To that list, I would add a crosscutting economic dimension wherein policy embodies affirmative steps to provide individuals an equal footing in occupational and other market transactions. Participatory citizenship is about the exercise of those rights and benefits through individual or collective political action, such as voting, signing petitions, writing letters, and lobbying. American pluralists commonly assume that legal and participatory citizenship go hand in hand. More participation—for example, through social movements—will yield more rights, which will in turn facilitate greater participation.

The book, however, challenges the easy, intuitive conclusion that legal and participatory citizenship are everywhere and always mutually reinforcing. While American history has been marked by a pattern of elites using ascriptive characteristics to exclude disadvantaged peoples from the halls of power (Keyssar 2000; Orren 1992; R. M. Smith 1997), women's groups have proved creative and nimble in gaining a seat at the policymaking table for marginalized women, including poor and minority women. This book offers systematic evidence that women's groups turned the logic of disadvantage on its head to construct compelling claims to access and authority. American women used creative political jujitsu to use the grounds of their exclusion as a basis for democratic voice.

At the same time, the book challenges the easy assumption that more inclusion necessarily leads to more participation. After all, the alternative metaphors for women's political development—the wave metaphor and the branching river metaphor—embody different assumptions about the relationship and anticipate different patterns of participation as women gain incorporation. The wave perspective would predict that participation would spike in periods when women are seeking greater legal citizenship rights, while the river metaphor would see rights movements as just one of many forms of collective action that flow and branch over time. Likewise, wave theory would predict that policy victories that enhance legal citizenship would be followed by a decline in collective participation (the wave crashes), while the rivers perspective would see engagement holding steady or gaining momentum. Thus, we have very different sets of predictions about the impact of participation on policy and of policy on participation.

The relationship between legal and participatory citizenship is both undertheorized and insufficiently tested. This study makes progress on both fronts by bringing to bear new systematic evidence of women's policy engagement over a 120-year period that encompassed both great rights movements and supposedly quieter times. The relationship between participatory and legal citizenship may be positive, but it need not be. If the assumption that they must go together does not hold true for women, who led some of the most transformative rights movements in American history, one must wonder about the overall validity of the assumption.

How Policy Shapes Participation

It is well documented, even axiomatic, that participatory citizenship has influenced the policies that define legal citizenship. Movements of politically engaged women brought suffrage in 1920 and women's rights advances in the 1970s. Social scientists are accustomed to thinking of policy in this way—as a goal or target of collective engagement. However, policies that enhance civic inclusion also have the power to feed back and shape participation. To use the scholarly vernacular, policy is not only a dependent variable but also an independent variable.

Policies may affect participation directly or indirectly via feedback effects. In the case of women, the direct effects are straightforward: The 19th Amendment, which guaranteed women the right to vote, expanded their participation at the ballot box. Meanwhile, laws and court rulings opened to women other forms of participation, such as jury service (Kerber 1998). The indirect effects of policy are less well understood. In a groundbreaking work, Paul Pierson (1993) identified two categories of mechanisms—resource effects and interpretive effects—by which policy may feed back into participation. Resource effects refer to endowments that increase individuals' capacity to engage politically. When government and nongovernmental institutions provide tangible assets such as money, positive experiences with programs, and educational access, individuals' civic skills and organizational capacity grow; with that, their political participation rises. Interpretive effects relate to citizens' "perceptions of their role in the community, their status in relation to other citizens and government, and the extent to which a policy affected their lives" (Mettler 2002, 352). When people feel more included or greater status as citizens, their participation in public life is predicted to grow.

Suzanne Mettler and Joe Soss (2004) have identified four variants of interpretive effects—that is, mechanisms by which policy affects participation. First, public policy defines political membership, including people's understanding of their rights and obligations. Second, public policy creates identity groups and shapes public ideas about their moral worth. Third, policies "frame the meaning and origins of societal problems, by identifying target groups for government action and defining solutions" (62). Finally, policies stimulate participation by defining "the universe of participants and demand makers" and by creating arenas for their collective action (63). In sum, interpretive effects involve policy's role in constructing people's ideas about their place in the polity and in creating a normative context in which they act on those understandings. Policy helps us to answer a variety of questions: What is my proper role as a citizen? When and in what kinds of issue debates will policymakers take my engagement seriously?

The political and economic incorporation of women over the past century makes them an ideal case for examining feedback effects on civic engagement. Since the late 19th century, women have gone from being largely excluded from the rights and obligations of political citizenship to being largely included. For example, laws and traditions that once kept women from voting, serving on juries, and running for elective office have gone by the wayside. At the same time, practices that contributed to women's economic marginalization—such as discrimination by employers, creditors, and public programs—have been outlawed. And social welfare policies, such as child-care tax credits and federally guaranteed family leave, have facilitated women's integration into the occupational sphere.

Women have been the focus of a great deal of policymaking over the past century, altering their relationship with the state in ways that might also change the nature of their participatory citizenship. While many studies have examined the generally positive effects of these laws on women's life opportunities and well-being, we know less about the direct and indirect ways that such policies might have influenced the form, rhetoric, degree, or substance of women's political participation.

On the one hand, we might assume that these effects were strongly positive. For example, we know that policies expanding individual rights, opportunities, and social protections often enhance the capacities, resources, and psychological orientations that encourage civic engagement. Such participation-enhancing factors include education, income, political interest, internal and external efficacy, self-confidence and dignity, sense of belonging, civic skills, and embeddedness in voluntary organizations and networks (Campbell 2003; Mettler 2002; Mettler and Soss 2004; Verba, Schlozman, and Brady 1995). As public policy has increased women's stock of civically valuable resources and orientations, their political participation would be expected to rise (McDonagh 2002, 2009, 2010; Soss 1999).

On the other hand, studies of the U.S. social welfare state suggest that the connection between public policies affecting women in particular ("women's policies") and women's capacity fully to take part in public life may be more complex than is commonly assumed. For example, feminist scholars have argued that welfare state programs may perpetuate traditional gender roles that consign women to the private sphere (Orloff 1993) and fail to compensate their unpaid care work (Sainsbury 1996). Others have suggested that the social welfare state has had a legacy of gender discrimination by providing dignified, reliable, "earned" benefits to men while subjecting women to means-tested or politically volatile state-level benefits (Fraser 1989; Katzenstein 2003; Mettler 1998).

Taken together, these studies suggest that the mere presence of policies that enhance civil, political, or social citizenship is not enough to put women on a path toward greater participatory citizenship. Instead, the design of such policies matters, for policies instruct groups about their place in the public sphere. This instruction, what Soss (1999) terms "political learning," may set the parameters of political organization, including its form, tactics, and policy agendas. The policy context also may influence the nature of the moral claims and narratives that groups use to ground their public engagement. Equally important, the policy context has the potential to define the parameters of groups' political authority in the eyes of voters, lawmakers, and other targets of collective action. In sum, even though the positive relationship between legal citizenship and participatory citizenship seems sensible—and in the case of policies such as the franchise, even axiomatic—the relationship may be more complex than assumed.

At root, then, policy structures the political context in which groups mobilize, formulate agendas, and argue their case, as well as the context in which policymakers view and assess those efforts. Women's citizenship is not simply about the legal regimen that defines the boundaries of their incorporation but is also about the ways that women themselves define and act out their public roles in keeping or in conflict with those boundaries. As women's groups have worked through legislatures, courts, and administrative agencies for greater legal and political inclusion, they have defined their civic place. Those definitions of place, however, have been profoundly shaped by the interpretive and resource incentives offered by existing public policies.

If we accept that legal citizenship has feedback effects on participatory citizenship, many theoretically and empirically interesting questions present themselves. These questions are especially compelling in the case of women, whose civic place has evolved so dramatically over the past century. For example, how do individual policies—or policy regimens, such as the cluster of equal-rights lawmaking that took place in the 1960s and 1970s—affect the level of women's collective engagement? The types of policies that women seek to influence? The way that women understand their interests and the ideational grounding of their political engagement? The perceptions of policymakers, patrons, and other external actors about where women's groups' authority lies and what sorts of policies they should pursue?

As others have, I argue that policy structures political engagement

(Campbell 2003; Mettler 2002, 2005; Mettler and Soss 2004; Pierson 1993, 1995; Skocpol 1992; Soss 1999, 2000). However, I elaborate on feedback theory by examining several questions that are heretofore underexplored. For one, while most of these studies have examined feedback effects on individuals (typically recipients of government aid), I examine how feedback effects operate on organizations—specifically, social movement organizations and interest groups. Second, I examine not simply whether engagement rises or falls but also how policy feeds back onto other dimensions of engagement, such as the rhetorical grounding of groups' advocacy and the types of issues that they choose to embrace. Likewise, I examine how different types of feedback effects interact to affect the scope and nature of groups' policy engagements. Finally, I look at how feedback effects play out and influence the political behavior not just of one clearly defined constituency group at one point in time but of a diverse population over a broad swath of history.

The Agenda: Ways to Capture Women's Collective Participation

Based on a policy feedback perspective, this book examines the evolution of American women as communities of shared interests and as an interest group community organized primarily (though not exclusively) around gender as a political identity. Three sets of questions animate this study.

(1) How has women's collective participation in the public sphere evolved since the late 19th century? Is it accurate to think in terms of waves of mobilization that build toward achievement of expanded rights and then recede once those rights have been achieved? To answer these questions, I explore multiple dimensions of the evolution of women's participatory citizenship, including their prominence in key national legislative debates, the types of organizations representing women, the types of policy issues these groups seek to influence, and the narratives they deploy.

(2) What role has legal citizenship played, either directly or indirectly, in structuring the participatory citizenship of American women? What factors other than policy might account for the observed changes in the scope and substance of women's policy engagement?

(3) In what ways do the observed patterns in women's participatory citizenship matter for their voice in American democracy and for development of the American state more generally? How has incorporation affected women's participation regarding their own interests or the interests of other social groups and humanity at large?

The answers to these questions about the level and form of women's participation and the narratives that have animated their work provide powerful insights into women's relationship to the state and the polity. That is, women's civic engagement sheds light on women's citizenship both as they understand it and as public policy has defined it for them.

Yet while this is a book about American women, its themes and conclusions shed light on larger questions that transcend gender. One question concerns how communities of interest evolve over time. Scholars have devoted considerable attention to the formation of collective action frames, yet we know relatively little about how such frames change and the implications for groups' policy agendas and political influence. Why do certain groups take hold of and mobilize around certain issues? Why do political elites (legislators, judges, bureaucrats) then come to see these groups as authoritative spokespeople for their chosen issues? And why, once groups have come to own issues within a particular policy niche, do they sometimes appear to disown the issues and abandon the niche?

What Happened? A Preview

From the last decades of the 19th century to the dawn of the 21st, American women led two major social movements for equal rights, sought and gained access to employment and education alongside men, challenged traditional gender roles at home, and acquired leadership positions in major institutions, such as the U.S. Congress, that were once all-male preserves. Yet as women have deepened and broadened their roles as citizens, their patterns of collective policy engagement have unfolded in surprising, often counterintuitive ways.

Women's groups' engagement expanded from the late 19th century through suffrage and into the postwar period before beginning a steady decline that lasted at least until 2000 and was interrupted only by a brief uptick during the height of the second wave women's movement in the late 1970s. These patterns show up in largely consistent ways across two categories of engagement: (1) prominence, as measured by the absolute and opportunity-adjusted quantity of appearances before congressional committees and the number of organizations testifying; and (2) policy agendas, as measured by the range of interests that women's groups advocated. As I show in the next two chapters, these are very different patterns from those that many conventional histories of American women would lead us to expect.

Equally interesting if less surprising were changes in the discourse that women's groups used to establish their political and policy bona fides. These narratives have evolved in ways that make sense in the context of women's movement from the home to the workplace. Yet the narratives, designed to influence public policy, were also profoundly shaped by it. Moreover, narratives rooted in women's disadvantaged status as political subordinates and outsiders proved remarkably versatile in allowing women's groups entrée to some of the most important public policy debates of the day.

At the risk of oversimplification, this study documents the rise and fall of America's first public interest lobby. From the time of suffrage onward, women's citizenship evolved from a phenomenon rooted in participatory, communitarian notions of women's civic place to one rooted in rights-oriented, Lockean liberal claims. As gender hierarchies have flattened, women as a public interest community have come to sound more like a collection of "special interests" traditionally associated with male-dominated organizations, such as business, trade, and veterans' groups. As women's groups have become more like men's, adopting orientations toward the state, republican citizenship norms and practices have lost some of their most authentic leaders and dedicated foot soldiers.

How Policy Orients Participation

No parsimonious explanation can account for the observed evolution in women's collective engagement in national policy debates. However, clues in the data and in broader theories of political change suggest a central role for the state itself in shaping the evolution of women's civic place over the 20th century. In spotlighting the state—in particular, public policies that it has promulgated—this book builds on policy feedback scholars' findings that policy shapes the contours of political participation. The trends in women's national policy engagement—the rise and decline of women's organizations' congressional presence throughout the 20th century, the proliferation of women's groups, the focusing of women's policy agendas, and the evolution in organizational narratives—result in large part from changes in public policy that have splintered the "public interest" community in general and shaped women's civic place in particular.

Policies create opportunities for new interpretations and incentives for the development of civic place. In the case of American women, two sets of policies drove their transformation: the 19th Amendment to the Constitution, ratified in 1920, which provided the foundation of women's political inclusion, the right to vote; and a series of administrative and legislative policies enacted in the 1960s and 1970s that provided a statistical, legal, and organizational foundation for women's equal treatment in the economic sphere. Policies enacted in both eras promoted women's inclusion but did so in different ways, with different effects on women's participation. Suffrage allowed for an encompassing interpretation of women's civic place that included sameness, difference, and hybrid understandings of women's identities, which mapped onto the full range of public issues. The rights revolution that began in the 1960s provided for a narrower conception of women's identity oriented around economic inclusion. These policies encouraged participation in the market sphere first and foremost and in the political sphere only to safeguard and expand those protections. While the 19th Amendment had encouraged participatory citizenship based on group- and other-oriented claims, later women's rights policies invited group claims without necessarily encouraging a broader conception of participatory citizenship. Thus, as I demonstrate, policy feedback effects are contingent on the type of inclusion they envision.

Why Care about Women's Groups?

Since ratification of universal female suffrage in 1920, women as individuals have made enormous strides in terms of participation in public life, gaining in both absolute terms and relative to men. Women go to college and vote at higher rates than men do. In the three most recent presidential administrations, a female has served as secretary of state as well as in other important executive positions. In 2008, a woman, Hillary Clinton, came close to being her party's nominee for president. From 2007 to 2011, a woman, Nancy Pelosi, served as Speaker of the House, presiding over a burst of lawmaking that included the realization of long-elusive goals such as fundamental health care reform. In the Senate during this era, two independent-minded women from Maine often decided key votes. While women remained quite underrepresented in both the House and the Senate (holding roughly 17 percent of the seats in the 111th Congress), the number of female members of Congress rose impressively throughout the 1990s and 2000s. Women are doing well, it seems.

Women's success in traditionally male spheres forces us to confront an uncomfortable question: Why should we care about the fate of single-sex organizations? After all, women have never had more opportunities to participate in public life as individual voters, donors, and policymakers and as members and leaders of nongendered organizations. To many young women, female-only associations seem like a relic of a bygone era when women had to organize in a "separate sphere" of collective action to have any influence. Is the declining prominence of women's groups and their concomitant specialization in feminist issues cause for concern?

For several reasons, I suggest that the answer is yes. As this book demonstrates, women's groups traditionally have been and remain important drivers of female civic engagement. Gender, together with its associated narratives and rituals, provides solidary and purposive incentives that offset the free-rider problem (Olson 1965; James Q. Wilson 1995). Women's organizations are particularly adept at providing practical skills training that women can carry into politics and public affairs (Burns, Schlozman, and Verba 2001, 230). Furthermore, women's groups matter because women remain vastly underrepresented in positions of political leadership, whether in legislatures, statehouses, and cabinet agencies or in citizens', professional, industry, business, trade, and educational associations (Shaiko 1996, 1997; see also chapter 8). Even when women do lead, they must be attuned to other interests in and around their positions—voting constituencies, party bosses, the president, congressional committees, boards of directors, donors, and so forth. Simply put, female leaders in mixed-gender settings cannot serve as single-minded champions of women's concerns.

If women's organizations are still relevant to women's political voice, then it matters how those organizations conceive of and represent their constituencies. The move away from broad policy interests and other-regarding difference rationales threatens women's groups' ability to represent the full spectrum of women's interests and perspectives. In a careful and pathbreaking study, Dara Strolovitch (2006; 2007) has shown that many women's groups do a poor job of representing marginalized women with bread-and-butter concerns, such as income maintenance.[7] But the question of representation may be even broader. Surveys suggest that while men and women agree on most issues, there are certain clusters of social and foreign policies in which women, as a group, have different opinions and priorities than do men (Goss and Skocpol 2006).

The equality orientation of women's organizations may limit their capacity to engage in the wide range of policy debates—including those where there is a gender gap—in the same way that these groups did when they were able to call on the full range of women's civic identities. When women's groups had the flexibility to draw on other-regarding civic identities, it was easy to adapt organizational agendas to engage in the issues of the day. In contrast, when women's groups limit themselves to civic identities centered on gender equality, policy advocates must locate a self-evident, compelling connection between women's rights and the policy at hand (say, nondiscrimination in employment) or sit back and wait for Congress to see the "feminist angle" as integral to the policy proposal. I hypothesize that as women's groups moved from maternal and civic orientations to feminist ones, they had increasing difficulty staking out central roles in many policy debates.

Looking Ahead

The following chapters tell the story of how a diverse constituency group, American women, has acted collectively to try to influence national public policy from shortly after the end of the Civil War through the dawn of the 21st century. Chapter 2 explores American women's collective action from the Gilded Age through the 1950s. I review the conventional and revisionist accounts of these decades and then evaluate them in light of the data on women's presence on Capitol Hill, including both the volume and policy orientation of their testimony and the nature of the organizations representing women's interests and perspectives in the halls of power. Chapter 3 picks up the story, presenting the conventional and alternative accounts of the feminist movements spanning the 1960s through 2000 and evaluating these different stories in light of the data. Chapters 4 and 5 take a closer look at the components of these historical developments. Chapter 4 examines three dimensions of change: the types of organizations appearing before Congress, the ways they established their political bona fides, and the issues they sought to influence. Chapter 5 zeroes in on foreign policy and health care testimony to track the evolution in women's civic place. The next two chapters unravel the reasons behind these observed changes. Chapter 6 systematically weighs the evidence for a host of possible explanations, laying to rest some (e.g., changes in Congress) while finding limited support for others (e.g., the movement of women into the paid labor force and the emergence of interest groups in issue niches that women's groups once dominated). Chapter 7 offers the book's core argument: that public policy, interacting with and reinforced by some of these larger social and political developments, shaped the evolution of women's groups' policy advocacy. Finally, Chapter 8 reflects on why the fate of women's organizations matters for women's citizenship and for democracy at large.

TWO

Suffrage and the Rise of Women's Policy Advocacy

In 1924, four years after American women had won the constitutional right to vote, the president of the newly formed National League of Women Voters reflected on what women's political incorporation had meant. "When we worked for suffrage," Maud Wood Park said, "I doubt that many of us believed that there was anything wonderful in being able to put some marks on a piece of paper and drop it into a box three or four times a year." Rather, she suggested, the vote was a means toward a larger end: "We thought of the ballot as a tool with which great things were to be done" on behalf of "the human welfare side of government." Working for policies that advanced the general welfare, she argued, "is a glorious thing to be doing" (Stuhler 2003, 111–12).

Maud Wood Park's reflections and aspirations offer a useful starting point for analyzing the evolution of women's public engagement in America. First and foremost, she clearly articulates the notion that policy (in this case, suffrage) is more than a goal or culminating achievement of social movements; policy also has the potential to unleash its beneficiaries' potential to advance broader issue agendas. In contemporary parlance, policy structures civic engagement. Second, Park's quotation previews women's policy agenda broadly speaking. Women's groups, such as the League of Women Voters, would advocate on behalf of policies that put the government in the business of advancing "human welfare," much as women were advancing human welfare through family, church, and charity. Newly enfranchised, women were going to make the state act more like a woman (McDonagh 2010).

Ratification of the 19th Amendment serves as the centerpiece of this chapter, which examines the evolution of women's participatory citizenship from 1880 to 1960. Suffrage occurred exactly halfway through this period, allowing us to examine women's collective engagement both before and after the extension of this fundamental political right. In the conventional wave narrative, women's engagement is said to have grown in the decades leading up to 1920, crested with ratification or shortly thereafter, then fallen in the aftermath, ultimately bringing the tide of women's mobilization to its lowest ebb by midcentury. However, some historians have argued that rather than fading away, women's activity after the first wave continued—if not at movement levels, at least at respectable ones. This chapter allows us to evaluate the merits of these two competing accounts and to begin to address how women's collective engagement has evolved over time.

First, I provide a brief overview of two distinct female-led movements that operated in the decades leading up to ratification of the 19th Amendment: the "woman movement" for wide-ranging social reforms and the movement for state and national suffrage. The suffrage movement, with its growth before 1920 and its purported crash thereafter, forms the first incarnation of the wave narrative. I then review the two decades that are said to exemplify the crashing-and-ebbing phase of the wave narrative, the 1920s and the 1950s. I also review revisionist arguments that see women's engagement as more of a continuum—rivers of engagement that may branch in different directions but nevertheless embody powerful currents of ongoing activism.

After laying the historical groundwork, I present systematic evidence of women's organizational engagement from roughly 1880 to 1960, a period that encompasses both the gathering-and-cresting and crashing-and-ebbing periods. By at least three metrics—volume of congressional testimony, number of groups testifying, and breadth of issue interests—the traditional account of women's postsuffrage quiescence is not just off base but flat wrong. The 1920s–50s actually was an unusually busy period for newly incorporated American women, who greatly expanded their civic place. Women's groups worked in female-led and mixed-gender coalitions to advocate not only for traditional concerns such as women's and children's well-being but also for emerging issues and those we might consider the province of men.

Women's Activities before Suffrage

Women have traditionally occupied different private and public roles from men, and these differences have shaped the two sexes' different paths toward political incorporation and full citizenship. The "cult of true womanhood," developed in the 19th century, identified women as morally virtuous and altruistic (Welter 1966). This conception gave rise to a "doctrine of spheres," in which women had dominion over a private, family realm, while men occupied the public realm of politics and market (Muncy 1991). In this world of separate spheres, women sought to exercise their voice and influence through moral reform societies, churches, and charities, which occupied a space between the private/female and public/male arenas (Baker 1984).

The doctrine of spheres and the ideational and legal framework that reinforced it seemed to afford women little latitude to venture into the halls of policymaking. However, by the Gilded Age (roughly 1870–90) and particularly in the Progressive Era (1890–1920), educated women had found a way to broaden women's sphere to legitimate their engagement in the public world of politics and to shape issue agendas. The rhetorical trump they used was "municipal housekeeping," a term attributed to the settlement house and peace activist Jane Addams to connote the notion that communities were merely extensions of the home and thereby constituted appropriate targets for women's special skills and virtues. A key mechanism that women used to perform municipal housekeeping was the locally rooted, often nationally federated mass-membership association (Skocpol 1992). Years before they had the constitutional right to vote, women had created a "female dominion" within the policy sphere that included bureaucrats, educators, settlement house workers, lobbyists, and millions of members of women's voluntary associations (Muncy 1991).

In the latter decades of the 19th century, "women's organizations increased so rapidly in number and variety that by 1900 no one had any idea how many or how many different kinds of associations there were" (A. Scott 1991, 81). The rapidly expanding female voluntary sector encompassed millions of civically resourceful women. By 1920, the National Congress of Mothers and Parent-Teacher Associations claimed 200,000 members.[1] The Woman's Christian Temperance Union, founded in 1874 and led for many years by the indomitable Frances Willard, claimed 500,000 members.[2] The mighty General Federation of Women's Clubs, organized in 1890, was the largest of all, with 1.5 million members in 12,000 clubs.[3] Its African-American counterpart, the National Association of Colored Women, had 100,000 members as of 1917, when it testified before Congress to demand an investigation of the racially motivated murders of African Americans in East St. Louis, Illinois.[4]

These and other women's groups—such as the Association of Collegiate

Alumnae (founded in 1882), the National Consumers League (founded in 1899), and the National Women's Trade Union League (founded in 1903)—engaged in campaigns to promote human welfare through both governmental and nongovernmental approaches. Among the issues on women's agenda in these years were Prohibition, prison reform, minimum-wage and maximum-hour laws for factory women, sex education in schools, peace, antilynching laws, women's pensions, and children's health (Bordin 1981; A. Scott 1991; Skocpol 1992). Thus, before suffrage, women's organizations were vigorously organizing around women's specific rights and needs and around other-oriented goals—what Willard referred to as the "Do Everything" agenda (Bordin 1981).

Alongside the "woman movement" for social reform was an equally vigorous, more focused movement for female suffrage. What scholars now call the first wave of feminism traced its origins to 1848, when abolitionists, including Lucretia Mott and Elizabeth Cady Stanton, gathered in Upstate New York for the Seneca Falls Convention to articulate the desperate need for the long-overdue incorporation of women citizens into the American polity. The convention produced a Declaration of Sentiments laying out foundational principles, grievances, and political demands on behalf of women. Self-consciously echoing the Declaration of Independence, the drafters asserted, "All men *and women* are created equal" and "are endowed by their Creator with certain inalienable rights" (1889, 70–71; emphasis added). The Declaration stated that men had maintained "an absolute tyranny" over women and had inflicted "repeated injuries and usurpations" on them. Among these wrongs, men had deprived women of the right to vote, stripped married women of civil standing, and compelled all women to submit to laws that they had no voice in formulating.

The women who attended the convention had cut their activist teeth in the abolition movement, which had taught them the basic skills of mass mobilization—organizing, holding public meetings, and running petition campaigns (Flexner 1959). "As abolitionists they first won the right to speak in public, and began to evolve a philosophy of their place in society and of their basic rights" (41). Although the groundwork was laid in 1848, the suffrage movement did not organize in earnest until after the Civil War, with the formation in 1869 of two organizations: the American Woman Suffrage Association, based in Boston and led by Henry Blackwell, Henry Ward Beecher, and Lucy Stone; and the more radical National Woman Suffrage Association, based in New York and led by Elizabeth Cady Stanton and Susan B. Anthony. In 1890, the groups merged to become the National American Woman Suffrage Association. Later, Alice Paul's more radical Congressional Union (1913) and Woman's Party (1916) emerged as prominent suffrage movement organizations.

The equal rights framework, first expressed in the Declaration of Sentiments, dominated the early decades of the suffrage movement (Kraditor 1971). But in the 1910s, a second line of argument came to prominence: The vote would enable women to apply their special skills and sensitivities to the improvement of government, policy, and society. The "expediency" rationale (Kraditor 1971) helped to broaden the base of the suffrage movement by drawing elements from the "woman movement" of social reformers. For example, the Woman's Christian Temperance Union's Willard referred to suffrage as "the home protection ballot," meaning that enfranchisement would advance the cause of Prohibition and thereby help women, children, and families (A. Scott 1991, 96). The expediency rationale resonated in an era of early state building, when localities and to some extent state and national governments had begun to assume social welfare functions that had been the province of female-led voluntary societies and charities (Kraditor 1971). If the state was performing womanly functions, wouldn't it benefit from women's experience and insights?

As the final congressional debate over female suffrage approached, women's organizations were engaged in two separate yet mutually reinforcing movements. Both asserted through word and deed an important role for women as citizens, contributing alongside men to democratic governance. Both movements also strategically balanced competing ideas about women's place in the public sphere. Women were both the same as men, endowed with equal God-given rights, and different from men in the possession of distinctive caregiving experiences and moral sensibilities. Eileen McDonagh (2010) has argued that the ability of Progressive Era women to combine these two understandings of women's place was critical to their influence in early state-building efforts. In sum, the years leading up to 1920 constituted the gathering-and-cresting era in the first wave of American feminism. However, history suggests that the suffrage wave gained strength from other female-led social reform movements unfolding at the same time. This insight—about how women's movements understand "women's issues"—is central to unraveling the puzzles of women's engagement.

The 1920s: A Long Postsuffrage Crash?

The notion of waves of mobilization directs our attention to a gathering force and a heightening presence—the part of the wave that rises. But as anyone who has ever lain on a beach to watch the surf knows, waves also crash. Social scientists focus on the gathering and cresting stages, which are both perplexing and exciting, while often viewing the crashing stage as axiomatic—an afterthought worthy of limited interest or inquiry. And so it was with the early studies of the first wave women's movement for suffrage.

Predictions that women's political engagement and influence would drop with enfranchisement began even before suffrage was ratified. Indeed, the threat of waning influence was one of the core arguments of the antisuffrage movement, whose leaders and foot soldiers were largely women. Antisuffragists argued vociferously that enfranchising women would undermine women's efforts to mobilize collectively for social reform by eliminating the separate, nonpartisan sphere in which women found the moral and organizational grounding for their public work (Jablonsky 1994; S. Marshall 1997). The thought was that women would be absorbed into the political parties, where their demands would be diluted and dismissed (Kraditor 1971).

Modern scholarship has lent credence to this tenet of antisuffragist doomsaying. To many contemporary historians, 1920 marked the beginning of a gradual downward spiral in women's capacity to organize and speak with a collective voice. The story of the 1920s usually begins with the observation that newly enfranchised women did not vote as a bloc or even vote at all, thereby undermining the imperative for elected officials to attend to female preferences. Because the 19th Amendment's "results had not matched expectations" (Lemons 1973, 228), women's "standing in the eyes of politicians dropped precipitously" (Chafe 1972, 29), and "women's access and influence in the political arena after 1925 were greatly reduced" (Klein 1984, 14). Barbara Ryan (1992, 37) concludes that there "was no clear direction after the suffrage victory." Women's organizations were not equipped to mount successful lobbying campaigns among newly enfranchised females (Harvey 1998), and the political climate of the 1920s "proved to be bad for women's organizing" (Banaszak 2006, 6). Furthermore, by "adopting formerly male values and behavior," newly enfranchised women "lost the basis for a separate political culture," leaving them without uniquely "women's issues" around which to organize and prompting their political fragmentation (Baker 1984, 644–45). While perhaps not lapsing into inactivity, women's groups "instead became more diverse and disunited" (Costain 1992, 26, citing Cott 1987).

By 1924, "little remained of a nationally organized women's movement" (Ferree and Hess 2000, 1). Instead, women's collective engagement foundered on "the monumental unresolved issue of the suffrage movement—

whether women would fare better in society if they had the same legal rights and responsibilities as men or whether their biological and social differences from males required laws tailored to meet their special needs" (Costain 1992, 27). Unable to settle on sameness or difference as the ideational basis for collective action, some scholars argued, women's groups lost their ability to pool their collective influence. By 1930, one such account asserts, women had "ceased to engage in autonomous political action on behalf of expanded state responsibility" (Sklar 1993, 77). By another account, the "woman movement as a whole was dead. . . . The sisterly feeling between women's organizations, and the vague unifying ethic accompanying that feeling, did not survive the 1920s" (O'Neill 1971, 263). Women were said to have abandoned collective action on matters of public concern and turned to private pursuits such as marriage and family (Kaminer 1984).

Nancy F. Cott (1992, 154) effectively summarizes what she terms the "composite portrayal of women's politics in the 1920s":

> After the achievement of the vote, the large coalition movement among women disintegrated; now insiders rather than outsiders, women (ironically) lost influence within the political process. Suffragists' predictions of transformation in politics through women's contributions were not realized. No longer operating from strong women-only voluntary organizations nor avidly showing their strength as unified voices, women were not as aggressive as men in pursuing political advantage in a still highly male-dominated system.

While elements of the declensionist story are plausible, skeptical historians have taken issue with the portrait of women as making laggardly contributions to politics and policy in the 1920s. For example, Paul Kleppner (1982) has suggested that larger political forces played an important role in the declining voter rates that are often blamed on women; indeed, he finds that, if voting had remained a male preserve, one-third of states would have seen statistically commensurate declines in turnout observed after suffrage. Kristi Andersen (1996) documents the incorporation of women into political parties and local and state elected offices. These studies, then, suggest that suffrage at best had underappreciated benefits for women's political participation or at least did not cause undue harm to America's participatory spirit.

Even stronger critiques of the declensionist narrative come from studies that have focused on women's traditional domain—the informal sphere of politics encompassing voluntary action through pressure groups. It should not be surprising that evaluating the effects of suffrage on individual measures of political participation—voting, running for office—may underestimate the effects of suffrage on women's engagement. After all, women were not accustomed to operating as free agents; rather, they were accustomed to working together, pooling their skills and voices through voluntary associations. Thus, it seems rather curious to evaluate the effect of suffrage on unfamiliar political activity while ignoring the more plausible scenario that inclusionary policies would have their greatest impact on forms of engagement with which women were already comfortable and experienced.

Along these lines, Cott has suggested the existence of a great deal of continuity in the scope and volume of women's collective engagement after 1920. Women's groups immediately retooled for the new era of women's politics. In 1920, the National American Woman Suffrage Association transformed itself into the National League of Women Voters to pursue multiple aims, including the "political education of women," the dissemination of disinterested information on parties and candidates, the advancement of "better legislation on matters for which women should be primarily responsible," and the unification of "the country's woman power into a new force for the humanizing of government" (Stuhler 2003, 37). The League also played the leading role in creating a large advocacy coalition, the Women's Joint Congressional Committee, which by 1924 included 21 women's organizations with a combined membership of 12 million women (Jan Wilson 2007, 21). The committee sought to bring the suffrage movement's "spirit of unity and cooperation" to bear on an ambitious policy agenda, including a national maternal and child health program, the federal government's first major foray into the financing of health care (19, 26).

In his seminal 1928 book, *Group Representation before Congress*, Pendleton Herring observed that women's lobbies were the second-most-common form of interest group, after trade associations (cited in Truman 1951, 100). Women's groups also were active on the state level, racking up numerous policy victories that belie the conventional story of women's waning influence (Andersen 1996). In the 122-year period covered in this study, the League of Women Voters—the organization that suffrage bequeathed—has appeared more times before Congress than any other women's group.

The 1950s: Retreating into Domesticity?

After a brief mobilization to support the troops during World War II, women are often portrayed as falling into a cult of domesticity. Wifely and maternal obligations are said to have hindered women's potential to engage fully in the rights and responsibilities of citizenship. Betty Friedan's seminal work, *The Feminine Mystique* (1963), described a world in which midcentury homemakers fixated on family and femininity while shunning positions of leadership in voluntary associations and other roles in the public sphere (235). Indeed, politically engaged women's voluntary associations of the sort featured in this study barely figured into Friedan's book—and then more as forums for the expression of female dissatisfaction than as vehicles for women's political empowerment (15–16).

Later scholars picked up this line, arguing that the conservative political climate of the 1950s "combined with a serious constriction of opportunities for women in education and the professions to severely limit the context in which women's organizations could function" (Levine 1995, 83). Perhaps as a result, "thoughts of political power . . . had no place in the 1950s' American housewife and mother image" (Ryan 1992, 36). A few accounts of "pockets" of women's political resistance notwithstanding, most histories of the 1950s "stress the postwar domestic ideal, the reassertion of a traditional sexual division of labor, and the formal and informal barriers that prevented women from fully participating in the public realm" (Meyerowitz 1994, 3). One scholar of the second wave movement declared the 1950s "stifling for women" (Davis 1999, 9). Barbara Ryan (1992, 36) suggests that, after three decades dominated by the "mythical ideal" of traditional family relations, "most people never even knew there had been a women's movement" in the late 19th and early 20th century.

And yet, as with the 1920s, evidence shows that women were more active in the 1950s than the standard *Leave It to Beaver* narrative of female domesticity would suggest. Robert Putnam (2000) sees the 1950s as the apex of 20th-century public engagement, with women occupying a central role as civic caretakers. This observation is backed by a 1956 nationwide survey of members of the League of Women Voters finding that 85 percent belonged to at least two other organizations and more than one-third belonged to five or more (Ware 1992, 284). Two years before she published *The Feminine Mystique*, portraying women as prisoners of the cult of domesticity, Friedan reported that the real source of women's frustration was an overload of volunteer activities (Ware 1992, 290). In his famous study of interest groups at midcentury, David Truman (1951, 100) reported that women's associations were "both influential and numerous." While dwarfed in number by business groups, women's groups constituted the largest segment of what might be called the "citizen group" sector. And, if their chapters are counted, the number of women's groups—estimated at 100,000—dominated business, labor, and civic organizations (Truman 1951, 58).

Underscoring Truman's evidence, feminist historians have sought to bring to prominence the political activities of midcentury women. In the run-up to World War II, small yet vocal right-wing groups, such as Mothers of Sons Forum, the Women's National Committee to Keep the U.S. Out of War, and Mothers of the U.S.A., campaigned against the lend-lease program to aid Britain and for U.S. isolationism generally (Jeansonne 1996). Later, groups such as the General Federation of Women's Clubs and Minute Women of America took up the charge of anticommunism (Brennan 2008). Women's groups at the center and on the left of the political spectrum were also active during these years. Amid the "social climate of antifeminism" of the 1950s, the National Woman's Party advanced the cause of the Equal Rights Amendment (Rupp and Taylor 1987, 18). The Young Women's Christian Association championed racial justice by lobbying for civil rights legislation targeting lynching and the poll tax and by institutionalizing education programs to encourage cross-race friendship and understanding (Lynn 1994). Working-class women joined labor unions in droves—membership tripled between the late 1930s and the early 1950s—and began to agitate at local, state, and national levels on policies such as maternity leave, child care, and equal pay (Cobble 2004).

The League of Women Voters, whose membership grew by 44 percent from 1950 to 1958, created myriad opportunities for women to engage in local, state, and national policy advocacy and to prepare themselves for elective office in later life (Ware 1992; Young 1989). The American Association of University Women offered similar opportunities to elite women (Levine 1995). By the early 1960s, Women Strike for Peace had organized in 100 communities to agitate for nuclear disarmament (Swerdlow 1993). And Costain (1992) documents significant women's rights–related advocacy by traditional women's groups from 1950–55. Ethel Klein (1984, 18) argues that, by the 1950s, women's groups were "an established lobby" with "greater political sophistication" than they had demonstrated during more outwardly activist periods.

Thus, in both the 1920s and 1950s, anecdotal evidence challenges the view that women's activism crashed and ebbed after suffrage. Yet the narrative of women's retreat from politics has a powerful hold on the imagination: The 1920s woman is the flirty flapper in a speakeasy; the 1950s woman is Betty Crocker in the kitchen. The suffrage movement unfolded over 50 years and culminated in only the ninth change to the U.S. Constitution since the founding period. How could collective momentum in the face of such a consequential victory possibly be sustained? What went up before the 1920s, it seems, had to come down.

Does Legal Citizenship Boost Participatory Citizenship?

The contested narratives about the postsuffrage era present three obvious hypotheses about the relationship between legal citizenship (policy), on the one hand, and participatory citizenship (advocacy), on the other. The first hypothesis is that the expansion of political rights will be followed by a decline in collective engagement, as unity and urgency of purpose dissolve and as conservative tides sweep in. This is the hypothesis underlying the wave narrative as well as of popular accounts of the 1920s and 1950s. A second hypothesis is that policies of civic inclusion will be accompanied by little or no change in the target group's participation in politics. This perspective is embedded in arguments that women's organizing exhibited more continuity than change after suffrage. A third hypothesis is that policies of civic inclusion will expand civic participation by delivering resources and creating a sense of belonging among the beneficiary group. This is the story that policy feedback perspectives offer (Mettler and Soss 2004). Here, movements continue to have an impact through the civil, political, and social rights that they have seen enacted into law. These policies both structure opportunities and agendas for further engagement and shape the beneficiaries' sense of inclusion—their civic place. In sum, feedback theorists believe that public policy and public engagement are locked in a virtuous circle of self-reinforcing dynamics.

What Happened? Women's Policy Advocacy on Capitol Hill, 1920–1960

From the 1920s through 1960, the federal government's policy endeavors grew. So, too, did American women's organizations. Contrary to narratives of decline through the "docile" 1950s, women's organizations ramped up their participation in national policy debates. The impressive growth in their public participation shows up in any number of ways. I focus on five measures, all of which tell basically the same story. These measures are (1) the number of appearances as witnesses before congressional hearings;

(2) the number of appearances adjusted for number of hearings; (3) the likelihood of testifying on important legislation; (4) the number of groups testifying; and (5) the range of policy domains covered.

Appearances at Congressional Hearings, 1877–1960

Figure 2.1 presents the simplest snapshot of the periods before and after suffrage: total appearances before Congress as well as the number of appearances adjusted for the number of hearings that congressional committees and subcommittees held. Beginning at the turn of the 20th century, women's groups began a steady, though not monotonic, rise in prominence on Capitol Hill.

As the figure shows, the peak came in 1945–48, when women's groups were working on, and Congress was considering, a wide range of issues arising from the New Deal and the war, including housing, health insurance, foreign aid, European reconstruction, and the Equal Rights Amendment. The breadth of the women's agenda accounts for the magnitude of their presence, but before turning to that argument, I will dispense with another intriguing explanation—that women's groups' robust engagement at midcentury resulted from what Dorothy Sue Cobble (2004) has identified as

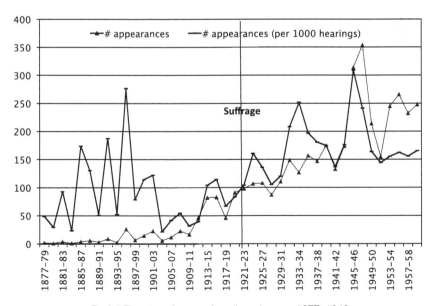

Fig. 2.1. The rise of women's policy advocacy, 1877–1960

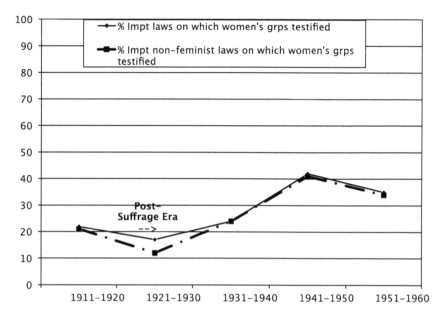

Fig. 2.2. Rise in women's groups' engagement with landmark laws.
(Data from Stathis 2003; relevant hearings identified by author using
Lexis-Nexis Congressional.)

a boom time for working-class women's activism. While labor women no
doubt made a difference at the local level and within the labor movement,
as Cobble persuasively argues, women's unions did not drive the midcentury increase in women's presence before Congress. Indeed, women's
unions constituted fewer than 3 percent of all women's group appearances
in the 1940s and 1950s, and nearly all of labor women's appearances were
by two groups, the International Ladies' Garment Workers' Union and the
Women's Trade Union League. The flourishing of women's associational
activity at midcentury, at least in national legislative circles, was not a product of union growth.

The figure also shows the rise in women's advocacy before Congress
adjusted for the total number of hearings held in any given Congress. This
view provides a sense of women's prominence relative to the opportunities to take part. The two patterns tell a broadly similar story: a steady yet
punctuated rise in women's appearances that peaked in the second half of
the 1940s. After adjusting for the number of hearings, however, two differences emerge: greater prominence in the late 19th century (most of which
was agitation for suffrage) and a dip in prominence in the 1950s. Nevertheless, whether one does or does not adjust for number of hearings, the data

clearly show that women's organizations did not fade away after suffrage. Rather, they continued to press their claims at a rate of roughly 1.5–3 times presuffrage levels.[5]

Much the same pattern appears when one considers women's organizations' participation in hearings on important legislation. Figure 2.2 shows the percentage of landmark laws on which at least one women's group testified during the corresponding hearings, either in the Congress in which the law was passed or in the prior Congress. Once again, there was a steady rise in the 1920s–40s with a leveling off in the 1950s. It is a measure of the importance of the women's lobby that groups were invited to offer their input on more than 40 percent of the nation's most important policy questions in the 1940s and 34 percent in the 1950s, eras when women are misleadingly portrayed more as helpmates for male endeavors than as autonomous and authoritative political actors.

Number of Women's Groups Appearing at Hearings, 1870s–1950s

Figure 2.3 offers yet another way of evaluating the pattern of women's national policy engagement before and after suffrage: the number of groups testifying on Capitol Hill. Between the 1910s and the 1950s, the number of women's organizations appearing at congressional hearings grew by 135 percent—and by close to 75 percent from the 1920s. These findings

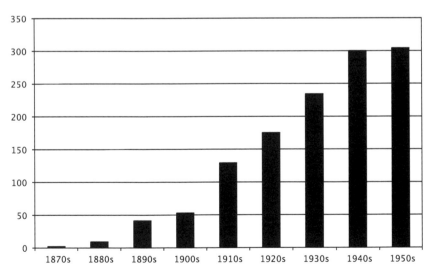

Fig. 2.3. Rise in number of women's groups testifying, 1870s–1950s

underscore Ethel Klein's (1984, 18) observation that the 1940s and 1950s saw the emergence of "an experienced women's lobby" that "provided an organizational context for maintaining or increasing pressure for women's rights in the future." However, these findings challenge her accompanying observation that women's activism "plummeted" at midcentury even as "their access to political decisionmakers grew" (18).

Cott (1992, 166) has argued that "the level of organization among American women after 1920 thus appears to compare very favorably with that before," and these data suggest that, if anything, she underestimated the boom. Cott observes that these groups increasingly organized around specialized constituencies (e.g., professional women, religious women, mothers, women of a particular political orientation) or for specific issues (e.g., birth control, education, peace). Chapter 4 considers the shifting composition of women's organizations, but suffice it to say here that Cott's observation has a good deal of merit.

Scope of Women's Groups' Issue Agendas, 1870s–1950s

Finally, a fifth and very important measure of women's policy engagement is the range of issue domains in which they were invited to testify. Figure 2.4 charts that number. In the 1910s, women's groups testified on legislation spanning 43 issue domains. Data limitations prevent us from figuring what percentage of all 228 possible domains Congress was attentive to at the time (the Policy Agendas Project does not code hearings prior to 1946). However, given the fairly limited scope of the federal government in the pre–New Deal era, it is reasonable to assume that women's groups were active in a good portion of the policy domains in which Congress was legislating. The scope of women's groups' engagement in the 1910s is remarkable given that women did not yet have the constitutional right to vote and were denied many other privileges of citizenship. That said, engagement by women's groups broadened dramatically in each decade after suffrage, reaching 93 issue domains by midcentury. Congress in the 1950s held hearings in 197 policy domains, meaning that women had a voice in nearly half of them.

This measure is fairly generous insofar as it counts women's groups as engaging in a policy domain even if only one group did so over a 10-year period. A more precise and meaningful measure of the scope of women's groups' policy advocacy is the number of issue domains in which women's groups posted at least 10 appearances over the decade. This measure eliminates the "one appearance here, another there" domains and calls our atten-

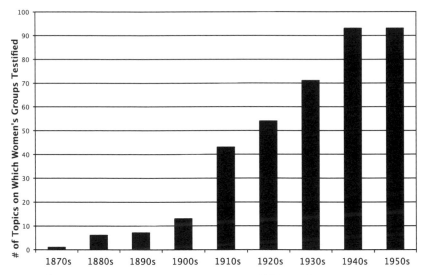

Fig. 2.4. Women's groups' issue interests widened, 1870s–1950s. (Counts based on policy topic codes from Policy Agendas Project; n = 225.)

tion to the domains in which women's groups had a deeper level of interest. By this more stringent measure, a similar pattern emerges: a steady rise through the 1940s, with a slight decline or leveling-off in the 1950s. Under the more stringent measure, women's organizations were still displaying an impressive breadth of policy engagements, with 25–32 issue domains covered in the three to four decades after suffrage.

Summing Up

This chapter began with three competing versions of women's collective engagement after suffrage. One version, the wave narrative, held that suffrage was in some senses a pyrrhic victory, delivering an important political right but leading to a decades-long unraveling of women's collective action that reached a nadir in the placid 1950s. Another version, slightly more sanguine, suggested that suffrage did not deliver a big boost to collective action in the short term but did have spillover effects in other realms, such as state-level policy change and access to political parties (Andersen 1996). This version also held that women's collective action, if not increasing dramatically, did continue at a healthy level. Finally, there is a third possibility, one predicted by policy feedback theory though not fully articulated in conventional histories of women's postsuffrage engagement: that the scope and volume of women's political engagement would rise dramatically once basic political and civil rights were secured. This vision is consistent with the river metaphor, in which women's activism flows and branches across a broad policy terrain. The data indicate that this third possibility most accurately captures the experience of American women's organizations in the period from 1920 to 1960. Simply put, far from retreating into some traditional, apolitical "feminine" sphere after suffrage, women got to work, not only in the public squares of their local communities but also at the highest levels of American government, the committee rooms of Congress.

What Issues Were Women's Groups Working On?

Table 2.1 shows the expansion of women's groups' policy reach from suffrage through midcentury. The table includes all issue domains in which women's groups testified at least 20 times during the decade—that is, issues that might reasonably be termed the "women's issues" of the day. These issues reflect a broad understanding of women's civic place: as rights-bearing citizens, as caretakers of vulnerable populations (including women themselves), and as stewards of the national interest.

TABLE 2.1. Issue Domains With at Least 20 Hearing Appearances by Women's Groups (number of appearances in parentheses)

1910s	1920s	1930s	1940s	1950s
DC affairs (31)[a]	DC affairs (85)	DC affairs (106)	DC affairs (191)	DC affairs (245)
Alcohol abuse and treatment (48)	Child health (43)	Alcohol abuse and treatment (69)	Gender discrimination (85)	International organizations (90)
Voting rights and issues (96)	Alcohol abuse and treatment (35)	Immigration and refugee issues (68)	Manpower, military personnel, dependents, military courts (85)	Defense alliances, security assistance (84)
	Education (general) (35)	Consumer safety and consumer fraud (59)	Agriculture (general) (80)	Manpower, military personnel, dependents, military courts (48)

TABLE 2.1.—*Continued*

1910s	1920s	1930s	1940s	1950s
	Gender discrimination (28)	Gender discrimination (57)	Low and middle income housing (45)	Government operations (budget) (44)
	Immigration and refugee issues (20)	National parks, memorials, historic sites, and recreation (36)	Price control and stabilization (40)	Juvenile justice (30)
		Regulation of drug industry, medical devices, and clinical labs (32)	Labor, employment and immigration (general) (34)	Agriculture (general) (28)
		Manpower, military personnel, dependents, military courts (23)	Elementary and secondary education (30)	Elementary and secondary education (28)
		Corporate mergers, antitrust (21)	Military readiness (28)	Elderly issues (incl. Social Security) (27)
		International organizations (21)	Tax policy (25)	Water resources (25)
			International organizations (22)	Foreign trade (general) (22)
			U.S. foreign aid (22)	U.S. foreign aid (20)
			Immigration and refugee issues (21)	National parks, memorials, historic sites, and recreation (20)
			National parks, memorials, historic sites, and recreation (21)	
			Farm subsidies, disaster insurance (20)	

[a] In each of these decades, women's groups were actively engaged on behalf of the District of Columbia, which lacked home rule and was therefore dependent on Congress for appropriations to run its schools and other public agencies. The appearances on behalf of DC offer a window into the sorts of issues that women's groups were engaging at the local level across the country: public education, crime control and law enforcement, good government, and so forth.

The table offers a general sense of the issue domains in which Congress considered women's groups to have authoritative standing to impart useful policy and political intelligence. That said, the table tells us very little about which dimension(s) of these multifaceted policies women's groups claimed as their own. For example, in the 1930s, women's groups took on the issue of immigration. A closer look at the hearings in question reveals that women's groups were speaking to both broad questions of national interest, such as whether to grant citizenship to foreign-born individuals who conscientiously objected to war, and more narrow feminist questions, such as the right of American women to maintain their U.S. citizenship when they married noncitizens. That testimony on women's rights and well-being issues in many cases will be counted in non-rights-specific policy domains (e.g., immigration, tax policy) raises the possibility that simply counting issue domains in which women's groups have testified will overstate the breadth of their interests. In other words, if women's groups testify in increasing numbers of domains but are always speaking to women's rights or well-being, are their policy interests truly widening in any way that matters?

To examine that question, I coded each of the roughly 10,400 appearances according to whether the women's organization was primarily advocating for women's interests, which I defined as their legal rights, professional status, economic well-being, or physical welfare. Such issues are often feminist issues, but they need not be. Antifeminist groups might take positions—for example, against suffrage, legalized abortion, or the Equal Rights Amendment—because they see these policies as antithetical to women's well-being.

Figure 2.5 charts the percentage of appearances in which the women's group testified primarily on non-women-specific issues (with women's rights, status, or well-being mentioned either not at all or only in passing). The early decades saw an oscillation between testimony on two major feminist issues (suffrage and protective labor legislation for women) and broader moral and patriotic issues that had traditionally been in the domain of "virtuous" womanhood (such as the regulation of vice, protection of children, and honoring of the national heritage). After suffrage passed, women's groups' interest in morality and patriotism continued, but they also moved assertively into a broader range of social, economic, and foreign policy interests. As the figure shows, women's groups continued to press for women's rights, status, and well-being, but a growing share of their testimony concerned nonfeminist issues.

There are many possible explanations for why women's groups in the

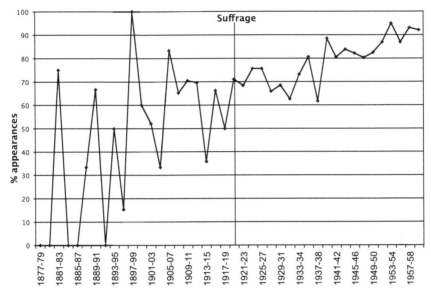

Fig. 2.5. Testimony on non-gender-specific issues, 1877–1960

postsuffrage era spent an ever larger share of their time before Congress advocating for universalistic community, national, and international interests and a smaller share of their time advocating for women's rights, status, and well-being specifically. I take up these explanations in chapter 7.

The Decline of Women's Coalitions?

Arguments about the collapse of the first wave women's movement tend to focus on the unraveling of formal coalitions created after suffrage to press particular legislation. For example, in 1920, the National American Woman Suffrage Association transformed itself into the National League of Women Voters, with an ambitious agenda of educating women for good citizenship and engaging them in multi-issue advocacy. Although it inherited up to 2 million members, the League's roster had dipped to only 79,000 members by 1930 (Kraditor 1971, 5; League of Women Voters 2009). The Women's Joint Congressional Committee, a coalition of nearly every major women's organization, was created in 1920 to carry the momentum of the suffrage movement into a national legislative advocacy. It succeeded in accomplishing its first task, passage of the Sheppard-Towner Maternity and Infancy

Protection Act of 1921. However, by 1930, the committee had largely dissolved (Jan Wilson 2007). These high-profile examples leave the impression that women's organizations were unified before and immediately after suffrage but had difficulty sustaining their collective work. Cott (1992, 168) argues that "although women formed groups of probably greater number and variety in the 1920s than they had ever before, it did not necessarily mean that they could work together nor could any particular group claim—without being countered—to speak politically for women."

That women did not speak with a unified voice is most certainly true. But women's lack of unity was also present before suffrage: Conservative women actively mobilized against the vote, and prosuffrage organizations such as the National American Woman Suffrage Association and the National Woman's Party were deeply divided over goals and strategies. Once the 19th Amendment was ratified, antisuffragists turned their attention to battling Progressive women in a host of policy arenas. Issues such as the Equal Rights Amendment, Prohibition repeal, and entry into war and international organizations splintered women's organizations in the first half of the 20th century and beyond.

Likewise, divisions among women did not preclude their joining formal coalitions or informal networks relating to specific legislative proposals. Women's groups such as the League of Women Voters, the General Federation of Women's Clubs, and the National Congress of Mothers/ PTA—the three most prolific women's groups on Capitol Hill—carried the Progressive banner well after the Progressive Era by testifying in favor of better poultry inspection, more humane treatment of Native Americans, enhanced federal maternal and child health programs, the development of federal parks, federal regulation of firearms, and public support for the United Nations. Although not as numerous or prolific, conservative women's groups also were prominent and well organized, testifying in unison against national health care legislation and "world government," for example, and in favor of limiting the president's power to engage in treaties with other nations.

It is difficult to use aggregate hearing data to measure precisely organizations' work in coalition. One rough proxy, however, is to find hearings where at least one women's group has appeared—that is, hearings that have some connection to women's interests—and to calculate the average number of women's groups that appear at such hearings. To that end, I calculated the average number of appearances, over time, by the 10 most prominent women's groups from 1920 to 1960; all of these groups tended to be on the same side of issues (meaning they were likely coalition partners). The average number of appearances per hearing by these big groups in the 1920s and early 1930s fluctuated between 1.5 and 2; in the 1940s and 1950s, the average was around 1.5—hardly overwhelming evidence for the end of women's groups' capacity to come together around core issues.

Thus, in the postsuffrage decades, women's groups worked in coalitions in numerous issue domains. Those domains included traditional concerns—such as women's rights and alcohol regulation—but also included a broad swath of domestic and foreign policy.

Crest and Crash? Reassessing the Wave Narrative after Suffrage

A linchpin of the crashing-wave narrative is the notion that after suffrage, women's groups fell into disunity. The ratification of the 19th Amendment had left them bereft of the one policy aspiration that had held many of them together, and, with such a long-fought and transformative move toward gender equality, women's groups felt wary about continuing to mobilize based on gender separatism and difference. Women's collective action is portrayed as having collapsed under the weight of its own success in incorporating women into the polity.

In some ways, the women's rights component of the woman movement declined after suffrage. Figure 2.6, the converse of Figure 2.5, shows the fraction of women's group appearances for women's rights, status, and well-being from the two decades leading up to suffrage through the 1960s. The figure looks a bit like a crashing and ebbing wave: a drop in the first years after suffrage followed by a bottoming out of women's political engagement in the 1950s.

However, even as suffrage groups collapsed, the women's organizational sector as a whole expanded and diversified. Prominent groups such as the Woman's Christian Temperance Union and the General Federation of Women's Clubs continued to appear before Congress at a steady pace, but they were joined by new groups—some small and destined to remain that way, others (such as the League of Women Voters) going on to great stature. In her excellent study of large women's organizations at midcentury, A. Lanethea Mathews-Gardner (2005) suggests that after suffrage, traditional women's groups underwent a transformation in identity from "civic" groups to "political" groups. The transformation showed up in changing organizational strategies. Where traditional women's groups had focused on "outside the Beltway" activities, such as organizing local clubs for nonpartisan civic engagement or attempting to mobilize public opin-

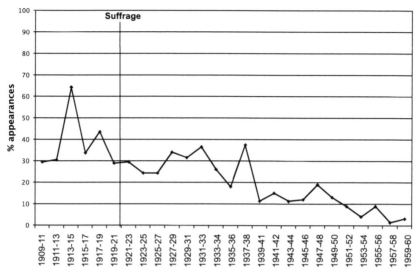

Fig. 2.6. Testimony on women's rights, status, well-being, 1909–60

ion around policy agendas, by midcentury these associations had shifted to more overtly political strategies, such as building up professional lobbying staffs in Washington. Mathews-Gardner (2005, 549) argues that "postwar women's associations were pioneers of experimentation with the sorts of organizational structures, identities, and strategies that would come to define modern-day interest groups, helping to pave the way for new forms of female activism in the latter half of the twentieth century." In this way, midcentury groups were breaking down traditional gendered understandings of citizenship in which women were "civic" but not overly "political" (555).

The other aspect of the crashing-wave narrative holds that women's groups fragmented. I have already suggested that this is not true—women's groups continued to work in coalition on issues such as women's rights, alcohol policy, education, and foreign affairs. But there is a deeper issue with the fragmentation-equals-decline equation. It implies that women as a group are strong politically only when they are collectively focused on a handful of issues. The data here suggest the opposite. Women's organizations' policy priorities did not so much fragment as diversify, allowing women to develop expertise and a unique voice on the broad range of issues of concern to a large and heterogeneous population of newly enfranchised citizens. The sheer number of policy questions over which Congress considered women's groups to be authoritative sources of political and policy information speaks to their centrality in the Washington pressure group community.

Thus, the data challenge the decline narrative, both in terms of its empirical reality and in terms of the arguments that have been offered for it. Bringing in the civic advocacy of the postwave era addresses the inaccurate conflation of feminism and gendered advocacy and the assumption that women's citizenship is necessarily about securing rights and status for women. Focusing on nonfeminist advocacy allows us to see postwave periods in a new light. Rather than a period of quiescence, the decades between suffrage and the revival of the women's movement in the 1960s witnessed a flourishing of women's engagement on important public issues.

The Legacy of Suffrage: Women's Groups, 1920–1960

Women fought for more than 70 years for the constitutional right to vote. That policy victory, which brought women the most fundamental form of political inclusion, was followed by rapid growth in women's presence on Capitol Hill. Women's groups testified more frequently, in greater numbers, and on a broader range of issues than had ever before been the case. As a highly visible and practically meaningful public policy, suffrage itself legitimized and encouraged this expansion in women's civic place. To some feminist historians, the proliferation of women's groups and policy agendas after suffrage signaled a threat to the cohesion of the woman movement. But the data here illuminate how the diversification of women's interests was accompanied by an expansion of their presence in national policy debates.

Let us now consider what happened in the four decades after 1960, a period that witnessed the emergence and flowering of the second great women's rights movement. Would the policy victories achieved by second wave feminists give way to a comparably robust increase in women's collective engagement? Would women's organizations in the postwave era of the 1980s and 1990s find a similarly versatile set of rationales in which to ground their collective action? The answer, it seems, is no.

THREE

The Second Wave
Surges—And Then?

Just as the period from the late 1870s through the 1950s encapsulated a major women's movement, so too did the period from 1960 to 2000. The first wave movement coalesced around suffrage and later around a maternal and child health bill. The second wave movement coalesced around a raft of policies to protect women from institutionalized discrimination and facilitate their access to nontraditional gender roles. The second wave took root in the mid-1960s, reached its heyday in the 1970s, and, depending on the account, either petered out or was institutionalized in the early 1980s. The second wave movement encompassed different ideological strands, such as radical, socialist, cultural, maternal, and liberal (Echols 1989); different notions of women's distinctiveness from men; different temporal incarnations, such as an older branch and a younger branch (Freeman 1975); and different organizational foundations, such as a collectivist mode and a bureaucratic mode (Ferree and Hess 2000; Rothschild-Whitt 1979). Before, during, and after the second wave, women's roles as mothers, workers, and advocates were transformed. As in the suffrage era, the second wave gave birth to a lively debate about whether those transformations and the policy victories that accompanied them would have lasting effects on women's voice and influence in public affairs.

In this chapter, I examine women's organizations' engagement in national policy debates—as measured by congressional hearing testimony—for the 1960–2000 period. I assess whether the wave theory of women's collective engagement, which originated in this era, fits the observed patterns or whether an alternative account—stressing the continuous rivers of post-movement participation—better depicts the reality of women's political history. Three distinct phases unfold in this period: the early 1960s, which began with three major national policy victories advancing women's rights and status; the late 1960s to the early 1980s, when women organized and sustained the second major national female rights movement, which pressured policymakers and social institutions to end the unequal treatment of women in employment, the market, education, government, and the family; and the 1980s–90s, when the women's movement was alternately said to have institutionalized or to have faded away.

Thus, the period from 1960 to 2000, with its massive organizational effort by women and its many feminist policy advances, offers a second opportunity to explore the relationship between the expansion of rights and the scope and nature of political participation. The last chapter showed that contrary to many accounts, the extension of full voting rights to women in 1920 was followed by a steady expansion in their presence on Capitol Hill. Women's groups flourished after suffrage. Their numbers proliferated, their agendas broadened, their prominence at hearings increased, and they played a growing role in important policy debates. For four decades after suffrage, a period that includes the purportedly stifling 1950s, women's groups took full advantage of their newfound constitutional rights to enlarge their voice in American democracy.

The experience of women in the postsuffrage decades raises an obvious question: Was the expansion of women's rights in the period centered on the 1970s likewise followed by an expansion in women's collective engagement in national policy debates? In terms of the familiar wave theory of women's mobilization, the question is whether the women's liberation and rights movements would maintain their momentum or whether they would crash on the shoals of victory, burn out, or endure a backlash. Not surprisingly, as was the case with the postsuffrage era, historians disagree about what happened to second wave feminism. Early popular assessments in the news media and in some scholarly works, proclaimed that the second wave movement had died by the 1980s, and some observers went so far as to claim that feminism itself, as an identity frame for collective action, had likewise fallen into disrepute. By these accounts, the wave crashed. More recently, however, scholars have argued that feminism as a movement and an identity did not fade away but merely changed forms. The wave rolled on; it just looked different.

I evaluate these competing perspectives with evidence from women's groups' appearances on Capitol Hill, together with supporting evidence from secondary sources. First, I introduce the early 1960s, which marked a lull in women's organizational engagement but witnessed the enactment of important public policies that would shape the movement to come. I then briefly review the period from the mid-1960s through 1980, when the women's movement flourished in its more public form. I show that, indeed, the early policy victories of the 1960s eventually were followed by an expansion in women's organizational engagement. Finally, I look at the postwave period from 1980 to 2000, where the pattern is very different. The feminist victories of the 1970s were followed not by an expansion in women's collective engagement on Capitol Hill but by a dramatic retrenchment. I conclude by pointing to the puzzling and perhaps counterintuitive connection between women's status and women's voice at the end of the 20th century.

Early 1960s: The Policy Origins of the Second Wave Movement

Looking back, Americans have come to view the 1960s as a transitional decade, a bridge between the postwar 1950s and the social movement foment of the 1970s—hence the expression, "Most of the 1960s happened in the 1970s." Women's groups both drove and got caught up in those social changes.

Women's move away from traditional roles had begun during World War II and accelerated in the 1950s, a decade, ironically, that popular culture and mythology associate with the essence of traditionalism. In fact, however, female labor-force participation among the iconic "middle American woman"—a white, married female aged 35–44—rose sharply in the 1950s and 1960s (Goldin 2006, 4). Labor-force participation by women with preschool-aged children rose by more than 50 percent in the 1960s (Klein 1984, 39). By 1970, nearly half of married white women were working outside the home. These demographic trends were reinforced by opinion data showing liberalizing attitudes toward female employment. Fully 44 percent of the public supported employment by married women in 1967, up from just 25 percent two decades earlier. Public support for giving women, regardless of situation, the same job opportunities as men also doubled during that time (Klein 1984, 90–91).

In a further move away from traditional roles, women of the postwar decades began marrying later and having fewer children—fertility rates declined by 25 percent over the 1960s (Klein 1984, 55). The divorce rate doubled between 1960 and 1975 (Klein 1984, 73). Women also grew more educated; the fraction of college graduates who were female rose by roughly 10 percentage points during the 1960s (Wolbrecht 2000, 151). As Claudia Goldin (2006, 14) has observed, "These changes altered the identity of women and shifted it from a family- and household-centered world to a wider one that was more career oriented."

The demographic changes that began in the 1950s and continued or even accelerated in the 1960s laid the groundwork for significant political and policy attention to women, particularly employed women. These policy developments in turn laid the groundwork for the second wave movement. Three early policies in particular facilitated the development of the second wave movement: the creation of commissions on the status of women; the Equal Pay Act of 1963, and Civil Rights Act of 1964.

Commissions on the Status of Women

Even before the 1960 presidential election, the major political parties had grown aware that women constituted a potentially important bloc of voters (Costain 1992, 33). In the 1950s, President Dwight D. Eisenhower had urged Congress to pass equal pay legislation and endorsed the Equal Rights Amendment (ERA) (Costain 1992, 35). Having narrowly won the 1960 presidential election, John F. Kennedy quickly turned his attention to strategies for consolidating the female vote. Acting on a suggestion from one of his advisers, Esther Peterson, he created the Presidential Commission on the Status of Women.

Established in 1961 in part to quell agitation for the ERA, the commission consisted of prominent figures from government, labor, academe, and women's organizations. In 1963, it issued a high-profile set of recommendations to advance women's equality and access. The proposals included a ban on sex discrimination in government employment and federal contracting, the appointment of more women to federal policymaking positions, the passage of "equal pay for comparable work" policies, enactment of special group benefits such as paid maternity leave and more generous widows' benefits under Social Security, and greater flexibility in employment and academic environments to accommodate women with domestic responsibilities (Carabillo, Meuli, and Csida 1993, 4–5).

Feminist scholars have long recognized the commission's role in providing resources, networks, legitimacy, and a political opportunity for the emergence of the second wave movement (Costain 1992; Davis 1999; Klein 1984; Wolbrecht 2000). Christina Wolbrecht (2000, 136) notes that, to the average woman, "the massive evidence uncovered by the Kennedy

Commission . . . led to the realization that women experience systematic and widespread inequality." To participants in the 1960s social movements, the wake-up call was the "disparity between the ideals of those movements and the treatment of female activists" (Wolbrecht 2000, 136; see also Evans 1980). After the commission had completed its work, several national councils and state-level commissions carried forward its work. I discuss their impact on women's organizations in chapter 7.

The Equal Pay Act of 1963

In 1963, Congress passed the Equal Pay Act, which required employers subject to the Fair Labor Standards Act to establish equal pay scales for men and women. Women's groups, including the National Federation of Business and Professional Women's Clubs and the General Federation of Women's Clubs, had long favored equal pay legislation, and President Eisenhower, a Republican, had endorsed it in his 1956 State of the Union address (Costain 1992, 33).

Peterson spearheaded the act from within the Labor Department, enlisting the efforts of Morag Simchack, a lobbyist for the United Rubber Workers (Carabillo, Meuli, and Csida 1993, 6). At the bill's signing, President Kennedy was flanked by representatives from leading traditional women's groups, including the Young Women's Christian Association, the National Council of Jewish Women, the National Federation of Business and Professional Women, and the National Council of Catholic Women. The president noted that this measure was just the start of help for working women and expressed hope that Congress would pass budget proposals providing $8 million for day care centers and a tax-law amendment that would permit deductions for child care (M. Smith 1963).

The 1964 Civil Rights Act

The year after the Equal Pay Act passed, a third landmark women's rights policy was enacted. Title VII of the Civil Rights Act of 1964 barred sex discrimination in employment more broadly. The provision is often portrayed in histories as a political fluke. In December 1963, with the Civil Rights Act heading to the floor for debate, the National Woman's Party contacted Representative Howard W. Smith (D-VA), a longtime sponsor of the ERA, to ask him to introduce an amendment barring discrimination against women, which he did on February 8, 1964. Feminist Congresswoman Martha Griffiths (D-MI) said that he later told her he had introduced the amendment as a joke, and other male members took it as such (Carabillo, Meuli, and Csida 1993, 9–10). The mocking tone and clear sexism of the debate galvanized female members, and the amendment passed and stayed in the final version of the bill, which cleared the House two days later (10–11). Under pressure from the business and professional women's clubs, the Senate passed the companion bill in June 1964, the House passed the Senate version, and the bill was signed into law on July 2, 1964 (10–11).

Key to the development of second wave feminism was the provision creating an enforcement body, the Equal Employment Opportunity Commission (EEOC), which was officially established in 1965. The only female member at the time, Aileen Hernandez, said that its meetings "produced a sea of male faces, nearly all of which reflected attitudes that ranged from boredom to virulent hostility whenever the issue of sex discrimination was raised" (Carabillo, Meuli, and Csida 1993, 13). One important EEOC meeting in California was held at a private club that barred women (13). The EEOC's early rulings on women's top priorities proved unsatisfying. In September 1965, the commission ruled that sex-segregated job ads in newspapers were legal, and two months later, the commission refused to invalidate antiquated state-level protectionist laws that many women workers considered discriminatory (14–17).

How Three Seminal Policies Helped Spur the Second Wave Movement

Although backed by traditional women's groups, these measures did not come at the behest of a massive, well-organized campaign for women's rights. Unlike suffrage and many of the second wave victories to come, these early achievements were largely the result of political entrepreneurship by individual policymakers within the federal government: President Kennedy and Peterson, his Women's Bureau director, in the case of the President's Commission; Representative Edith Green (D-OR) in the case of the Equal Pay Act; and Representatives Smith and Griffiths in the case of Title VII of the Civil Rights Act. Later, feminists within government—including Griffiths, President's Commission member Pauli Murray, and Department of Justice lawyer Mary Eastwood—complained publicly that the EEOC had failed to take women's discrimination complaints seriously. The two EEOC commissioners most sympathetic to feminist appeals, Richard Graham and Hernandez, "privately suggest[ed] the need for an organization to speak on behalf of women in the way that civil rights groups had done for Blacks" (Hole and Levine 1971, 82; quoted in Carabillo, Meuli, and Csida 1993, 19). Women in the U.S. Department of Labor were also quietly leaning on their sisters in organized labor to create "an NAACP for women" (Carabillo, Meuli, and Csida 1993, 20).

These recommendations were realized in 1966, when the National Organization for Women (NOW) was established at the third annual meeting of women's commissions. NOW was the product of feminist anger at the EEOC's recalcitrance as well as a more immediate frustration that the male-dominated Department of Labor was controlling the conference agenda and stifling dissenting voices and the introduction of resolutions from feminist representatives (Carabillo, Meuli, and Csida 1993). NOW emerged from a meeting in a hotel room occupied by feminist author Betty Friedan, whose *The Feminine Mystique* (1963) had argued that the cult of female domesticity was ruining women's lives. The 28 women present established the basics of the organization: temporary chair (Kathryn Clarenbach), status (voluntary); name (NOW); policy goal (equality for women, starting with the elimination of sex-segregated job ads); strategy (action organization); and membership dues (five dollars per month) (Carabillo, Meuli, and Csida 1993, 25). By October 1966, 300 women and men had become charter members, a board of directors had been elected, an action plan had been approved, and a statement of purpose had been adopted (29–31).

Anne N. Costain (1992, 122) has aptly observed that "government played a key role in determining the course of the American women's movement." Buttressing her observation, these seminal policy victories occurred during a lull in women's presence on Capitol Hill—a low not seen since the 1920s. Women's roles and gender consciousness were in flux, as were their policy agendas. Traditional mass-membership organizations remained very much present, though some once-prominent groups clearly had begun to fade. At the same time, the feminist groups that would lead the second wave movement were not yet well established—the earliest of these groups organized in 1966–68 but did not become respected forces within Washington until the 1970s. At that point, these two types of groups joined forces to push a robust feminist agenda, with the older groups providing guidance, resources, networks, and political contacts to aid their newly formed sister organizations (Klein 1984).

In the next two sections, I lay out the evolution of women's policy advocacy on Capitol Hill. First, I examine, for the period from 1960 through 1982, five indicators of women's organizational engagement—the number of women's groups' appearances on all issues; the number of those appearances as a share of all hearings; the frequency of women's groups' testimony on particularly important issues, the number of women's groups testifying, and the range of issues that these groups advocated. This period covers the lull following the active 1940s and 1950s as well as the emergence and flourishing of the second wave movement in the 1960s and 1970s. I then examine the period after 1982, when the ERA finally failed and the women's movement either fell into disarray and dissolved—or institutionalized as a permanent, vibrant advocacy community in Washington.

What Happened? A New Wave of Feminism Lifts Women's Advocacy

When NOW was formed in 1966, it had an ambivalent attitude toward conventional politics. Many rank-and-file feminists within NOW and other emerging second wave groups feared that a focus on national legislative advocacy would lead to organizational hierarchy and centralization, betraying feminist preferences for flat organizational structures and local control (Costain 1981; Mansbridge 1986). In its early years, NOW moved quickly toward public protest and alliances with radical feminist groups (Costain 1992). However, by the early 1970s, NOW and most major women's groups had opened Washington lobbying offices, and the movement's "public presence shifted from confrontation to organization" (Costain 1992, 2). Anne N. Costain and W. Douglas Costain (1987, 197) refer to the 1970s as the "routinizing period" of the women's movement, in which the movement consolidated and broadened its political tactics. By the late 1970s, most major women's groups had hired full-time lobbyists (Costain 1992; Costain and Costain 1987).

At the same time, Washington developed a new openness to women's movement claims as "a less ideological group of politicians, holding ambitions for higher office, began to view equal rights for women as an innovative issue with the potential to further their presidential aspirations" (Costain 1992, 133). Anne N. Costain (1992, xv) argues that the "crumbling of the New Deal coalition ushered in a period of political uncertainty in the late sixties and early seventies and the potential electoral impact of a women's bloc of votes began to attract attention." In response, "strategically placed politicians saw the value of making a serious effort to attract women's support. This attention allowed the women's movement to gain early legislative victories without possessing many resources or tactical skills."

Women's groups got an added boost from President Jimmy Carter, whose administration (1977–81) "can be characterized by its unprecedented level of presidential commitment to equality for women" (Costain

1992, 93). Carter and his aides met often with women's organizations to plan strategies for advancing women's rights (93, 95) and appointed record numbers of women to high-level posts. Carter also lobbied hard for the ERA by leaning on governors in states that had not ratified the amendment, by enlisting members of Congress to sway public opinion, and by helping to coordinate ERA activity (93).

These efforts were mirrored on Capitol Hill when Congress introduced a raft of feminist legislation. Between 1965 and 1982, 1,244 bills and resolutions—an average of roughly 140 per session—were introduced dealing with women (Costain 1988, 159). Most revolved around the ERA. In the 1970s, these legislative introductions began to bear fruit. Some 78 women-oriented laws were enacted between 1971 and 1982, six times as many in the preceding 12-year period (161).

Appearances at Congressional Hearings, 1960–1982

The early 1960s marked a doldrums period for women's organizational advocacy as traditional mass-membership groups began to lose force and the second wave movement was in its infancy. However, by the second half of the decade, when movement groups began to form and traditional groups joined the cause, the number of hearing appearances rose steadily. The institutionalization of second wave feminist organizations is clearly visible as a pronounced bump in women's presence on Capitol Hill during the second half of the 1970s and the early 1980s, as figure 3.1 shows.

The rise is impressive, though less so after controlling for the number of hearings. As the lower line shows, women's groups posted only a modest recovery from the declines of the early 1960s, with the exception of two particularly active sessions toward the end of the period.

Turning to women's involvement with particularly important legislation, organizations participated at a steady rate from the 1950s through the 1970s. While women's groups participated in hearings on a slightly smaller fraction of important legislation in the 1970s (32 percent) than in the 1950s (35 percent), the difference is substantively insignificant. However, it is perhaps surprising that women's engagement in the 1970s was not higher, given that this period included four landmark gender-equality laws, compared to none in the 1950s (Stathis 2003).

This evidence suggests that even as women's engagement fell off in the 1960s and only partially rebounded in the 1970s, engagement on important matters remained steady throughout these decades, particularly when feminist laws are included.

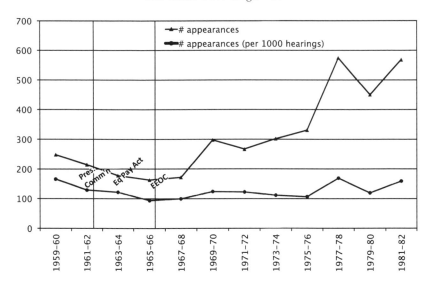

Fig. 3.1. The rise of women's policy advocacy, 1960–80

Number of Women's Groups Appearing at Hearings, 1960–1982

Another measure of women's national policy engagement is the number of organizations testifying on Capitol Hill. Here, the impact of the women's movement is evident, as are the fragmentation and diversification of the interest group universe. Whereas at midcentury roughly 300 groups testified per decade, dipping a bit in the 1960s, by the 1970s, the data show a burst in the number of women's groups speaking to legislative proposals on Capitol Hill. Figure 3.2 shows this growth.

The movement was born in the 1960s, but it became institutionalized as a policy advocacy community in Washington in the 1970s. The late 1960s and early 1970s witnessed a boom in births of second wave organizations, among them NOW (1966); Federally Employed Women and the Women's Equity Action League (1968); the Interstate Association of Commissions on the Status of Women (1970); the National Women's Political Caucus, Women's Rights Project of the American Civil Liberties Union, NOW Legal Defense and Education Fund, and Women's Action Alliance (1971); and Equal Rights Advocates, the Women's Rights Project of the Center for Law and Social Policy, and the Women's Lobby (1972). In addition, most professional associations had created women's caucuses by the early 1970s (Rosenberg 1993, 254). Debra C. Minkoff (1997) estimates that the

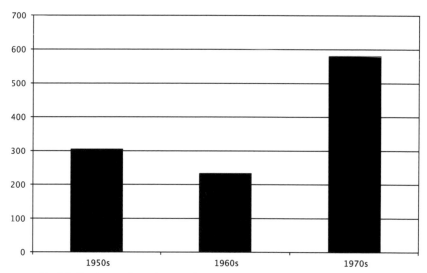

Fig. 3.2. Rise in number of women's groups testifying, 1950s–70s. (Local, state, and national units counted separately.)

number of national women's organizations grew from 43 in 1960 to 334 in 1980, a nearly eightfold increase.

Many of these groups pushed hard throughout the 1970s and 1980s for legislation to protect women from discrimination in the workplace, in higher education, in pension programs, and in credit markets. In some cases—for example, Title IX, which banned sex discrimination in federally assisted higher education programs—women's groups lay low while the bill was being debated in Congress to avoid arousing opposition but worked in strong, vigorous coalitions to defend the law after it was enacted (Davis 1999, 212). Although much of the work of the women's movement took place outside the Capitol's corridors, these new feminist groups developed a strong congressional presence during the 1970s.

In many cases, the new feminist groups worked alongside the older mass-membership associations that featured so prominently in congressional hearings at midcentury—the League of Women Voters, the PTA, the American Association of University Women, and the National Council of Jewish Women, to name a few. These groups continued to advocate for non-gender-specific public policies, but they also took up the mantle of gender equality. In the mid-1950s, the League of Women Voters had quietly abandoned its opposition to the ERA, allowing the group to become an important force in the ERA coalition of the 1970s by bringing in $2.5 million and galvanizing League members (Young 1989, 159). One League lobbyist "observed that she had never seen so much unity and excitement within the League as on the ERA issue" (Costain 1992, 51). In embracing the second wave feminist agenda, traditional groups were able to attract younger members who otherwise would have been unlikely to join (51). Roughly 60 groups, including most of the major traditional women's organizations, joined the fight over implementation of Title IX in the early 1970s (Gelb and Palley 1996, 100).

To the second wave struggle of their younger sister organizations, these traditional groups brought financial resources, networks of politically astute activists in every congressional district, and assistance in setting up Washington lobbying operations (Costain 1981, 107, 109; Costain 1992, 50–51). Costain (1992, 50) notes that the lobbyist for National Council of Jewish Women "used her entrée as an ally of organized labor to help get the new groups included as witnesses in committee hearings." These traditional groups were important allies for another reason: They had many more members than the new second wave groups. For example, Joyce Gelb and Marian Lief Palley's (1996, 25–26) survey of seven traditional women's groups counted a combined membership in excess of 2.5 million in 1980, more than seven times the 350,000 membership reported in 1985 by nine leading feminist groups (four of which had no membership base at all).

Figure 3.3 shows how traditional multipurpose voluntary organizations embraced the making of feminist claims. In the 1950s and early 1960s, their testimony almost never revolved around women's rights or needs, but by the mid-1960s, it started moving in that direction. Throughout the 1970s and early 1980s, in any given Congress, roughly 10–30 percent of traditional groups' testimony was feminist in nature.

Costain (1981, 108) argues that the traditional women's groups became natural partners because of their feminist origins: the American Association of University Women, the Federation of Business and Professional Women, and the League of Women Voters were "founded out of concern for participation by women in society," while the National Council of Jewish Women and United Methodist Women "began out of feminist protest." Most financial resources came from these traditional groups, while the newly founded feminist groups "brought new recruits and fresh ideas" (Costain 1992, 51–52; see also Klein 1984, 29). Thus, with the combined forces of traditional and new groups, "significant resources were now available to mount an effective challenge to the status quo" Costain (1992, 51). Karen Beckwith (2005, 589) has asked whether "feminist movements are

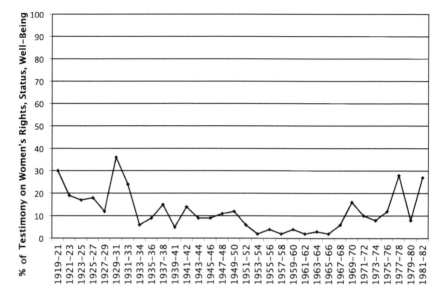

Fig. 3.3. Feminist claims by traditional groups. (Groups: AAUW, LWV, WCTU, YWCA, GFWC, PTA, NCJW.)

presaged by women's conventional political participation." These findings suggest that conventional women's groups based on female solidarity are indeed eager to mobilize for explicitly feminist causes.

Scope of Women's Groups' Issue Agendas, 1960s–1970s

The final measure of women's organizational engagement is the scope of their issue agendas as measured by the Policy Agendas Project subtopic codes. The data show a continued widening in the range of issues on which women's groups testified. While women's groups in the 1950s testified on roughly 40 percent of issue areas covered by the subtopic codes, that rate had topped 60 percent by the 1970s. Figure 3.4 charts the breadth of women's groups' issue agendas over this period.

Secondary analysis suggests that the widening in women's issue interests reflected the feminist movement's growing understanding of the pervasiveness of gender inequities within existing public programs and the potential for policymakers to remedy inequities in all spheres of life. The Policy Agendas Project's 228 codes cover a broad range of topics but tell us little about the extent to which gender issues were explicitly raised at hearings. For example, a hearing on Social Security at which a feminist group

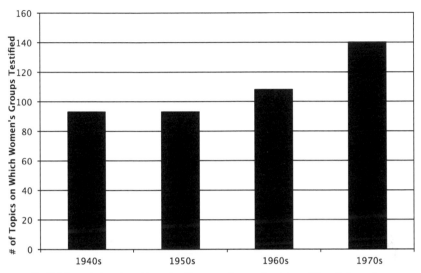

Fig. 3.4. Issue interests widened with second-wave feminism. (Counts based on policy topic codes from Policy Agendas Project; *n* = 225.)

testified about gender inequities would be coded as a "social welfare" hearing, not a "gender and sexual discrimination" hearing.

My secondary coding of the substance of the women's group's testimony helps to refine the analysis. I found that women's groups represented women's rights, status, and well-being in 82 issue areas in the 1970s, up from just 26 issue areas in the 1960s. Women's groups suddenly were advocating for women's interests in entirely new policy areas—vocational education, small business programs, and the media, among others. Some evidence from case studies shows that the diversity of women themselves drove this expansion as feminists identified common interests amid their different experiences. For example, white radical and liberal feminists joined with African American feminists to advance antirape policies and programs (Bevaqua 2008), while predominantly white female peace activists joined with predominantly black welfare recipients to argue for the redirection of defense spending into antipoverty programs (Estepa 2008).

Thus, in the 1970s a diverse set of women's groups representing a wide variety of women's experiences applied a feminist critique to existing and proposed policies spanning a broad range of policy domains. As Dara Z. Strolovitch (2011) has noted, many New Deal policies omitted protections for jobs disproportionately occupied by women and otherwise treated women unequally. Much of the second wave movement's agenda was to redress the inequalities in "universal" social welfare policies. As women's groups demanded that Congress consider the effects of policy on females, these groups won a seat at an expanding number of witness tables.

These findings dovetail with those of Wolbrecht (2000) that the range of feminist issues in congressional bills widened. In the mid-1950s, legislation addressed three key issues—equal pay, pensions, and the ERA (148). By the late 1970s, legislation covered a dozen issues, including those three as well as questions of women's health, education, reproductive rights, military service, and protection from violence (149). Although Congress's feminist policy agenda grew throughout the 1950s and 1960s, the big jump came in the 1970s, with a slight expansion in the 1980s and early 1990s. To supplement Wolbrecht's findings, my analysis shows that, in the 1970s, women's groups increasingly managed to find a "women's angle" on the topic at hand, and members of Congress and their staffs were open to hearing that perspective. Of course, during the 1970s, traditional groups pursuing not explicitly feminist concerns continued to testify, meaning that women's groups covered a broad swath of the policy landscape.

Would the Second Wave Recede or Surge in New Directions?

Women's organizations greatly expanded their issue engagement after the passage of the 19th Amendment. That amendment both reified the notion that women should have equal standing with men in the public sphere and invited women to use their particular wisdom and sensibilities to advocate on behalf of the issues that concerned them. By some measures—most notably, appearances at congressional hearings—women's groups peaked at midcentury. However, as was evident in measures such as the number of groups speaking before Congress and the range of policy areas over which they sought influence, women's collective presence reached an all-time high in the 1970s. The second wave feminist movement was a catalyst for expanding women's engagement on Capitol Hill. The wave metaphor aptly depicts women's activism in this era.

These findings are not surprising. They are consistent with assertions that the women's movement—particularly the liberal, equal rights wing—institutionalized during the 1970s and shed its early wariness about legislative advocacy on Capitol Hill. As Ethel Klein has noted, women's rights legislation had been introduced in the 1960s, but the women's movement of the 1970s was central to getting those bills passed and signed into law. She reports that 71 women's rights bills were passed in the 1970s, more than seven times the number passed in the 1960s (1984, 30). By 1980, report Gelb and Palley (1996, 209), "a wide cross-section of Washington activists perceive[d] the feminist community as a continuing effective force, with no sign of abated influence." Indeed, a top Republican staff aide said that feminist groups were "a force that's listened to" that is "cohesive, intelligent and effective."

Costain (1992, 79) puts the high point of the women's movement at 1975. By my measures, the apogee occurred a bit later, in the early 1980s. Regardless, by most accounts 1980 marked a turning point for the feminist movement. Conservative Ronald Reagan was elected president on a pledge to rein in the sort of government spending and regulation that had fueled liberal advocacy groups for close to two decades, an agenda that included a particular goal to "defund the left" (Berry and Arons 2003, 81). Especially important to the feminist movement was the loss of the ERA, whose ratification period expired in 1982. The ERA was "the key issue that allowed women's groups to unite, to build public support, and to demonstrate significant political power" (Costain 1992, 76). When the deadline passed with the amendment several states short of the 38 necessary for ratification, the feminist movement was deflated.

Did the Wave Crash?

The end of the ERA presented a question: Would feminism as a movement, or at least a collective ideology, carry on? Even though the ERA's loss demoralized activists, forces were gathering to breathe life into the movement. The Reagan administration created a threat around which left-leaning women's groups could rally activists and raise money. Feminist bureaucrats were well ensconced in the federal government, allowing for a certain continuity of feminist interest representation across election cycles. A gender gap had arisen in the 1980 presidential contest that put women's votes in play. Traditional women's groups remained active in spheres having nothing to do with women's rights. A new generation of conservative women's groups arose to challenge the feminist Left. (For an overview of these developments, see, e.g., Banaszak 2010; Costain 1992; Davis 1999; Ferree and Hess 2000; Mansbridge 1986.)

Moreover, by the early 1990s, political and cultural events seemed to presage a resurgence of feminism. Susan Faludi published *Backlash* (1991), a best-selling book detailing systematic threats to women's gains and making the case for the continuing imperative of the feminist struggle. The

Clarence Thomas–Anita Hill controversy sparked a national conversation about women's treatment in the workplace and helped elect a bumper crop of feminist women to Congress. And popular culture featured strong, feminist women in prominent roles—for example, in the movie *Thelma and Louise* and the television shows *Roseanne* and *Murphy Brown* (Henry 2004). Nearly two-thirds of women (and half of men) believed that a women's movement was still necessary to effect changes to benefit women (Sapiro 1991). For these reasons, we might expect the 1980s and 1990s to have been robust years for women's presence on Capitol Hill, even without the lodestar of the ERA.

Women's Participation and the (Greatly Exaggerated?) Death of Feminism

However, some observers viewed the 1980s and 1990s as far less propitious. Beginning in the 1970s and continuing into the 1990s, a narrative of feminism's decline took hold in the media, political discourse, and the academy. The first widely acknowledged obituary for the second wave movement came in the form of a 1976 *Harper's* magazine cover story, "Requiem for the Women's Movement" (Hawkesworth 2004). From 1989 through 2001, at least 160 articles in English-language newspapers referred to the death of feminism or the "postfeminist" era (963). The narrative of decline took at least three forms. Feminism had (1) lost its appeal among younger women; (2) ignored and thereby alienated working-class and minority women; and (3) fallen victim to a conservative backlash aimed at defunding feminist advocacy groups and giving voice to organizations representing traditional women.

We often hear that younger women do not want to call themselves feminists. Ask a woman in her 20s or 30s—even a liberal woman—and you may well see an embarrassed shrug of the shoulder or hear an emphatic "No." Many younger women are uncomfortable with the term or at least with the labeling exercise. Yet young women located in places where feminist activism has traditionally been strong, such as blue-collar workplaces and elite colleges and universities, seem to be more amenable to adopting the feminist label. National polls bear out these mixed findings, as I discuss in chapter 6. Regarding young women's posture toward feminism, we also hear that the second wave was so passé that young women had to invent a "third wave"—one that would sex up and open up the constricted approach of their foremothers. Even as third wave women delighted in sexual expression and demographic inclusion, their efforts neither developed a mass following nor produced a robust cadre of social movement organizations, as the second wave had. Indeed, the third wave has been roundly criticized for failing to assemble a policy agenda around which to mobilize younger women—or any women, for that matter (Henry 2004; Quindlen 1994; Rowe-Finkbeiner 2004).

The second charge is that second wave feminism lost its appeal because it paid insufficient attention to bread-and-butter issues affecting working mothers and disadvantaged women. In interviews with more than 100 female activists, Marilyn Gittell and Nancy Naples (1982) found deep divergence between the policy priorities of community-based female activists, who were focused on education, employment, housing, and child care, and feminist leaders, who were focused on sex discrimination and professional advancement. Pamela Aronson (2003) found that working-class women and women of color were much less likely than middle-class white women to self-identify as feminists. Seeking to explain the phenomenon, Martha Burk and Heidi Hartmann (1996) observed that the conservative mobilization against abortion forced feminists to fight a rearguard action that prevented them from mobilizing around issues of work and family. These authors argued that "women's organizations in the short space of twenty years lost political power and came to be perceived as irrelevant (or even hostile) to the common woman" (19). Some working women, they suggest, blamed the feminist movement for longer hours and job insecurity. Lending credence to this critique, the Women's Legal Defense Fund, a second wave group founded in 1971 to fight job discrimination, in 1998 changed its name to the National Partnership for Women and Families and shifted its agenda toward policies, such as paid sick leave and broader access to health care, that facilitate work-family balance, particularly for nonelite women. Likewise, a chapter-based organization, MomsRising, emerged in 2006 to advocate in favor of family-oriented policies, including the provision of paid leave and flexible work schedules, enhancement of food and product safety, and reduction of childhood hunger.

A third assertion is that feminism fell victim to the conservative politics of the 1980s. Reagan's election in 1980 constrained the political opportunities for women's groups to advance their policy agendas. One of the administration's early acts was to defund liberal organizations that had benefited from federal social programs enacted in the 1960s and 1970s (Berry and Arons 2003). Not surprisingly, Kay Lehman Schlozman (1992, 357) found that nearly 8 in 10 women's rights groups (like most public interest groups) believed that the Reagan election had made their work more difficult.

The so-called Reagan Revolution also gave energy to an emerging movement of conservative women. Epitomized by Phyllis Schlafly and her organizations, STOP ERA and the Eagle Forum, this antifeminist backlash movement repudiated the second wave's social critiques, political ideology, and policy agendas. Schlafly galvanized homemakers and other tradition-minded women to stop ratification of the ERA, which had united women's federations and second wave groups on an unprecedented scale (Mansbridge 1986). When ratification failed, women's groups lost their center of gravity and retreated to their prior issue niches. Traditional groups, which were aging and losing vitality, continued to press public interest legislation in an increasingly crowded field of public interest advocates. Feminist groups, having secured a raft of broadly applicable legislation in the 1970s and now facing a hostile political environment, fought a rearguard action to defend gains and to champion the goals of specific, albeit important, constituencies (e.g., battered women).

Costain (1992, 105) summarizes the state of the movement at the dawn of the Reagan era: "Although national women's groups were able to increase their memberships in the early eighties as a result of the new conservative political reality in national politics, most groups seem[ed] to lack a unifying vision of what could be accomplished to further their cause. They were united in their determination to fight rollbacks in gains they had already made—most notably in abortion rights—but had few other sweeping political goals." NOW's media skills made it the de facto voice for the women's movement, but by the early 1980s "it was no longer a prominent force on Capitol Hill" (106) These findings about the state of the women's movement at the organizational level echo in a major study of civic engagement at the individual level. Based on their 1990 survey, Nancy Burns and her colleagues observed with surprise how rarely women were active in feminist causes (except for abortion). The authors noted that the "silence when it comes to women's issues is particularly striking" because at the time, Congress was considering major legislation to facilitate women's claims of gender discrimination (Burns, Schlozman, and Verba 2001, 124). These scholarly findings would seem to lend some credence to assertions in the popular press that, as an orienting principle and a social movement, feminism was in decline in the 1980s and 1990s.

Women's Activism Takes a Different Form?

Yet numerous scholars have taken issue with the feminism-in-decline narrative. While public protests clearly declined after the 1970s (Staggenborg and Taylor 2005; Wolbrecht 2000), this development may simply reflect feminism's transformation into a different kind of movement, one less dependent on outside agitation and more reliant on fomenting change from within government (Costain and Costain 1987; Wolbrecht 2000). Jennifer Leigh Disney and Joyce Gelb (2000, 66) suggest that "the transformation from an autonomous women's movement to a women's lobby . . . has in many respects brought many of the 'outsider' issues 'inside' the beltway, thus gaining greater legitimacy, getting into the public discourse, and altering the political agenda."

Considerable evidence supports the proposition that the women's movement continued to flourish in both old and new forms. One body of evidence concerns the proliferation of feminist groups. Minkoff (1997) found that while the number of national women's groups dipped from their 1980s high, slightly more were in existence in 1995 (n = 246) than in the movement heyday year of 1975 (n = 242). Disney and Gelb (2000, 40) found that the number of women's organizations active in Washington nearly doubled from 75 to 140 between 1982 and 1997. Many of these groups focus on specific subpopulations of women or narrow issue concerns. Women's groups have proliferated within African American, Latina, Asian, and Native American communities (Staggenborg and Taylor 2005). Indeed, Becky Thompson (2010) notes that as the white feminist wave was receding, new feminist groups rooted in critiques of privilege were on the rise, bringing together women of color, lesbians, poor women, and others who questioned the limits of women's shared experiences. At the same time, groups have arisen to advocate on behalf of women's health, prevention of rape and domestic violence, and protection of reproductive rights (Gelb and Palley 1996, xviii). For example, the Older Women's League, founded in 1980, increased its local chapters by 70 percent and its membership by 75 percent in the mid-1990s (Disney and Gelb 2000, 60).

Other skeptics of the feminism-in-decline narrative have noted that the movement has institutionalized outside the Washington interest-group community. Feminist organizations have permeated global civil society (Hawkesworth 2004), and transnational networks of feminist women have arisen to meet the challenges of globalization (Staggenborg and Taylor 2005). Feminists have also organized to advocate on behalf of women's interests within existing entities, including social movements (Meyer and Whittier 1994), philanthropic foundations (Hartmann 1998), the Catholic Church (Katzenstein 1998), and the military (Katzenstein 1998). Costain (1992, 105) notes that feminism became integrated into state, local, and organizationally based women's units, such as women's studies programs, women's caucuses within professional associations, and unions—not necessarily the types of groups that have a major presence on Capitol Hill.

Scholars who conceive of the feminist movement in broad terms—beyond its public presence in street protests and so forth—are considerably more sanguine about its staying power. Writing in the late 1980s, Mayer N. Zald predicted that "of all the social movements on the current scene . . . because of its specialized organizations and constituencies . . . the feminist movement appears to have the best chance for continued high levels of mobilization and activity." (1988, 13; cited in Disney & Gelb 2000, 40) Eight years later, Gelb and Palley (1996, xvi, xix) validated that prediction, concluding that the women's rights policy network in Washington "remains vibrant" in a way that "defies all predictions of the 1980s."

What Happened? Women's Collective Engagement, 1982–2000

Scholars are divided on the question of what happened to the second wave movement. Did it fade away as a force for women's advocacy in Washington, or did it institutionalize and continue to work, perhaps out of the national media spotlight, for women's rights and equality? The congressional testimony data allow us to adjudicate between these two perspectives. If indeed feminism institutionalized, we would expect to see its presence in the ultimate inside-Washington venue, the congressional hearing room. Likewise, we would expect to see it rebound when Democrats retook the White House in 1992. Sadly for feminists, I find strong support for the argument that feminism as an advocacy movement is in serious trouble. But the trouble extends beyond second wave feminism. Traditional women's groups, which had represented women so prominently through the 1970s, dropped off the map in the 1980s and 1990s. Even the major women's occupational groups were in decline. Indeed, the data suggest that by the late 1990s, serious questions had arisen about the relevance of women's groups as players on Capitol Hill. The declining relevance of women's groups leads inexorably to a deeper question about the relevance of gender as an organizing principle.

Appearances at Congressional Hearings, 1982–2000

As pundits and some scholars began bemoaning the decline of feminism in the conservative 1980s, Congress was showing increasing openness to the consideration of women's rights issues. The number of hearings on women's rights expanded throughout the 1980s before falling back slightly in the early 1990s (Baumgartner and Mahoney 2005; Wolbrecht 2000, 148). During that time, the range of feminist issues in congressional legislation also widened (Wolbrecht 2000, 148). "While women's rights no longer commanded the public's attention as it had in the 1970s and early 1980s, elite-level decision makers and interest organizations continued to wrestle with questions of public policy related to women's rights" (Wolbrecht 2000, 140). And, as discussed, women's groups were prepared to testify: Costain and Costain (1987) refer to the late 1970s through mid-1980s as the "institutionalizing period" in which legislative lobbying became emphasized.

Given this relative openness to women's interests, it is surprising that testimony by women's organizations dropped beginning in the early 1980s. Figure 3.5 shows the stark decline in the absolute number of appearances.

Figure 3.6 shows women's group appearances per 100 hearings over the period of study. By bringing in the pre-second-wave era, this graph affords a panoramic view of women's public engagement on Capitol Hill. As documented earlier, women's engagement grew rapidly after suffrage, peaked at midcentury, and then bottomed out in the 1960s. While the feminist movement brought women's engagement back from the doldrums for a brief period, the downward spiral began again in the early 1980s and has yet to recover. By the late 1990s, women's groups were less prominent on Capitol Hill than they had been in the years immediately preceding suffrage.

Congressional hearings became shorter in these latter decades, which could raise questions about the trend line that adjusts for number of hearings per Congress. However, as I show in chapter 6, the decline in women's appearances is not simply an artifact of shorter hearings or of other changes in congressional treatment of outside interests: Appearances by women's groups declined relative to those by other interest groups and all types of witnesses.

My findings dovetail with those of Matt Grossman (2012), who studied interest group participation in hearings in the 1995–2004 period. He counted hearing appearances by organizations representing 15 different social and political groups, including women. He found that, relative to the size of their combined membership, women's groups were in the middle of the pack in terms of prominence at hearings. However, relative to the number of organizations, they were near the bottom, ranking 13th out of 15. Unions, environmental groups, conservative organizations, and consumer groups testified at a rate between three and four times that of women's groups. Only religious and ethnic groups testified at lower rates.[1] Likewise,

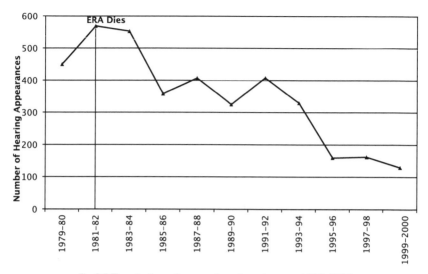

Fig. 3.5. The decline of women's policy advocacy, 1980–2000

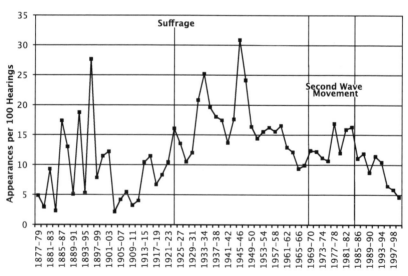

Fig. 3.6. Women's group appearances, 1877–2000 (adjusted for number of hearings)

the patterns of women's organizational engagement depicted in figures 3.1 and 3.6 parallel Amenta et al.'s (2009) depiction of the density of abortion rights and feminist groups and of *New York Times* coverage of feminist and abortion rights issues. Both the media coverage and group density measures "rise dramatically in the mid-1960s and peak around 1980" (645). Costain (1992, 101) charts a similar decline from the late 1970s through the mid-1980s in *New York Times* coverage of women's events. Thus, various studies lend external validity to my data suggesting a dramatic decline after the early 1980s in women's organizations' presence in political debates on Capitol Hill.

The decline in women's groups' appearances also shows up in the data on landmark legislation. Women's groups' engagement in hearings on important bills rose dramatically in the four decades after suffrage. In the 1920s, women's groups were present at hearings for roughly 20 percent of such bills, but by midcentury, that figure had doubled, to 40 percent. However, in the 1970s, that number dropped to roughly 30 percent, where it remained through the 1990s.

Number of Women's Groups Appearing at Hearings, 1982–2000

The story of women's organizational decline is evident, though later and less pronounced, in the count of women's groups appearing on Capitol Hill. Figure 3.7 shows that as the feminism-in-decline narrative was taking hold in the 1980s—and as the number of women's group appearances was falling—the number of groups testifying actually rose a bit before falling in the 1990s.

This paradox lends credence to assertions that women's groups indeed proliferated and specialized during the 1980s, but it suggests that many of the groups were not the large, politically influential interests likely to be called again and again to testify. I will later elaborate on this point, showing the declining presence of major national women's organizations in the 1980s and 1990s.

The proliferation of groups on Capitol Hill in the 1970s and 1980s and the drop-off in the 1990s is reflected in Minkoff's (1997) count of national women's organizations. She finds that the number of national women's groups more than doubled between 1970 and 1975, then fell by nearly 25 percent between 1985 and 1995. Reinforcing these trends, Costain (1992, 96) shows that membership in selected women's groups rose steadily through the early 1980s, reaching a peak of roughly 800,000, then fell precipitously through 1986 (where her series ended) to roughly

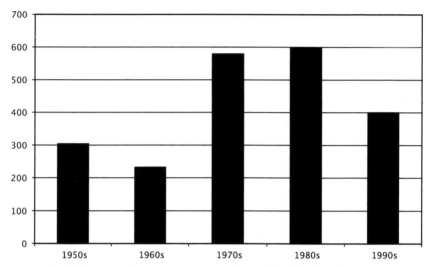

Fig. 3.7. Number of women's groups testifying, 1950s–90s. (Local, state, and national groups counted separately.)

550,000. Thus, it appears that while the women's movement indeed institutionalized in the 1980s, its organizational foundation was fragile. Nevertheless, the decline in women's groups' hearing-adjusted appearances fell far more quickly than did either the number of women's groups testifying or the number of women's groups in existence. Thus, the observed decline in women's organizational presence on Capitol Hill in the 1980s and 1990s is not a simple artifact of the decline in women's organizations overall.[2]

Scope of Women's Groups' Issue Agendas, 1980–2000

One argument against the decline-of-feminism narrative is that the women's movement broadened its agenda in the 1980s, in part as a reaction to critics who saw it as too focused on legislation promoting equal treatment under law. Critics suggested that such legal changes disproportionately furthered the professional ambitions of white middle-class women while neglecting deeper economic, social, and policy inequities affecting disadvantaged subgroups—older women, minority women, poor and working-class women, divorced women, single mothers, and so forth. By the early 1980s, women's organizations responded by highlighting the ways in which broader issues such as the economy and Social Security affected women (Costain and Costain 1987, 205–6).

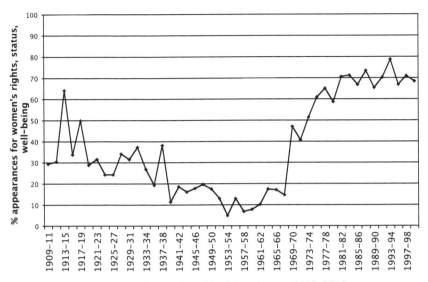

Fig. 3.8. The fall and rise of feminist advocacy, 1909–2000

To assess this assertion, I examine the range of issues that women's groups addressed in their hearing testimony. This chapter presented evidence that feminist groups in the 1970s indeed were expanding the range of issues to which they brought a feminist perspective. This trend extended into the 1980s and reached a plateau in the 1990s. In those decades, women's groups inserted themselves into debates about more than 60 percent of the policy issues coded by the Policy Agendas Project.

That said, while the range of issue domains was broad, the interests represented narrowed throughout the period. Recall that I coded all of the roughly 10,400 hearing appearances according to whether the organization was advocating primarily for women's rights, status, or well-being or for other constituencies, including the broad public interest. Figure 3.8 shows the fraction of hearing appearances, going back to the decade before suffrage, that was dedicated to women-specific interests.

As the figure shows, a stunning reorientation of women's organizational energies took place between the 1940s–60s and the decades of the second wave movement. In the middle decades, women's groups advocated for women's rights, status, and well-being roughly 10–20 percent of the time; by the 1980s and 1990s, that figure had risen to closer to 70–80 percent of the time. These findings suggest that in the last third of the 20th century, women became a collection of specialized interests. Their days as a public interest lobby were largely behind them.

Women's Voice and the Second Wave: An Assessment

The second wave women's movement elevated women's standing in Washington. After a slowing of participation in the 1960s, women's organizations in the 1970s marched in droves to Capitol Hill to air a newly formulated set of grievances and to demand policy remedies. The second wave women's movement birthed scores of new organizations oriented around women's rights under law and later around a broader array of feminist issues and constituency interests. The effect of the women's movement is clear. Women's groups testified more often, in greater numbers, and in a broader array of issue domains during the 1970s than in the preceding decade.

By the latter half of the 1970s and certainly by the 1980s, pundits and scholars began weighing in on what the second wave movement had meant and whether it was over. One school of thought held that feminism had faded as an organizing principle and as a vibrant movement. Another perspective held that although the headline-grabbing protests may have faded, the movement was continuing in an institutionalized and arguably more effective form.

The evidence from Congress provides support for both views. The large number of groups present at hearings and the broad range of issue domains in which they offered testimony support the proposition that the women's movement did not fade away but simply changed form. Strong support exists for the notion that the women's movement institutionalized itself into a permanent advocacy community in Washington that promotes feminist perspectives on a wide array of issues. At the same time, the decline-of-feminism narrative finds support in the sharp drop in women's group appearances before Congress beginning in the early 1980s. Indeed, by the late 1990s, women's groups were less prominent in Capitol Hill hearing rooms than they had been in the decade before suffrage. Rather than branching into rivers of activism, the wave of activism surged and then crashed.

This startling finding presents some obvious puzzles. By many accounts, women's voices on Capitol Hill should have been more rather than less prominent in the late 20th century than in earlier decades. After all, in part because of the women's movement itself, women's status and political resources, such as education and income, had grown. Likewise, women's groups had proliferated and become well entrenched in Washington. In a recent study of 37 constituency groups (e.g., lawyers, veterans, farmers), women were tied for 6th in number of organizations, ranked 5th in combined membership, and came in 17th in size of political staff (Grossman 2012, 33). Furthermore, women's groups possessed many of the attributes found to be correlated with a strong presence at congressional hearings, including having been long established in Washington (Grossman 2012, 154), having relatively large memberships (Grossman 2012, 154; Kasniunas 2009; but see Leyden 1995), and having relatively large political staffs (Grossman 2012, 154). With these advantages, why should women's collective engagement on Capitol Hill be in decline, their voices increasingly muted?

The Story So Far

I have presented some surprising and counterintuitive findings about women's collective engagement in national policy debates over the late 19th and 20th centuries. This period witnessed a broad expansion in women's legal rights, including the constitutional right to vote, and access to economic and political institutions once dominated by men. Yet the relationship between women's rights and women's political voice is by no means straightforward. The decades after suffrage were associated with a broad expansion in women's organized presence on Capitol Hill and in the range of issues they tackled, while the decades after the second wave women's movement saw no such expansion—and, in some cases, witnessed a pronounced decline in women's groups' presence before Congress.

Before examining possible explanations for these puzzling patterns, I take a closer look at these developments by utilizing both the data on women's group appearances and a second dataset of transcripts from their testimony in two policy realms, foreign relations and health care, that recurred throughout the 20th century. Using a scientific sampling of women's groups' testimony on these issues, I trace the evolution in the types of groups involved, the sources of their political authority, and the civic identities on which women's groups rested their policy claims. The analysis shows a fundamental shift in the way that women—as represented by women's organizations—understood their civic place.

FOUR

From Public Interest to "Special Interests"

After their great victory for women's rights, suffrage leaders were poised to use their political inclusion to accomplish great things for human welfare. When feminists convened nearly a half century later to pick up the women's rights banner, they proclaimed their desire to bring women into "full participation in the mainstream of American society" as part of a "worldwide revolution of human rights" (Carabillo, Meuli, and Csida 1993, 159). These promises were lofty and inspiring and sought to enlarge women's engagement in new and exciting ways.

But beneath the similar rhetoric lay important differences in the organization and expression of women's voice and aspirations. The postsuffrage statement came from the League of Women Voters, the national federation of civic-minded women that emerged from the suffrage movement to train newly enfranchised women in the practices of thoughtful citizenship and effective public advocacy. The second statement was part of the founding credo of the National Organization for Women (NOW), whose agenda was more targeted: to expose and eradicate sexism wherever it was found. While these groups shared core principles, including a commitment to grassroots democracy, they also laid out different trajectories for women's collective engagement.

The role of women's organizations on Capitol Hill underwent profound changes over the 20th century. These changes included the rise and fall of appearances before congressional committees and a concomitant expansion and contraction (however slight) in the number of groups appearing and in the policy domains they engaged. Let us scratch beneath the surface of these patterns to examine what is driving them and how they might be related. Who gets to speak for women? How do women establish themselves as forces to be reckoned with? What exactly *is* a "women's issue" anyway? And, most important of all, how have the answers to these questions changed over time?

The data afford several ways to approach these questions. First, I look at the types of organizations that constitute the women's interest group universe. I document the rise and fall of multipurpose voluntary organizations; the proliferation of occupational groups; the establishment of second wave feminist groups, often focused on single issues; the emergence of antifeminist backlash organizations; and the proliferation of organizations representing women of color. Second, I examine the organizational characteristics, including membership and internal procedures, that female advocates use to establish their political authority. Finally, I explore the policy agendas of women's groups over time.

These three transformations—in organizational types, authority claims, and policy agendas—tell us how half the population has evolved as a politically relevant class since the late 19th century. The data document profound changes in women's participatory citizenship and allow us to derive a straightforward account of the up-and-down, widening-then-narrowing pattern that characterizes women's collective policy engagement. The straightforward account holds that women's political evolution is the product of the characteristics of the groups representing them. This chapter explores the evolution of the "women's lobby" from one composed of broad-based, multipurpose organizations to one rooted in professionally managed niche lobbies. And yet, if changes in women's organizations are driving the evolution in women's policy advocacy, we are left with a prior question: What underlying forces are driving those changes? I take up that question in chapters 5 and 6.

"Membership to Management"

Theda Skocpol (1992, 1999, 2003) has argued that federated voluntary organizations—those with national, state, and local affiliates—played a critical role in the development of democratic citizens and in the construction of the early welfare state in America. Organizations such as the Woman's Christian Temperance Union, the General Federation of Women's Clubs, and the National Association of Colored Women's Clubs mobilized women around a wide variety of local, state, and national policy endeavors, particularly in the late 19th century and the first half of the 20th century. Skocpol has documented the decline of these groups as thriving hubs of civic activity for everyday citizens and the concomitant rise in professionally staffed expert advocacy groups based in Washington and has aptly described this pattern as the shift from "membership to management" (Skocpol 2003).

While Skocpol and others have captured these shifts through membership counts and organizational censuses, here I show how the changing composition of the women's associational universe affected women's public voice. Changes in organizational structures and missions altered the types of authority claims that women's groups could make before lawmakers and the types of policy proposals they could legitimately seek to influence.

The data support the observation that tiered organizations are declining as a force for women's advocacy in the United States. Until the 1970s, they constituted roughly 80 percent of appearances by women's organizations, but that share had dropped to a little more than 50 percent by the 1990s. This is a generous measure, for it includes chapter-based groups as well as organizations that have geographically rooted affiliates. Nevertheless, chapter-based organizations have far from disappeared from the Washington scene, as I discuss shortly.

Figure 4.1 presents another way of assessing the decline of federations. Here I chart appearances by the seven traditional federated women's associations, all formed in the late 19th or early 20th century, that testified the most over the course of the dataset.[1] As the figure shows, beginning in the 1970s, these groups became an ever smaller organizational presence on Capitol Hill. In the 1950s, these seven groups were responsible for 50 percent of all women's group appearances; by the 1990s, that number had dropped to just 8 percent. A similar pattern holds in the absolute number of appearances. These seven groups appeared five times as often in the 1950s as in the 1990s, even though Congress held 5,000 fewer hearings in the earlier decade.[2]

These findings in part reflect the declining memberships of these groups. Data assembled by Robert Putnam show that 8 out of 10 large, traditional women's groups suffered significant membership losses— generally from 60 to 90 percent in population-adjusted terms—between 1966 and 1996 (Goss and Skocpol 2006).[3] The groups that lost ground included such historically prominent associations as the Federation of Business and Professional Women (–84 percent, in terms of the fraction of the relevant population who belonged); the American Association of University Women (–80 percent); the General Federation of Women's Clubs

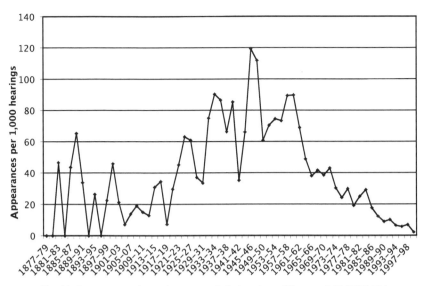

Fig. 4.1. Appearances by major women's federations. (Groups: AAUW, LWV, WCTU, YWCA, GFWC, PTA, NCJW.)

(–73 percent); the Woman's Christian Temperance Union (–91 percent); and the League of Women Voters (–63 percent). If women's organizations are any indication, traditional volunteer-based citizens' federations indeed appear to be fading from the political scene.

The Rise of Women's Occupational Groups

One type of tiered organization on the rise in Washington is the occupationally based association. Women's labor unions, farm and agricultural organizations, professional associations, and occupational support entities constituted roughly 10–25 percent of women's groups' appearances until the 1970s. With the second wave movement and women's advancement in white-collar professions, these groups proliferated over the next three decades, constituting nearly 60 percent of all appearances by women's groups in the 1990s. Occupational organizations, which often have state and local chapters, helped maintain the presence of tiered organizations before Congress as traditional women's civic groups faded.[4]

The occupational sector evolved in much the same way as the larger interest group sector did: More and more organizations appeared, representing ever more specialized interests. For example, appearing on Capitol

Hill were organizations representing roughly 30 nursing constituencies. In addition, the feminist movement was taking root within the occupational sector, as organizations arose to represent the particular interests of women in different jobs—everything from construction to farming to professional philanthropy to office work. The proliferation of women's occupational groups, then, reflects women's movement into the labor force and their recognition that their work roles gave them unique perspectives, experiences, and claims to make in policy debates.

The Proliferation of Feminist Advocacy Groups

Another sector of the women's group universe that posted growth evident from 1960 through the 1980s is the feminist sector. At least two explicitly feminist groups, the National Woman's Party and the American Association of University Women, arose in the suffrage era and survived for decades afterward. The National Woman's Party, which championed the Equal Rights Amendment during the "doldrums" years (Rupp and Taylor 1987), testified 68 times between the 1920s and 1980s; the American Association of University Women, which worked on an array of issues, including advancing women's educational access, testified more than 300 times between 1920s and the 1990s and continues to thrive. But those two exceptions notwithstanding, feminism found its voice on Capitol Hill in the second wave era.

Between 1966, when NOW was established, and 2000, more than 600 new second wave feminist groups appeared before Congress. These included national advocacy groups and their local affiliates, such as the National Women's Political Caucus and the Lincoln, Nebraska, chapter of the Older Women's League; state organizations such as the Pennsylvania Breast Cancer Coalition; local service providers such as the Minneapolis Women's Center; and women's occupational groups advocating for women's concerns, such as the Massachusetts Women's Bar Association. Contrary to the stereotype of the second wave as an elite women's movement, many of the groups appearing on Capitol Hill represented disadvantaged subpopulations: older women, blue-collar women, victims of domestic or sexual violence, and minority women. While hundreds of feminist groups spoke before Congress in those years, most testified just once. Only 25 of these second wave groups (4 percent) testified more than 10 times, and only 2 (the National Organization for Women and the Women's Equity Action League) testified more than 100 times. These figures indicate that the women's movement was broad and diverse, rooted at all levels of government, and quite active on Capitol Hill, though not operating through the sorts of mass-membership peak associations that had dominated congressional testimony in earlier decades.

The proliferation of feminist groups in the 1960s, 1970s, and 1980s is also reflected in data on organizational foundings. My analysis of data from three directories of national women's organizations discovered that in 1963, just 24 percent of women's groups focused on women's rights, status, and well-being, but by 1993, that number had doubled. At the same time, the share of women's groups focused on society at large was 50 percent in 1963 and just 23 percent in 1993 (Goss and Skocpol 2006, 342). The shift is more striking in light of the founding of different types of groups. Of women's groups established before 1960, 22 percent focused on women's rights, status, or well-being; of those founded after 1960, that number more than doubled to 57 percent. Likewise, groups started in the prefeminist era were far more likely to focus on society at large (50 percent) than were the groups founded in 1960 and after (13 percent) (Goss and Skocpol 2006, 344). Between 1970 and 1993, 359 national women's groups were established; 96 percent of them were focused on women's advancement (345). Most of the national groups worked on a broad array of issue concerns, but some focused on single issues (e.g., the National Battered Women's Law Project, the National Coalition for Sex Equity in Education, and Women against Pornography) or subpopulations (e.g., Black Women United, the Disabled Womyn's Educational Project, and the Older Women's League).

Feminist groups differed in another important respect from the traditional federated voluntary associations that had dominated women's advocacy in Washington before the second wave. Feminist groups were far less likely to have active memberships that financed the organization and formulated issue agendas. To be sure, some second wave groups were membership-based, including NOW, which has a strong tradition of internal participatory democracy (Barakso 2004), and occupation-based organizations, such as the Coalition of Labor Union Women and the Women's Caucus for Political Science (Carden 1977). However, most feminist groups formed to influence policy relied on individual, foundation, and sometimes government contributions rather than membership dues and turned to professional staffs and elite board members to set organizational agendas. They reflected Skocpol's (2003) "membership to management" transformation. For example, Carden (1977, 10) found that only 4 of 22 national second wave groups formed to pursue specialized goals had members. Reflecting this reality, combined membership in feminist groups was only a small fraction of membership in the old-fashioned women's organi-

zations. Joyce Gelb and Marian Lief Palley (1996) found that four prominent feminist groups had a combined membership of just 250,000 in 1978;
by contrast, the four largest traditional women's groups had about 10.7 million members that year, or 43 times as many (Goss and Skocpol 2006, 347).

While the leading feminist groups were visible on Capitol Hill, especially in the late 1970s and early 1980s, they never reached anywhere near
the same prominence (measured by hearing appearances) achieved by the
mass-membership women's associations of old.

The New Right: Conservative Women's Groups

The feminist movement spawned a backlash by conservative women, who
argued that too much equality would be bad for their sex. These New
Right groups were founded to push back against the policy priorities such
as the Equal Rights Amendment. The interplay between feminist and conservative women's groups was an important part of the emergence of the
"culture wars" of the 1980s and 1990s.

Three prominent conservative women's groups appeared with some reg-
ularity on Capitol Hill in the 1980s and 1990s: the Eagle Forum, founded
by Phyllis Schlafly in 1972; Concerned Women for America, founded by
Beverly LaHaye in 1979; and the Independent Women's Forum, founded
by three conservative women in 1992 in response to the Clarence Thomas
hearings. These three groups appeared 57 times between 1979 and 2000, or
roughly 5 times per Congress. The three most prolific feminist groups—
NOW, the Women's Legal Defense Fund, and the National Women's
Political Caucus—appeared roughly 5 times as often in that time frame.
Thus, while conservative women's groups brought important new perspectives to national debates in the feminist era, their prominence on Capitol
Hill should not be overstated. In her study of modern conservative women,
Ronnee Schreiber (2008) suggests that these groups are founded on a
paradox: They seek to eradicate identity politics while relying on gender
identity as a basis of recruitment and organization. The tension between
ideological and organizational imperatives may hinder the growth of these
movement groups and limit their prominence in institutionalized forms of
politics.

A Voice for Women of Color in the Modern Era

Women of color also made strong gains in the era of women's rights. The
1970s and 1980s witnessed the birth of a wide range of feminist organiza-

tions specializing in advancing the interests of African American, Native American, Hispanic, and Asian American women. Groups that debuted before Congress in the 1970s included the Black Women's Consciousness Raising Association, the Chicana Caucus of the National Women's Political Caucus, and the Alaska Native Sisterhood. In the 1980s, newly appearing groups included the American Association of Black Women Entrepreneurs, Pan Asian American Women, and the Coalition of Hispanic American Women. These groups joined older associations, such as the National Association of Colored Women's Clubs, which remained in existence but whose presence (like that of other traditional women's groups) was fading.

One organization—the National Council of Negro Women, headed by Dorothy Height—was responsible for 43 percent of all appearances by minority women's groups. (The vast majority of other minority women's groups appeared just once or twice each.) Mary McLeod Bethune formed the Council in 1935 to bring African American women's groups together around common agendas. By the early 1970s, its 25 allied groups and 145 local sections claimed 4 million members.[5] The Council's reach grew rapidly in the 1960s and 1970s, when it undertook a wide variety of antipoverty, civil rights, and women's rights projects (Height 2003, 207). The Council's congressional appearances reflected the broad interests of a membership whose life experiences were shaped by the intersections of race, gender, and class. Issues on which the Council testified included the minimum wage, housing, elderly assistance, juvenile delinquency, child care, pay discrimination, the status of black males, and television violence. The Council's appearances lend support to the finding of Dara Strolovitch (2007, 69–71) that groups representing "intersectionally disadvantaged" women had necessarily broad agendas reflecting the multiple concerns of members.

Figure 4.2 charts the presence of minority women's groups before Congress. As the figure shows, with three exceptions, they never constituted more than 4 percent of all women's group appearances in any given Congress. However, viewed in terms of the number of appearances, the data show general growth in the 1940s, when civil rights was moving onto the national agenda, and then a very steep increase in the 1970s, when second wave feminism took hold. Minority women's groups seemed to follow the same downward trajectory seen with other women's groups during the 1980s and 1990s with the exception of a "local peak" in the 1993–94 Congress, when lawmakers were considering national health care reform and legislation dealing with violence in music and the media.

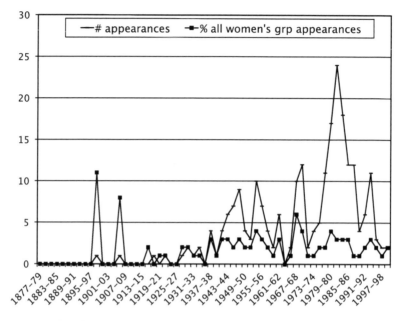

Fig. 4.2. Minority women's groups on Capitol Hill, 1877–2000

Political Authority: How Women's Groups Count

Scholars have suggested that the structural form that an organization assumes affects its political influence (Clemens 1997; Skocpol 1999, 2003). The mechanisms connecting form to influence are many. For example, Skocpol (2003) suggests that mass-membership groups build cross-class solidarity, providing a broad base of political support for generous social programs. Clemens (1997) documents how early-20th-century social groups appropriated familiar organizational forms, including "business methods," to gain acceptance and power. I build on these insights by illuminating, through qualitative analysis of women's groups' testimony, how they used organizational features to signal their political authority.

I define political authority as the demonstrated capacity of an organization first to speak on behalf of citizens who are attentive to an issue and second to reward friendly elected officials or punish unfriendly ones. Political authority relies on the transmission of political information, an important resource that interest groups can offer to legislators (R. L. Hall and Deardorff 2006; Heitshusen 2000; Wright 1996). By conveying political information—about the size of the attentive public, the direction and intensity of its interests, and the likelihood of its acting politically on those interests—pressure groups signal their political authority. Political authority is the organizational quality that tells Congress, "Listen to us." I distinguish political authority from policy authority, which involves a group's substantive expertise.

Different types of groups have different stocks of organizational resources and therefore different levels of political authority. Given women's traditionally disadvantaged place in politics, their authority could not be assumed; thus, women's groups have had to be explicit and intentional in establishing it. I examine women's groups' testimony at hearings in two policy realms (international affairs and government provision of health care) over a nearly 80-year span (1920 to 1996) to identify the specific types of evidence that women's organizations used to signal their political authority and how those evidence claims evolved. These issues were selected because they provided diversity to increase confidence in the robustness of the findings and because they drew concerted attention from women's groups throughout the 20th century.[6] Three sources of authority claims emerged as dominant: (1) the size and structure of the organization's membership; (2) the internal processes by which the organization arrived at its issue positions (for example, careful study, broad-based consensus building, democratic decision making); and (3) the group's capacity to mobilize members and/or the wider public for political activity. However, women's groups differed in their ability to draw on these sources of authority. As the women's group universe evolved from mass-membership associations to more centralized advocacy groups, explicit political authority claims evolved and in many cases faded away, with claims to *policy* expertise taking center stage.

Political Authority through Membership

One obvious source of political clout is an organization's membership. In an election-driven political system, members of Congress pay attention to organizations that command attentive voters (Fiorina et al. 2007). Not surprisingly, number of members is a positive predictor of a group's being invited to testify before Congress (Grossman 2012; Kasniunas 2009). For the first two-thirds of the 20th century, women's groups routinely drew on this source of power, touting their legions of dues-paying members and their affiliates in localities across the nation. In my sample of hearing testimony, membership figures appeared in 50–90 percent of appearances from

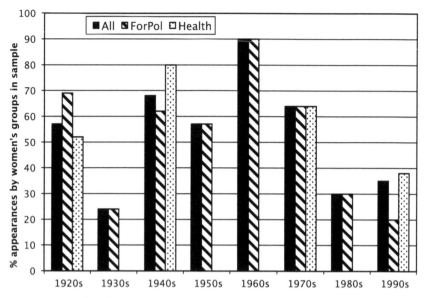

Fig. 4.3. Membership as source of women's groups' power

the 1920s through the 1970s, except in the anomalous 1930s. Then, in the 1980s and 1990s, the fraction of organizations that used their membership and affiliate figures dropped dramatically, to 20–38 percent. The upper-bound figure applies to health care testimony in the 1990s and is attributable to the nursing organizations and coalitions of women's groups that appeared to express their views on President Bill Clinton's health-reform plan. Figure 4.3 shows the trends across the two policy realms separately and combined.

What happened? The drop in the 1980s and 1990s was in large part a function of the rise of staff-run advocacy groups that have donors as opposed to engaged grassroots memberships (Skocpol 2003). But it is also true that mass-membership groups such as nurses' organizations sometimes forewent the opportunity to introduce membership figures. A careful reading of the hearings suggests that witnesses spent less time attempting to signal their political power in the 1990s than in the 1950s, and members of Congress ceased probing for such information.

For much of the 20th century, in contrast, the importance of mass organization was often made immediately clear. In the opening paragraphs of their statements before Congress, women's group representatives of the 1920s–70s nearly always provided the number of members in the organization and a description of their geographic distribution. To cite several of many examples, the National Council of Women claimed 11 million members in 1924; the General Federation of Women's Clubs, 3 million in 1948; the American Association of University Women, 154,000 in 1963; the National Council of Parents and Teachers, 12 million in 1963; and the League of Women Voters 157,000 in 1969.[7] By the 1960s, the American Association of University Women had more than 1,500 local units; the League of Women Voters had more than 1,100; and the National Council of Jewish Women and Hadassah had more than 300 each. Women's groups also acted in coalition. The Conference on the Cause and Cure of War, active in the 1930s, represented 11 of the nation's largest progressive women's groups. The Citizens' Committee for UNICEF, active in the 1960s–70s, included roughly 10 women's groups among its ranks.

The significance of a large membership was captured during a House hearing on the 1965 foreign aid bill, when Representative James G. Fulton (R-PA) told the witness for the 12 million-member National Congress of Parents and Teachers, "You are one of the largest organized agencies on a voluntary basis of any that I have ever run into in my political career. I, therefore, think you should be listened to, and carefully. If we talk of every woman being able to control one vote besides hers, and consider half of your members are women, we already have 18 million votes which is almost as many as we Republicans got overall in the last national election."[8] Such exchanges were absent by the 1980s and 1990s, when membership figures were mentioned by way of background (if at all) and then never addressed again.

Political Authority through Internal Democracy

From the 1920s through the 1960s, women's groups commonly signaled their electoral power to Congress by portraying themselves as minidemocracies, with mass memberships engaged in elaborate and thoughtful processes of deliberative decision making. Traditional women's groups, such as the American Association of University Women, the League of Women Voters, and the National Congress of Parents and Teachers, often took pains to describe their democratic procedures, in which local units intensively studied policy questions, reached consensus on them, and then voted for national policy positions through resolutions presented at national conventions.[9] Organizational witnesses frequently introduced the full text of these resolutions into their testimony and hence into the record of the hearing proceedings. The General Federation of Women's Clubs was typical in using internal democracy to buttress political authority in its 1950 testimony on the United Nations Charter:

> The General Federation makes its policy through its resolutions which are sent to all its member organizations 2 months before the convention, for study, and so that their delegates to the convention may be instructed. Then they come to the convention, and at that time both sides are presented, for and against the resolution, if it happens to be of a controversial nature, and then the resolution is either adopted or discarded; and, if adopted, it becomes the policy of the federation.[10]

Although complex and cumbersome, these rules and procedures afforded several advantages to influence-seeking organizations. First and most obviously, legislators intimately understood and respected their parliamentary language and rituals, for, as Skocpol (2003) has noted, they mirrored those of Congress. Second, the rules and procedures allowed witnesses to go before Congress and claim credibly that their organizations were true representations of attentive issue publics; after all, thousands of members had carefully considered the position and presumably become attuned to its fortunes on Capitol Hill. Third, the processes of careful study, deliberation, consensus-building, and formal passage of resolutions inoculated women from the stereotype that their positions were based on emotion rather than reason. As Patrice DiQuinzio (2005) has argued, emotional or experiential arguments may be less than credible or effective in a classical liberal democracy, such as the United States, that enshrines notions of rational citizenship.

Frequently from the 1920s through the 1940s and from time to time thereafter, members of Congress expressed interest in the process by which an organization had arrived at its position. Friendly legislators sought the information to help the organization shore up its credibility during the proceedings, while hostile legislators often introduced questions about internal processes in an effort to challenge a group's stature. In a remarkable series of exchanges during the national health insurance hearings of 1946–47, for example, Senator Forrest C. Donnell (R-MO) grilled all six witnesses from women's civic associations in an attempt to find weaknesses in their claims to represent attentive womanhood. In the case of the 40,000-member League of Women Shoppers, this grilling dominated the testimony. In the case of the American Association of University Women, a large portion was devoted to Donnell's prosecution-style efforts to get the

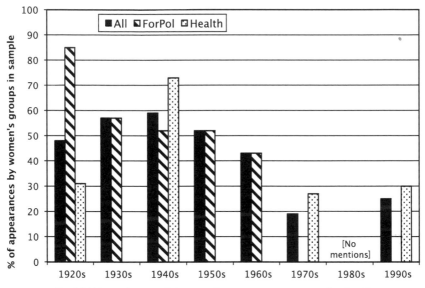

Fig. 4.4. Women's groups' democratic processes as source of authority

witness to concede that, contrary to the views of her organization's parliamentarian and widely used rules of order, a convention by mail does not constitute a convention. (She made no such concession and in fact argued that mail ballots were more democratic because they allowed for participation by smaller, poorer branches.)[11] Such questions from both friendly and hostile members of Congress helped election-minded legislators assess whether women were invested deeply enough in their policy commitments to reward or punish members based on their votes.[12]

Beginning in the 1960s and accelerating rapidly through the 1970s, 1980s, and 1990s ensuing three decades, internal democracy became less and less relevant as a signal of political authority. As figure 4.4 shows, such explanations typically were featured in 40–60 percent of appearances through the 1960s before falling off dramatically.

The changing composition of testifying groups accounts for this trend. As Skocpol (2003) has documented, the traditional federated organizations— those most inclined to utilize internal democracy—declined in prominence, while a newer breed of professional advocacy groups rose to the fore. Lacking the organizational characteristics that had proved politically useful for their predecessor organizations, these women's groups utilized policy expertise as a substitute for political influence. In other words, the source of their influence lay not in their ability to speak for mass, demo-cratically organized constituencies but in their ability to make a strong case based on professional expertise. Policy and political authority, in a sense, had become conflated.

Political Authority through Mobilization of Attentive Publics

The power of women's groups was rooted not simply in their status as barometers of thoughtful public opinion but also occasionally in their ability to mobilize attentive publics, whether associational members or the general population. Congressional statements make clear that members looked to women's associations for such services, as illustrated by three hearings spanning three decades.

In a 1949 House Foreign Affairs Committee hearing on the Marshall Plan, Rep. Richard Chatham (D-NC) told the League of Women Voters witness, "A group like this, backing the program, would be very important when the bill reaches the floor. There are people interested in the business interests which come out of this thing. I think when a group like [the League] gives their wholehearted support it will make it much easier for us to fight for the program." The witness, Kathryn H. Stone, replied, "I think that should be true when 630 leagues in 35 States are really follow-ing and discussing this issue. . . . You will be hearing individually from our league members and from our leagues as they feel impelled and moved to write to you."[13] That pledge of civic action prompted Representative Sol Bloom (D-NY) to quip, "I heard from your league members last Novem-ber 2 [Election Day]."[14]

The League of Women Voters was again pressed into service in the early 1960s to save President John F. Kennedy's controversial long-term foreign aid bill. In an extraordinary series of exchanges with members of the House Foreign Affairs Committee, witness Barbara Stuhler was asked to supply her assessment of public tolerance for the newly conceived proposal (by Representative Dante Fascell [D-FL]); to work through the League's 130,000 members and 1,100 local units to "sell" the controversial program to the American people (by Representatives Robert Chiperfield, [R-IL] and Lawrence Curtis [R-MA]); and to generate "letters from hundreds of citizens in support" (by Representative Harris McDowell [D-DE]).[15] Sev-eral members commented on the League's active citizenship. For example, Representative Robert Barry (R-NY) reported that he was "delightfully saturated" by having five times the average number of League units in his district.[16] Representative Barratt O'Hara (D-IL) called the League "one of the most potent factors in informing the American people as to the mutual aid program."[17]

Six years later, Representative O'Hara acknowledged the League's earlier influence: "I want to say this to you and to your membership. Some years ago our foreign aid program was in great danger. I have always thought that the League of Women Voters saved it" by holding bipartisan congressional forums around the country. "Public interest was aroused as never before, and the foreign aid program with all its blessing by our country and the world was saved."[18] The League's importance in the 1960s is exemplified by the appearance of Lyndon Baines Johnson and his wife, Lady Bird Johnson, at the organization's biennial convention in Pittsburgh in 1964. The president declared a League of Women Voters Week in September of that year and beseeched Leaguers to support his War on Poverty (Young 1989, 161).

The 1970s was a transitional decade. In foreign affairs, the mass-membership civic organizations continued to play an important role, notably by supporting appropriations for the United Nations Children's Fund (UNICEF) and the United Nations more generally. At a 1977 Senate hearing, the League of Women Voters touted its role as a "two-way communication link" whose project supporting the United Nations had found "a way to get information from citizens, as well as getting information to them."[19] In health care, women's organizations typically mentioned the number of members or affiliates, but only by way of introducing their organizations. In no case, however, did a witness suggest that its members were mobilized around national health insurance in a way that Congress people might perceive as an electoral threat or opportunity.

However, as was the case with membership numbers and internal democracy, by the 1980s, women's groups had become unlikely to tout their ability to mobilize the public for policy causes. While the potential to mobilize citizens never constituted a common authority-generating strategy, it faded in importance by the late 20th century. There were no such mentions in the 1980s and very few in the 1990s.

Again, lacking the promise or threat of mass mobilization, women's groups relied on professional expertise as their primary source of politically relevant authority.

Sources of Political Authority: A Summary

Skocpol (2003) has bemoaned the shift in the interest group universe from membership to management. She has suggested that traditional associations had important advantages—in their ability to bring people together across class lines, inculcate important civic skills, and mobilize broad publics for generous social programs. I would add another virtue: These organizations provided a mechanism for the development of citizen expertise, which gave everyday American women a credible voice in public policymaking. Before women developed policy expertise through professional roles or political clout through elective office, these federations made women players in Washington. Ample evidence from intensive questioning of witnesses and other hearing discourse demonstrates that members of Congress took seriously women's federations' authority even as individual women were politically and economically marginalized by patriarchal laws and social norms.

These political advantages, made possible by institutional design, allowed women to construct electoral power even as questions arose about whether a women's voting bloc existed in the electorate. These organizational features also allowed female citizens, who had yet to reach parity with men in political and professional life, to find an authoritative, collective voice that male legislators took seriously. However, as traditional federated mass-membership associations faded from the scene, these sources of political authority were less apparent in congressional testimony. By the last two decades of the 20th century, women's organizations rarely made explicit claims to political clout, instead relying on policy analysis, occupationally based expertise, and moral exhortation, without clearly signaling to Congress that the group had political resources to reward sympathetic legislators and punish laggards. The data do not allow claims to be made about the relative magnitude of women's political power in the pre-1980 versus post-1980 period. I merely suggest that, in later decades, women's groups were far less likely explicitly to signal their political resources.

What Is a "Women's Issue?"

Different types of groups choose to advocate on behalf of different policy proposals. Likewise, legislators routinely invite some groups but not others to testify on a given issue. Whether one advocates or is invited depends on whether the group has and is considered to have policy authority—substantive expertise about the causes, dimensions, and potential remedies for a given public problem. In Joseph R. Gusfield's (1981) terms, groups "own" issues or at least have an ownership stake.

One way to think about a group's ownership of an issue is to consider the policy domain in which the group is especially active. Farmers' groups have an ownership stake in agriculture policy, teachers' unions have an ownership stake in education policy, and so forth. Another way to think about ownership is to consider the policy dimension, or the specific facet of a proposal, that draws the group's interest. In practice, policy proposals often include many narrow provisions and thus affect a variety of group interests. Thus, groups that may not regularly engage in that issue's policy domain may weigh in on a narrow dimension of a particular proposal affecting the organization's constituency.

Here, I examine the evolution in both facets of women's groups' policy engagement. With respect to domains, I focus on one prominent shift: the move away from foreign policy as a focal point for women's collective action. With respect to dimensions, I focus on the shift toward women-specific interests. Both analyses help to answer the question, "What is a women's issue, and how did that definition change over time?"

Policy Domains: Women's Abandonment of Foreign Policy

From the 1870s through 2000, women's groups testified in every major policy domain and in 198 of the 228 subdomains (86 percent) identified by the Policy Agendas Project. The array of issues over which women's groups sought influence is indeed broad: trade and tariff policy, income tax reform, air and water pollution, home rule for the District of Columbia, survivor benefits for service members' dependents, food and drug safety, historic preservation, women's and African American rights, universal health care, world peace and multilateral engagement, affordable housing, education reform, juvenile delinquency prevention, foreign aid, working conditions for immigrants, farm policy, alcohol regulation, child labor, nurse training, gun control, Supreme Court nominations—the list goes on. Indeed, women's groups' policy agendas in many respects reflect America's. Women's groups have often played a central role in advocating the growth of the American state.

Surprisingly, the distribution of women's groups' policy interests across major policy domains remained fairly stable over time. From the 1900s through the 1990s, for example, the share of women's appearances devoted to agriculture-related topics generally hovered between 2 and 4 percent, the share devoted to labor, employment, and immigration was generally between 2 and 7 percent, and the share devoted to education was usually between 3 and 4 percent. In several policy domains, however, appearances by women's organizations waxed and waned in more noticeable ways. Sometimes, those oscillations appear to go with the issue-attention cycle—for example, health care consumed a disproportionate amount of women's groups' attention in the early 20th century (when maternal and child health proposals were on the agenda) and the last third of the 20th century (when nurses' organizations and others weighed in on national health reform proposals). Civil rights and liberties consumed a considerable portion of women's issue attention between the 1880s and 1910s, when suffrage was under consideration, dropped from the 1920s through the 1960s, then picked up again as Congress considered the second wave agenda in the 1970s and 1980s. While women's issue engagements sometimes coincide with issue-attention cycles, at other times the pattern seems less predictable. For example, environmental policy jumped as a share of women's groups' attention in the 1960s, when ecology came into vogue, but attention declined in the 1990s, when environmentalism was on the rise.

One broad and striking pattern is the demise of foreign policy as a "women's issue." Beginning in the World War I era, women's organizations took on war, peace, national defense, and international cooperation as core components of their policy agendas (Cott 1987). They remained engaged at least through the 1950s, when their participation began to drop. By the 1990s, women's groups were scarcely a presence in major congressional foreign policy debates. Women's groups' disowning of foreign policy occurred as Congress greatly ratcheted up its involvement in international affairs, holding more and more hearings (Goss 2009). Women's retreat also occurred, ironically, as foreign policy debates were moving away from domination by elites and toward the inclusion of lay citizens' voices (Lindsay 1994, 28; Tierney 1993; Uslaner 1995).

Figure 4.5 shows the number of women's group appearances in the areas of domestic policy versus international policy (international affairs and foreign aid). Women's groups' appearances at domestic policy hearings declined steadily throughout the postwar era, but the drop in appearances on international affairs issues was especially stark and dramatic from the 1950s through the early 1970s, after which it settled into a low equilibrium. The drop would have been even more striking if the foreign aid of the 1950s, largely military assistance, had been counted in the "foreign aid" category instead of in defense.

Another way of looking at the decline in the centrality of foreign policy among women's groups is to look at the share of their testimony devoted to international affairs and foreign aid. In the 1950s, that number reached roughly 30–45 percent in any given Congress before plummeting to 5–15

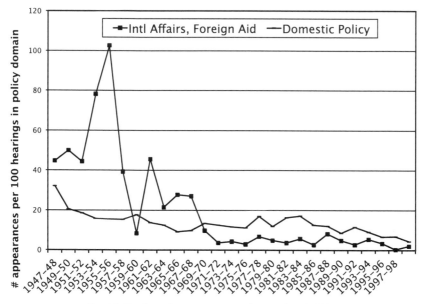

Fig. 4.5. Decline of appearances on international affairs

percent from the early 1970s through the 1990s. Women's groups appeared more often in absolute terms on foreign policy questions, including international affairs and defense, in 1923–25, just after enactment of national suffrage, than they did in any of the last three congresses of the 20th century.

Accompanying the quantitative drop in organizational appearances was an equally intriguing qualitative shift in the nature of women's foreign policy engagement. For most of the 20th century, women's groups were important advocates for the major international issues of the day, and they appeared en masse to state their positions before Congress. In the 1920s and 1930s, women's groups were preoccupied with urging U.S. participation in the Permanent Court of International Justice (the World Court), which they saw as an alternative to war in resolving international disputes. During the 1940s, women's groups played a prominent role in hearings on two of the most important items on Congress's agenda: the reconstruction of Europe after World War II and the creation of the United Nations. The 1950s represented the most active decade for women's groups on Capitol Hill, at least in the realm of foreign policy: They appeared more than 300 times during that decade. The vast majority of those appearances concerned aid to foreign nations, continued participation in the United Nations, universal military service and training, and the positioning of U.S. forces in Europe. During the 1960s and 1970s, women's groups continued to focus on foreign aid and international organizations—in particular UNICEF, created in 1946. The Citizens Committee for UNICEF spoke on behalf of 9–12 women's organizations as well as a handful of child-welfare groups in urging Congress to increase its appropriation to the international aid agency.

From the 1970s through the 1990s, however, the scope and nature of women's foreign policy interests changed dramatically. Women's groups' appearances were scattered across a larger range of issues, with less collective focus. In earlier centuries, if women's groups sought to testify at an international affairs hearing, they did not usually do so alone. Beginning in the 1970s, however, if a women's group appeared at an international affairs hearing, it was more likely than not to be there without the company of any other women's group. Instead, individual groups tended to testify on issues involving women's rights and professional status—discrimination against women in the Foreign Service, female athletes' participation in the Olympic Games, international trafficking in women. Another change involved the types of women's groups that were engaged in foreign policy debates. The big, multipurpose membership associations that had served as women's voice on Capitol Hill at midcentury had abdicated that role by the 1990s. Roughly one-third of all appearances by the League of Women Voters and by the American Association of University Women in the 1950s concerned international or defense policy. By the 1990s, many of the once-stalwart advocates had ceased to testify on foreign policy questions. These included the national League of Women Voters, the National Congress of Parents and Teachers (which had become the PTA), the American Association of University Women, the National Council of Jewish Women, the Citizens' Committee for UNICEF, the Daughters of the American Revolution, and the Women's International League for Peace and Freedom.[20] In their stead, a handful of new, specialized organizations represented women, most notably the Women's Commission for Refugee Women and Children and the Coalition for Women in International Development.

Policy Dimensions: Other-Oriented and Women-Specific Concerns

The second way of thinking about women's groups' shifting policy agendas is to examine the dimension of a given proposal that attracts their attention. One of the most striking patterns in the testimony concerns the waxing and waning of women's groups' advocacy of the rights, status, equality, advancement, and well-being of women as women. In chapters 2 and 3, I examined the wave theory of women's policy engagement. Here, in advocacy for women-oriented issues, the waves become apparent.

Regardless of the status of feminism as a social movement, Congress has considered feminist legislation in every Congress at least since the 45th (1877–79), when the Senate Committee on Privileges and Elections held a hearing on a constitutional suffrage amendment. Even during the decades that are considered feminism's doldrums, especially the purportedly domesticity-oriented 1950s, Congress held hearings on a number of women's issues, including women's interest in divorce litigation, an Equal Rights Amendment to the Constitution, and equal pay for female workers. Two longitudinal series capture congressional attention to feminist issues. Anne N. Costain (1988, 159–60) finds that the number of hearings and the percentage of bills concerning women's interests rose in the 1960s and 1970s, when the second wave movement was under way. Frank R. Baumgartner and Christine Mahoney (2005) find that women-related hearings peaked from the late 1960s through the early 1980s—roughly tracking the local uptick that I recorded in women's groups' testimony.

Not surprisingly, women's groups' participation in hearings explicitly devoted to women's rights proposals has risen and fallen as Congress has chosen to prioritize or deprioritize issues such as suffrage, the Equal Rights Amendment, and sex discrimination in education and the workplace. In the presuffrage era, between 35 and 100 percent of women's appearances were on civil rights bills, nearly all of them about female suffrage. Between the 1920s and the end of the 1960s, appearances on women's rights bills oscillated. Such appearances were not unusual in the 1930s and 1940s (roughly 9–14 percent) but were rare in the 1950s and 1960s (roughly 2 percent). With the second wave, the fraction of women's group appearances that concerned women's rights bills jumped to 30–33 percent in the 1970s and 1980s, when the number of women's issue hearings and bills greatly increased. Then, in the 1990s, when congressional hearings on women's rights issues declined dramatically, so did the number of women's groups' appearances on women's rights bills (to less than 4 percent of all appearances in that decade).

However, the testimony record makes clear that women's groups did not wait for Congress to "discover" feminism. Rather, they found a way to speak to "the feminist angle" on general policy proposals. This approach became particularly salient during the second wave. Thus, one major contribution of contemporary feminism was its ability to scrutinize existing

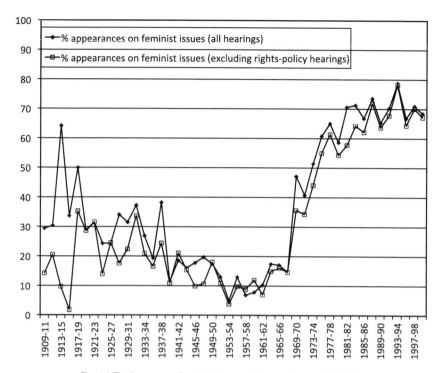

Fig. 4.6. Testimony on feminist issues (rights, status, well-being)

and proposed policies for their impact on women as a class. Women's groups identified systematic inequities in the law and then advocated legislation to redress them.

Figure 4.6 charts the percentage of women's organizational appearances in which the organization advocated solely or significantly for women-specific interests, defined as rights, status, or well-being. The figure shows women's advocacy on behalf of women's interests within all policy domains as well as in all policy domains excluding civil rights and liberties (where women's rights proposals are categorized).

As the figure shows, women's groups were attentive to women's rights, status, and well-being throughout the period. But the 1940s–60s indeed formed a doldrums period, with just 10–20 percent of appearances focusing on women's rights and status. When women's groups testified, they did so overwhelmingly on issues pertaining to the public interest (e.g., environmental conservation, national defense) or to specific constituencies other than women (e.g., children, the poor). However, in the early 1970s, with the second wave movement, women's groups turned their attention to the dimensions of broader policies that most directly affect women's rights, status, or well-being. This attention rose sharply in the 1970s and stayed high through the 1980s and 1990s, when roughly 65–75 percent of appearances focused on women. Examples of women's groups' attention to feminist dimensions of general policies included their advocacy for equity in Social Security, gender equality in the Foreign Service, equitable repayment for nursing services, payments for ex-wives of military service personnel, affirmative action in federal contracting and media licenses, and funding for breast cancer research. The attention to feminist concerns cut across policy domains.

At first blush, the waning presence of women's group on Capitol Hill raises questions about the vitality of the second wave movement in the 1980s and 1990s and about women's collective advocacy more generally. As we have seen, women's groups' appearances fell, as did the number of organizations testifying and the range of issues that they addressed. However, in the substance of women's groups' Capitol Hill advocacy, feminism remained strong throughout the 1980s and 1990s. Women's groups remained a vibrant force but exercised their influence in a more focused manner than had been the case in the first five decades after suffrage.

However, the flip side of this story is also important. With second wave feminism, women's organizations were far less likely to testify on general public issues or issues primarily affecting constituencies other than women. At midcentury, when women's groups were at their most prominent on Capitol Hill, nearly all of their testimony was other-oriented. They focused on issues such as U.S. participation in the United Nations, shortages in affordable housing, land conservation, water pollution remediation, public education, agricultural subsidies, African American civil rights, and taxes and tariffs, to name a few. By the 1990s, such other-oriented testimony was far less frequent—typically around 30 percent of all appearances. Furthermore, such testimony was concentrated in just a few policy domains. For example, in only six domains—health, agriculture, education, environment, government operations, and public lands—did women's groups testify at least 20 times on nonfeminist issues during the 1990s. When one considers women's citizens groups only, significant amounts of other-oriented testimony occurred across an even narrower range of domains: health, education, environment, and government operations.

The Case of the League of Women Voters

The three broad transformations described above—in organizational structure, authority claims, and issue agendas—are exemplified by the League of Women Voters. The League, founded in 1920 as the successor to the National American Woman Suffrage Association, is a particularly important organization. These two groups were present on Capitol Hill for the entire time period under study. Together with its state and local affiliates, the League testified more often (990 times) and on a broader range of issue areas (105) than any other women's organization. The League testified nearly twice as often as the second-most-prominent organization, the General Federation of Women's Clubs. Indeed, the League accounts for nearly 10 percent of all appearances by women's groups from the nation's founding through 2000. The League constitutes a particularly instructive case for understanding the evolution of American women's groups over the 20th century.

The League's Role in the Life of Elite Women

Like many other organizations founded in the early decades of the 20th century, the League is a federated association, with an organizational structure that mirrors that of the U.S. system of government. Through local, state, regional, and national Leagues, the organization performs citizen education and policy advocacy at all levels of government. Although it has never boasted nearly as many members as, for example, the General Federation of Women's Clubs, the League represents a particularly influential group of women—well educated, well connected, and politically attentive. In earlier decades, the League frequently served as an important training ground for women who wanted to run for public office (Kirkpatrick 1974).

Like many other organizations, the League floundered in the 1930s, but after the war, it grew markedly. In a period of residential mobility and baby boom fertility, college-educated women looked to the League as a place in the community to find other women like them—intellectually engaged citizens eager to make a public contribution beyond their roles as loving wives and mothers. In their classic study of midcentury trade policy, Raymond A. Bauer, Ithiel de Sola Poole, and Lewis Anthony Dexter (1963, 390) remarked with surprise that League members were "charming housewives who often turned out to be professionally trained economists!" As figure 4.7 shows, however, the League peaked in membership in 1969–70, just as the second wave movement was institutionalizing. The League's engagement on Capitol Hill had peaked roughly a decade earlier, then declined precipitously.

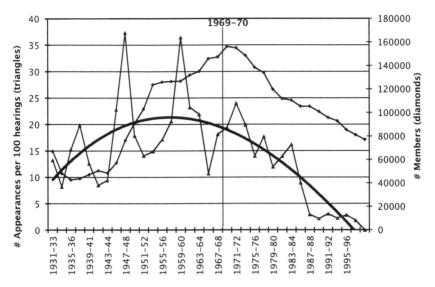

Fig. 4.7. The rise and fall of the League of Women Voters

The League's Sources of Political Authority

The League was formed with the earnest and enthusiastic mission of educating millions of newly enfranchised women for good citizenship and to represent their perspectives in public affairs. A 1921 brochure, *Why Join the League of Women Voters?*, stated that, among other contributions, the League "develops the intelligence of the individual voter," "works for better legislation on matters for which women should be primarily responsible," "provides a meeting ground for women of all parties and all groups, where they may . . . work together for things in which they have a common interest," and "unites the country's woman power into a new force for the humanizing of government" (Stuhler 2003, 37). The grassroots orientation was strengthened in 1946, when delegates to the national convention changed the bylaws to make local Leagues the core of the organization and empowered those Leagues to carry out a nation-spanning policy agenda (Young 1989, 147). In 1948, the League adopted the structural innovation of the neighborhood-based "unit," bringing members together for face-to-face discussions and decision making (147).

Thus, the League was structured to give priority to intensive study, deliberation, and consensus building. Internal procedures ensured that it carried out such aims. Before the organization can conduct policy advocacy on a local, state, regional, or national policy, members at the appropriate level vote to conduct a wide-ranging, objective study of the issue, debate and reach consensus on questions of policy arising from the study, and vote at an annual or biennial membership meeting whether to adopt the consensus position(s). Although parliamentary procedures allow for exceptions to the process, it is followed most of the time. At the national level, two years typically elapse between when the biennial convention delegates vote to formulate a position and when it is approved (or rejected). Although League members often voice frustration that the procedures are cumbersome and prevent the organization from jumping into a debate in a timely fashion, they have served the League's desire to give women's voice respectability, gravitas, and influence in the male world of politics. As the League's national president, Marguerite M. Wells, wrote in 1938, the League "involves harder work than most organizations demand of their members," making it "unique not only in its purpose but also, at least to a degree, in its methods" (Wells 1962, 9).

These organizational features have served the League well. The important, much-studied push for liberalization of foreign trade in the 1950s illustrates the League's comparative advantages. In the early 1950s, the League took a survey instrument designed by economists and the Federal Reserve and dispatched 3,500 of its members to conduct 11,000 interviews in more than 500 communities (Young 1989, 165; Bauer, Pool, and Dexter 1963, 390). The League hoped to use the survey interviews and results to illuminate the underappreciated extent and impact of foreign trade in local communities. Louise Young (1989, 165) notes that the "results provided a rich storehouse of data useful in communicating with Congress." When Congress held hearings around the country in 1955, one lawmaker "remarked with apparent surprise that people were better informed than he had expected" (166).

The League's engagement in foreign trade demonstrates how bureaucratic structures (such as cultivating a mass membership organized at the local level) and procedures (such as studious consensus and citizen education) can provide organizations with the political authority to speak on all sorts of issues. The League's declining prominence on Capitol Hill from the 1970s through the 1990s provides a window into the declining relevance of authority claims rooted in grassroots democracy.

"An Everywoman's Organization," with a Policy Agenda to Match

Nothing about foreign trade policy made it an obvious women's issue. The women of the League chose to embrace the issue because they considered it important to midcentury American prosperity. Although born of the first great movement for women's rights, the League defined its issue agenda expansively from the start. In her 1923 presidential address, Maud Wood Park argued that the League's "fundamental purpose" was to be an "everywoman's organization" (Stuhler 2003, 93). In the 1940s, the League was actively engaged in proposals to deal with a postwar housing shortage, price stabilization, and tax policy in addition to women's equal rights legislation. In the 1950s, the League was involved in debates regarding the United Nations Charter, water resources, and foreign aid. In the 1960s, its major concerns included water pollution, resource conservation, and (again) foreign aid. In the 1970s and 1980s, with the emergence of the second wave movement, the League joined the cause, testifying for equal employment opportunities for women and for child care programs while expanding issue advocacy in the areas of the environment, government accountability and performance, and poverty.

In the evolution of women's groups' issue agendas, the League was representative in some ways and anomalous in others. With the second wave movement, the amount of League testimony devoted to women's rights and advancement rose, reflecting women's groups' collective gravitation toward feminist concerns when the political climate was right. Yet the League was anomalous in that it did not switch off its attention to other-oriented interests even as women's groups seemed to be redefining women's issues as feminist issues. The League's diverse issue portfolio drew on a complex and variegated understanding of what a women's issue is.

The League of Women Voters, which has appeared on Capitol Hill more than any other women's group, struggled with and epitomized many of the transformations facing single-sex organizations over the 20th century. The organization began with a broad public agenda and a commitment to intensive, face-to-face democracy. Its membership and legislative presence rose through the 1960s but then began to founder as newer, more specialized advocacy groups came on the scene. The League's story offers clues regarding the puzzling patterns of women's collective engagement.

The Reorientation of the Women's Group Universe

Women's organizations have been a critical part of the Washington interest group community since before female suffrage. They have mobilized members, resources, and expertise to represent women's voice in a wide range of foreign and domestic policy debates on Capitol Hill. However, women's organizational engagement evolved in striking ways over the late 19th and 20th centuries. The previous chapters documented changes in the volume of testimony, number of groups, and range of issues. This chapter has offered a closer look at changes in the types of organizations testifying, their authority claims, and their issue interests.

Although seemingly distinct constructs, these three dimensions of change are in fact closely intertwined and point to a larger transformation in the expression of women's citizenship. In essence, what the 20th century witnessed—and what these three dimensions of change highlight—is the rise and decline of women as a grassroots public interest lobby. The mass-membership federations that were so prominent, particularly in the decades after suffrage, brought together women, particularly educated women, to develop their policy knowledge, leadership skills, and political savvy. These groups were typically organized at the local, state, and national levels; sought broad memberships at all levels; and exercised processes of internal democracy familiar to members of Congress. These characteristics gave the groups the authority to speak on behalf of a broad and important segment of the female electorate. The hearing transcripts make clear that women's groups strategically used these organizational features to amplify the force of their testimony, and members of Congress paid attention to these authority claims.

Most of the traditional women's organizations were intentionally broad in their issue concerns. Many of these organizations were born of women's exclusion from mainstream institutions or of the struggle for a greater voice in American democracy; thus, their origins primed them to speak on feminist concerns. At the same time, these women's groups represented a special female domain of voluntary action that existed alongside the predominantly male world of politics and sought to bring a uniquely female perspective to policy debates. Women's groups interpreted their mission broadly, embracing an expansive definition of women's issues. Their organizational form and internal procedures facilitated this inclusive interpretation. The evolution in women's organizational features and policy interests was accompanied by a striking evolution in the civic identities that grounded women's organizational advocacy.

FIVE

Sameness, Difference, and Women's Civic Place

In 1914, the Great War broke out in Europe. Three years later, under President Woodrow Wilson, the United States reluctantly entered the conflict. During that time, the American woman suffrage movement gained unprecedented steam; after decades of agitation, the vote appeared within reach. The intersection of these two great struggles—the war for democracy abroad and the quest for democracy at home—presented painful quandaries for American women. Once the war began, should they put their suffrage activities on hold to mount a movement for American isolationism and world peace? When American boys were being shot or gassed on distant battlefields, should women continue to protest for their right to put a piece of paper in a ballot box, or was such agitation inappropriate? Would a women's peace movement derail the female suffrage movement?

Women's groups vigorously debated these questions but ultimately found a way to link the two struggles and empower women's participation in both. Despite early misgivings, the National American Woman Suffrage Association quietly supported the creation of the Woman's Peace Party, founded by the famed social reformer Jane Addams in 1915. The association's more radical lobbying division, the Congressional Union, headed by the fiery Alice Paul, was among the founding members of the Peace Party, whose membership reached 40,000 by 1916 (Alonso 1993, 63, 65). As Harriet Hyman Alonso (1993, 64) has noted, the suffragists were united in their belief that, as "the mother half of humanity," women deserved "a share in deciding between war and peace." This fusion of women's rights and women's caregiving allowed activists with a wide range of sentiments and sensibilities to participate in both struggles.

In the 1960s, America was again embroiled in war, this time in Vietnam. Women Strike for Peace, founded in 1961 to oppose nuclear testing and proliferation, picked up the earlier maternal rhetoric by holding a mothers' march in Washington in 1966 and a demonstration at the Pentagon the following year (Swerdlow 1993). Displaying large photographs of Vietnamese children poisoned by napalm, the defoliant used by U.S. forces, the women's group declared, "Children are not for burning" (135). Such maternal pleas would fade the following year, when younger members applied a feminist lens to the organization's ideology. At one organizational congress, radical women from the New York chapter "carried a female dummy representing traditional womanhood across the stage, announcing that it would be buried formally that evening at Arlington Cemetery" (139). Younger women assailed the organization for perpetuating sexism. The Chicago contingent argued that "until women go beyond justifying themselves in terms of their wombs and breasts and housekeeping abilities, they will never be able to exert any political power" (140).

The public severing of maternalism from feminism in the 1960s and maternalism's very public burial ask us to take a closer look at the evolution of women's activism, not just in the realm of war and peace but across the policy spectrum. These antiwar anecdotes illustrate the different narratives that women's groups have used to establish the urgency and authority of their public voice. Women's testimony before Congress provides a more comprehensive, systematic source of information on women's rhetorical repertoire. An analysis of testimony can tell us a great deal about the role that women saw themselves playing in the polity and the sorts of symbols, metaphors, and analysis that they considered effective in swaying lawmakers. Here, I use women's testimony in two domains—foreign policy and health care—to examine how women's groups established women's civic place and how the notion of civic place changed over time.

As described earlier, civic place refers to the intersection of a social group's civic identity, mode of organization, and policy agenda. A civic identity signifies collective beliefs about citizens' claims against and duties toward their fellow citizens and the state. Rooted in individual experiences (e.g., motherhood), civic identities help to locate groups' roles in politics. Organizations use civic identities to develop rationales for their constituents' political authority and policy demands (e.g., mothers should be caretakers of society). Organizational leaders also develop structures (e.g., federations) and internal procedures (e.g., consensus-based decision making) to occupy and send value signals about a social group's civic place. Organizations directly reveal their constituents' civic place through advocacy of public policy issues (e.g., testifying for international cooperation).

To track the evolution in women's groups' civic place, I draw on an original dataset containing 368 pieces of witness testimony from 87 hearings or series of hearings on foreign policy and government provision of health care. Each transcript was analyzed to uncover the rhetorical strategies that women's groups used over the 20th century to connect their civic identities to their policy advocacy, thereby establishing their civic place. For each piece of testimony, I asked, "How does this organization establish its bona fides to speak on the issue at hand?" Three dominant women's group identities emerged: (1) a "maternal" identity, rooted in women's roles as caretakers of family and community; (2) a "good citizen" identity, rooted in women's roles as stewards of the national interest; and (3) an "equal-claimant" identity, rooted in women's experience of inequitable treatment. Organizations sometimes drew on more than one identity, but generally just one dominated each piece of testimony.

To structure the historical analysis, I elaborate on the familiar dichotomy on which much feminist theory and analysis is based: the so-called sameness-versus-difference dichotomy. Generally speaking, the maternal identity maps onto the difference understanding; the equal-claimant identity maps onto the sameness understanding; and the good-citizen identity constitutes a clever combination of the two. Women's groups linked each identity to a wide range of issues within the realm of health care and foreign policy. However, not every identity was equally amenable to every dimension of those very complex issues.

First, I briefly review the sameness-versus-difference question, paying particular attention to its uses by women's organizations over time. Then, I review the three identities that emerged from the testimony. For each case—maternal, good citizen, and equal claimant—I show trends over time and spotlight particular instances of its use by women's groups advocating policy interests. Together with the findings of the last three chapters, this exploration of the shifting civic place of women's organizations lays the groundwork for unraveling the story of the rise and fall of women's organizational presence on Capitol Hill.

Women's Sameness, Women's Difference

Understandings of women's civic identity have revolved around a core question: whether women are at root the same as or different from men. Sameness arguments characterize women as independent political actors "endowed by their Creator" with the same citizen rights enjoyed by men. The sameness paradigm was present in the first wave women's movement's 1848 Declaration of Sentiments, which adapted the Declaration of Independence to state that "all men *and women* are created equal" (italics added). The sameness paradigm also guided the rhetoric of the early suffrage movement (Kraditor 1971). Likewise, sameness was the underpinning of the brand of liberal, or equality, feminism that came to dominate the second wave movement in the 1970s. The doctrine infused the founding statement of purpose of the National Organization for Women (NOW), which stressed that women were "human beings, who, like all other people in our society, must have a chance to develop their fullest human potential" (Carabillo, Meuli, and Csida 1993, 159). And sameness was the lodestar of the uncompromising feminist strategy that characterized the Equal Rights Amendment struggles of the 1970s and early 1980s (Mansbridge 1986).

The notion that women were the same as men informed women's activists' understanding of their relationship with the state. In this understanding, the state has a duty to protect the rights claims of women, including equal political rights and the right to equal treatment under the law. When the state fails to treat women equally, women have the prerogative to voice their grievances and claims for redress through the political process. Sameness understandings, then, stress what the state owes to the citizen: equal political rights and equal treatment under law. This relationship puts the natural rights conception of citizenship front and center. Women join men as carriers of the classical liberal tradition in American political culture.

Conversely, difference arguments conceptualize women as distinctive, relational actors. This perspective holds that whether by nature, by nurture, or by some combination thereof, women demonstrate an "ethic of care" toward others (Lister 2003). This ethic of care, in turn, undergirds women's proper role in strengthening democracy. For example, the postrevolutionary period gave rise to the notion of "republican motherhood," in which women's public contribution was to train their sons to be good citizens (Kerber 1976). The difference paradigm also informed Progressive Era frameworks for collective action, such as social reformer Jane Addams's suggestion that communities were just extensions of families and that women consequently could bring their domestic caretaking skills to improving government performance—what has been termed "social feminism" (O'Neill 1971), "civic maternalism" (Koven 1988), and "municipal housekeeping" (Skocpol 1992). The difference paradigm also informed early-20th-century suffragists' arguments that giving women the vote would allow them to use their experiences in charitable and reform organizations to improve the performance of government (Kraditor 1971). And it informed women's peace movements from the early to mid-20th century (Alonso 1993; Goss 2009; Jeffreys-Jones 1995).

Like the equality framework, the difference framework serves as a basis for women's relationship with the state. In the difference framework, women assume the role of engaged members of the polity, bringing their special experiences and caring sensibilities—especially as mothers and dependents—to their civic work. Women's role in public life is to use what economists would call their comparative advantage. This understanding of women's role stresses what citizens owe or can contribute to the polity—and to the state, as the democratic embodiment thereof—as opposed to what the state owes to the citizen. The difference framework, as developed by 19th- and early-20th-century women, harks back to the founders' civic republican tradition, a subordinate yet important strain of American political culture emphasizing engagement, community, consensus, and civic virtue.[1]

The second wave women's movement had a complex and sometimes fraught relationship with the difference argument as articulated in the Progressive Era. Some offshoots of the feminist movement, such as ecofeminism and portions of the women's peace and antinuclear movements, were comfortable using a language of maternal care as a source of legitimacy and authority (Alonso 1993; Somma and Rinehart 1997). However, the core cadres of the feminist movement—first consciousness-raising groups and later rights-based advocacy groups—viewed difference feminism as a threat to women's liberation and equality. They feared that difference reinforced "damaging sex stereotypes" (Davis 1999, 146) that could be "co-opted by those hostile to women's emancipation to fuel arguments for their continued subordination" (Offen 1988, 154). As Nancy Fraser (1997, 99) writes,

> Equality feminists saw gender difference as an instrument and artifact of male dominance. What passes for such difference in a sexist society, they claimed, are either misogynist lies told to rationalize women's subordination . . . or the socially constructed results of inequality. . . . In either case, to stress gender difference is to harm women. It is to reinforce our confinement to an inferior domestic role, hence to marginalize or exclude us from all those activities that promote true human self-realization, such as politics, employment, art, the life of the mind and the exercise of legitimate authority.

As Fraser (100) notes, "The political task was thus clear: the goal of feminism was to throw off the shackles of 'difference' and establish equality, bringing women and men under a common measure."

One line of attack was on the female tradition of volunteer work, which fueled the philanthropic and social reform efforts that distinguished women's organizations in the Progressive Era. The flagship NOW in 1971 "issued a resolution telling women they should only volunteer to effect social change, not to deliver social services. . . . The new woman of the 1970s could be an activist; she could work for free to change an inequitable system but could not be a volunteer" (Kaminer 1984, 4). Women's peace advocates took this resolution to be a "denigration of volunteerism as female exploitation" (Swerdlow 1993, 158). Difference arguments made a bit of a comeback in the 1980s, when "cultural feminism" arose to reclaim femininity (Fraser 1997, 100), and when theorists such as Jean Bethke Elshtain (1981), Carol Gilligan (1982), and Sarah Ruddick (1989) argued that maternal experiences and women's relational orientation more broadly have the potential to contribute to a more moral, peaceful, and just society.

These scholarly efforts to reembrace difference notwithstanding, feminism's fundamental wariness of difference arguments persisted throughout the 1980s and 1990s. Many equality feminists perceived care rhetoric as a threat to women's advancement, particularly in the professional realm. To many women who did not or could not aspire to motherhood—and even to many mothers—difference arguments reduced women to one-dimensional and easily oppressed beings. By the early 1990s, Theda Skocpol (1992, 538) concluded that "in the United States today no such unproblematic connections of womanhood and motherhood, or of private and public mothering, are remotely possible—not even in flights of moralism and rhetorical fancy."

Thus, the sameness and difference constructs have "run like two currents through the stream of feminist theory and politics since the late eighteenth century" (Lister 2003, 96). Issue entrepreneurs have used accepted understandings about women's essence to frame women's collective action and to assemble issue agendas and legitimize women's authority to advance them. Understandings of sameness and difference have also been subject to debate and tension within women's movements, from suffrage through the second wave and beyond.

However, even as these understandings have been in tension, they have also provided a diverse repertoire of symbols, metaphors, and narratives from which women's advocates could draw as the political and social context warranted. Indeed, scholars have documented the many instances in which women throughout American history have moved between, conflated, combined, or sampled from these two supposedly dichotomous understandings to advance their political and policy goals. Such strategies have allowed women's leaders to fit innovative, hybrid narratives to changing times (Goss and Heaney 2010).

Such hybrid perspectives have been used to advance both explicitly feminist goals, such as women's rights and status, and more universalistic concerns. With respect to feminist goals, Eileen McDonagh (2009) argues that suffragists blended equality and difference rationales to win the vote.[2] Likewise, Progressive Era women's advocates pushed mothers' pensions as a means of caring for women as a group with particular needs (difference) and advancing women's equality (sameness) (Sarvasy 1992). Echoing that synthesis, second wave feminists of the 1980s advocated policies to protect classes of women who were uniquely vulnerable or underrepresented— pregnant workers, battered women—with an end of providing them with equal freedoms and opportunities (Costain 1988). In other cases, women's groups have synthesized sameness and difference understandings to mobilize women around causes that are not explicitly about women's rights or status. Such campaigns have included promoting environmental protection (Somma and Rinehart 1997), advancing gun control (Goss and Heaney 2010), and opposing war (Goss and Heaney 2010).

Hybridizing is possible because, as Joan W. Scott (1988, 38) has argued, "Equality is not the elimination of difference, and difference does not preclude equality." Both constructs acknowledge women's distinctiveness in the political realm, difference theorists because they find meaning in women's sensibilities, and equality theorists because they have embraced separatist strategies of feminist organizing and in some cases supported policies (such as those dealing with pregnancy) that must acknowledge women's difference to achieve their equality. Karen Offen (1988, 156) has suggested that it is time for women to claim a hybrid "relational feminism" that would "reclaim the power of difference . . . and . . . reweave it once again with the appeal to the principle of human freedom that underlies the individualist tradition." Joan C. Tronto (1993) has made a similar call for women to claim "an ethic of care" that sheds the baggage associated with traditional notions of women's morality. Likewise, Scott (1988, 43) suggests that it is to women's advantage to include both sameness and difference constructs in their discursive repertoire, for difference has been women's "most creative tool," while equality speaks to "the principles and values of our political system."

As this overview suggests, sameness, difference, and hybrid rationales have served as the foundation of women's collective work in the public sphere. They have informed frameworks of collective action, providing purposive and solidary incentives for women to join together in social movements and other voluntary associations. As I demonstrate, they have also formed the basis for women's claims to speak authoritatively before elected officials at the highest level. This analysis is not a simple tour through women's discursive repertoires. Rather, it provides a bird's-eye view of what turns out to be a significant evolution in women's civic place in the United States—an evolution with implications for their presence and voice in American democracy.

The Maternal Roots of Women's Civic Place

In the first four decades of the 20th century, in both the international and domestic realms, women's groups derived their authority from the special knowledge, skills, and civic responsibilities that women claimed by virtue of their roles as caretakers of the family and its traditions. In my sample of foreign policy and health care hearings, women were especially engaged in two policy debates: U.S. participation in the World Court (1920s) and its nationality convention (1930s); and the Maternity and Infancy Protection Act of 1921, better known as the Sheppard-Towner Bill, which provided federal aid to the states for health education programs aimed at lowering maternal and child mortality rates. Although these legislative proposals occupied different policy realms and appeared differently amenable to a maternal frame, women's groups in both cases capitalized on their authority as guardians of the family. Women's family authority took various forms rooted in biological motherhood, social motherhood, and family heritage.

Biological Motherhood

Passage of the Sheppard-Towner Bill constituted one of the top priorities for women's associations, which organized the Women's Joint Congressional Committee to advocate in support of the program. It is perhaps axiomatic that women's groups' authority over maternal and child health policy would derive from members' status as mothers. Women's groups such as the League of Women Voters and the National Consumers League rooted their advocacy in their "special experience and knowledge" of the health needs of women and children.[3] A representative of the National Congress of Mothers and Parent-Teacher Associations noted that her organization was "rather unique because we have rich and poor, wise and ignorant, and all of them working together for the good of the children." She suggested that the bill would give women "knowledge and proper care" to have "many healthy children," an aim reinforced by the Great War's "tragic wiping out of so many precious lives."[4] As scholars have argued, women's groups' "appeal to male politicians' reverence for motherhood was a powerful and shrewd political tactic" that gave women an opening wedge into a broader critique of the domestic social problems of the industrial era (Jan Wilson 2007, 45, 29; see also Ashby 1984).

Maternal authority also proved a powerful lever for women in foreign policy debates from the 1920s to 1950s. Women's groups lobbied for greater engagement in international institutions, such as the World Court and later the United Nations, as well as for European reconstruction aid. These debates unfolded against the backdrop of World Wars I and II; as the mothers of soldiers, women staked a collective claim on foreign policy questions. Women's patriotic organizations and military auxiliaries were more likely to employ maternal rhetoric than were multipurpose civic groups, but these groups also drew authority from mothers' sacrifices.

Women's groups used maternal authority both to justify and to oppose international engagements. In the 1920s, women's groups used motherhood arguments to lobby for U.S. entry to the World Court. Mothers had given up their sons for war, draining women's physical, economic, moral, and spiritual resources, argued an American Association of University Women representative.[5] Conversely, mothers' groups in the 1940s often opposed U.S. engagement in the United Nations by claiming to speak for the voiceless "loyal fighting men who are paying in what Mr. Churchill calls blood, sweat, and tears for this conflict"[6] and for the "millions of mothers and fathers of boys and girls now serving in the United States armed forces."[7] By the 1950s, mothers' groups were firmly on the side of international engagement. As a witness representing the World Organization of Mothers of All Nations (WOMAN) told the Senate Foreign Relations Committee:

> I am a mother of four sons, two of whom are war veterans. I know I am expressing the fears and bewilderment of millions of mothers, confronted with the obvious fact that although we stand today in the very shadow of onrushing atomic catastrophe, virtually nothing is being done by our Government and the government of our Allied Nations to stop this catastrophe.[8]

The group's chair used a family metaphor to describe the Cold War: "WOMAN does not maintain that communism and democracy cannot live in the same world. As women we are conscious of the infinite variety between members of the same family—in our own children."[9]

Social Motherhood

In the period from 1920 to 1950, women's groups located their authority not just in biological motherhood but also in the social caretaking that women performed as an extension thereof. For purposes of establishing policy authority, women were social as well as biological mothers. With respect to health care, the social conception of motherhood meant enlisting the government to supplement women's voluntary work, what Paula Baker (1984, 642) terms "the domestication of politics." Stating flatly, "the Government has a responsibility for things like the care of mothers and babies," Mary Stewart of the Women's National Republican Executive Committee argued that "the new times bringing women into politics have brought new ideas of Governmental responsibility," including federal support for maternal and child health care.[10] Conversely, conservative women's groups opposed to the Sheppard-Towner Bill argued that far from assisting women in family caregiving, the federal government threatened to undermine the family by taking over its functions. These women saw their political role as protecting their sphere of authority—the family— from what they branded as the paternalistic and socialistic designs of progressive reformers. Said Mrs. Albert T. Leatherbee of the Massachusetts Antisuffrage Association,

> The chief object of attack in the battle of socialism against our established Christian civilization is the family. Socialists know that so long as the legitimate legalized family remains the unit of society, they can never control the State. It is the first necessity to break up the family that amid the resulting chaos may endeavor to build a society based upon individualism in which children become wards of the State.[11]

In addition to threatening family cohesion, the bill would undermine families by invading the privacy of the home and by promoting birth control, according to opponents. Decrying the interference "with the domestic relations of private life" and the looming policy decision by "the National Government to supervise the pregnancy of the country," Leatherbee and other conservative witnesses connected family protection to the protection of core American values. In their view, women had a duty to use their moral authority as mothers to stave off threats to the family and hence to the nation. Progressive reformers used maternal rationales to counter such claims: "That a bill whose only purpose is the saving of life should be attacked as 'destructive of the family' seems fantastic. Nothing so certainly destroys the family as death."[12]

Family Heritage

A third way in which women's groups used family roles as their source of policy authority was by casting women as guardians of their ancestors' legacy of military service. Women's patriotic groups confine membership to women who can trace their heritage to soldiers who fought in 18th- and 19th-century wars. To these groups, female citizens must honor their ancestors' sacrifices by defending American values and institutions, particularly the Constitution. A representative of the Kentucky chapter of the Daughters of the American Revolution (DAR) called the Constitution "the greatest document that was ever written, and we love it."[13] Women's groups' authority to defend the Constitution was derivative, the product of family lineage. A witness for the Minnesota DAR acknowledged that her freedoms are "precious legacies I inherited from the young soldier from Virginia." She vowed that young soldiers would not have died in vain if modern-day women, "in whose hands the priceless gift of liberty has been placed . . . are true to that trust and preserve and strengthen our freedom."[14]

Maternal Rationales over Time

Figure 5.1 documents the presence of maternal rationales in women's groups' testimony over time. As the figure shows, women's groups drew on women's family roles frequently from the 1920s to 1950s, though they clearly had other rhetorical strategies at their disposal. Although scholars have suggested that suffrage rendered maternalism obsolete (Baker 1984; Cott 1987), the evidence indicates that women commonly used their family roles as a source of political authority at least through the 1950s.[15]

The maternal understanding of women's civic place was rooted in gender difference. With the emergence of second wave feminism, women's groups' use of maternalism dropped precipitously such that it was virtually obsolete by the 1970s. Why did maternal rationales rooted in women's role as family and community caretakers decline so dramatically in the feminist era? There are two possibilities: long-established groups shifted away from maternal rationales over time, or the types of groups using maternal rationales faded from the scene. A closer inspection of the data reveals that the latter explanation is driving most of the change. The types of groups that relied on maternal rationales—chiefly women's patriotic organizations

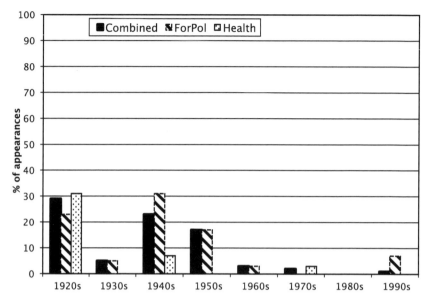

Fig. 5.1. Women's groups' policy authority rooted in maternal sensibilities

and women's clubs—had all but disappeared from congressional hearing rooms by the 1970s. Groups such as the League of Women Voters and the American Association of University Women used maternal rhetoric in the early decades and then shifted away, but their adaptation was not the major reason for the observed pattern. At the same time, by the 1970s and 1980s, the types of groups that were dominating health and foreign policy testimony were drawing on different female identities to make their case.

Women's Civic Place as "Good Citizens"

Beginning in the 1920s and continuing through the 1970s, voluntary associations afforded women a different basis for female policy authority: the good-citizen identity. In the wake of suffrage, women's leaders were eager to educate the newly enfranchised in the norms and habits of democratic citizenship. Furthermore, women's leaders were keen to prove that women were worthy of their inclusion in the polity—that they would be conscientious citizens and bring improvements to democratic governance. Like the maternal identity, the good-citizen identity was other-oriented.

It thereby provided a flexible platform from which to engage in a broad array of public issues. However, the good-citizen identity offered an even broader platform than the maternal identity, for the civic-minded woman could speak to issues not traditionally associated with or easily linked to maternal experiences. Women's groups used the good-citizen identity to weigh in on everything from civil liberties to water resources policy. The good-citizen rationale had three interrelated components. It dodged the sameness-difference question, stressed the effort required of thoughtful citizenship, and invoked the public and national interest.

Dodging the Question of Sameness versus Difference

The good-citizen framework avoided a head-on reckoning with the question of whether women were the same as or different from men. Reading through midcentury testimony, one is struck by how infrequently the large women's organizations explicitly referred to gender. Absent were sentimental appeals to women's particular virtues or claims to equal treatment. As Anne N. Costain (1988, 150) points out, women leaders "worked to erase the perception of distinctiveness" in hopes of being "accepted as equals of other voters." There were no female citizens and male citizens—just American citizens.

At the same time, women's group testimony was fraught with the implicit message that women were, in fact, superior citizens, more conscientious, less nakedly political, and more public-interest oriented—that is, different from men. To use a contemporary term in American politics, women's groups' difference rhetoric operated like a dog whistle, audible to those who were attuned. Women's groups emphasized their nonpartisanship, implicitly distinguishing their efforts from the self-interested pursuits of male-dominated parties, which after suffrage worked to exclude women from positions of authority (Sharer 2004). And women's groups drew on their expertise derived from voluntary work in the nonpolitical sphere. By withholding explicit appeals to female virtue while elaborating on the practices associated with care for others, women's groups cleverly elided the sameness-difference distinction. In so doing, they created a hybrid civic identity that captured the best of both.

Elaborating on Civic Effort

The second component of the good-citizen rationale was the frequent invocation of the laborious processes that women's groups undertook to develop their positions on policy issues. Women's groups discussed processes of careful, objective, nonpartisan study. They portrayed themselves as promoters of good policy, untainted by crass political considerations. A particularly rich but by no means unrepresentative example of such discussions came from Mrs. Harry C. Long of the United Church Women of Ohio, who testified before a Senate subcommittee in 1954:

> Since the inception of the United Nations and long before that, I organized study groups, led discussions, moderated panels, and have spoken with scores of church and club groups locally and over the State, on various phases of world affairs, with emphasis on world organization, and accent on the work of the United Nations. And as a member of the Christian world relations committee of United Church Women, I have visited the United Nations a number of times. This summer I was a member of a European seminar made up of writers, speakers, ministers, and teachers, who spent the summer on a study tour of social, political, and economic conditions of Europe. I visited FAO in Rome, UNESCO in Paris, and the European headquarters of the U.N. in Geneva. . . . I know something of the great humanitarian achievements and the social good accomplished by the specialized agencies of the United Nations.[16]

Many times throughout hearings, particularly at midcentury, congressional committee members took care to compliment the female witnesses on the thoughtfulness of their positions. Congressman Pete Jarman (D-AL), for example, responded to testimony by the Women's Trade Union League and the League of Women Voters on postwar aid for Europe by saying, "They impressed me equally well. To me it is outstanding that the women of this country, or at least those represented by the two ladies who have addressed us, and I imagine they represent a cross section, are far ahead in their thinking, I believe, either of the people in general, or of the Congress."[17]

Invoking the Public and National Interest

The third component of the good-citizen rationale was its reliance on appeals to the public interest generally and the national interest specifically. Against the backdrop of World War II and the Cold War, women sought out a civic place alongside men as defenders of the American way of life. In foreign policy, women's groups maintained their traditional interest in questions of war, peace, and international cooperation, but the maternal rhetoric that had dominated in the earlier decades was confined to small, conservative, isolationist mothers' groups. The larger women's groups, whether internationalist or isolationist in orientation, adopted gender-neutral language. In debates over the United Nations charter, for example, the conservative Ladies of the Grand Army of the Republic warned of "a very stealthy scheme for a One World Government, which if put into effect would abolish the United States of America,"[18] while the internationalist National Council of Jewish Women stated that the United States occupied a "position of leadership" in the world that necessitated full participation in the United Nations.[19]

The Good Citizen Rationale over Time

Figure 5.2 charts the percentage of women's groups' health, foreign policy, and combined testimony in which the witness couched her presentation in terms of defending the national economic or political interest. Such appeals became a declining share of all appeals as the 20th century wore on. As was the case with maternal rhetoric, this evolution was driven mostly by changes in the types of groups testifying over time as opposed to changes in rhetorical claims within the same groups.

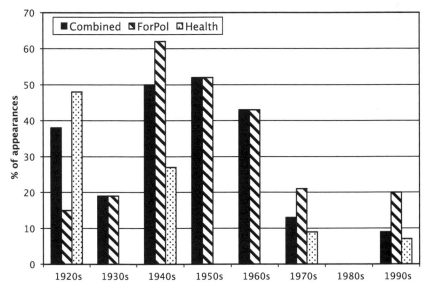

Fig. 5.2. Women's groups' policy authority rooted in national interest

Thus, women's groups reconciled the sameness-difference tension by continuing to organize as women in deference to their common experiences as mothers, wives, and politically marginalized citizens but at the same time by making relatively nongendered claims on behalf of the public good. Women organized as women but did not call attention to gender as the basis for collective action. Their approach to policy advocacy was rooted in principles of rational study and analysis. In short, women's contributions as citizens would be informed by the female experience but pursued on men's terms. The rise of the good-citizen framework as a basis for women's collective action may help explain the perception that the "woman movement" collapsed after suffrage. If women's groups downplayed the gendered nature of their work, it would almost by definition become less easily identified as women's collective action.

Embodying the Good Citizen: The League of Women Voters

The League of Women Voters was not the only organization to embrace the good-citizen framework, but as the women's organization that testified most frequently, it was the most prominent. The League's mission from the outset was to "develop the woman citizen into an intelligent and self-directing voter and to turn her vote toward constructive social ends" (Young 1989, 49). Because of the League's importance to women's advocacy and because the good-citizen rationale has not been well documented, I use the League to illustrate how this novel civic identity functioned in practice.

The first component of the good-citizen identity is ambiguity surrounding the question of sameness and difference. In the League's case, the ambiguity showed up as ambivalence about whether it was a women's organization. Even though *women* was part of the organization's name at its founding in 1920, within a year, president Carrie Chapman Catt advocated changing the name to the League of Voters and admitting men as members. She thought that sex integration was a signal of progress and that the League would be a fitting home for independent-minded males (Stuhler 2003, 40). A 1946 report on the League's history noted that members "do not think of their organization as a 'woman's organization,' but rather, as a citizen organization whose work is carried on by women simply because they happen to be able to organize their time and energies in a convenient working pattern" (Stone 1946, 16). This report also remarked that the "League has never been feminist in its thinking or approach."

Yet as much as it hesitated to identify as a women's group, the League's gender consciousness is reflected in its founding mission "to finish the fight" of suffrage; in its aim to incorporate women so as to provide "the *fresh challenge* needed to revitalize democracy"; in its ongoing interest in the equal rights of women; and in its devotion to the public interest (Stone 1946, 5–6, 15; *League of Women Voters in Perspective* 1994, italics added). "There is no male counterpart of the League of Women Voters," observed League leader Kathryn H. Stone in 1947 (83), "and few male counterparts of the various civic sections of many of the other women's organizations." Finally and most obviously, the League was an organization of women and by women. It refused to admit men until 1974, a half century after Catt had suggested doing so, and it did not elect its first male national board member until 2008. Well into the 21st century, its membership remains overwhelmingly female and its active members almost exclusively so. And *women* remains part of the name. Thus, the League exemplified the first component of the good-citizen rationale: a simultaneous denial and embrace of women's difference, allowing for women to be both undifferentiated from yet civically superior to men.

The League also embodied the second component of the good-citizen identity, the emphasis on intensive deliberation and participation. The League deploys elaborate internal rituals of study, consensus, and parliamentary procedure to formulate its policy positions. In the words of Marguerite M. Wells (1962, 11), the League's president from 1934 to 1944, "To consider well before undertaking action and to prepare well before beginning to act—this may be called a religion with the League of Women Voters." Such activities were directed outward as well. In its earliest years, hundreds of Leagues created "citizenship schools," lasting from days to weeks, in which experts in political science and public administration trained women in subjects from the "the mechanics of voting to the philosophy of representative government" (Stone 1946, 8). During World War II, when freedom was imperiled, the League began a "Wartime Service" in which "every member would educate the public about the importance of American democracy" (*League of Women Voters in Perspective* 1994, 22).

Massive campaigns continued in the 1940s, with the "Take It to the People" campaign to generate support for the United Nations, and in the 1950s, with the "Freedom Agenda" to combat McCarthyism by educating the public about civil liberties (*League of Women Voters in Perspective* 1994, 11, 24). In their seminal work on the politics of foreign trade in the mid-1950s, Raymond A. Bauer, Ithiel de Sola Pool, and Lewis Anthony Dexter (1963, 389–91) devote a chapter to "the Ladies of the League," who "must have been by several orders of magnitude the most active group to be found on either side of the trade controversy" and whose studies made news. The League's guiding philosophy was that women expressed their good citizenship through intensive study, deliberation, and civic education and in so doing set an example for the rest of the country to follow. As League president Percy Maxim Lee told the national convention in 1952, "The League within itself must be a vital force demonstrating democracy at its best. . . . To support democracy, we must *be* democracy" (Stuhler 2003, 251). The League's internal practices gave weight to its implicit claims to civic virtue.

Finally, through its broad policy agenda, the League self-consciously sought to speak for the public interest. In its early years, the League inherited a policy agenda of traditional women's concerns, such as child welfare and gender discrimination; within the first three years, state Leagues had successfully championed some 420 "women's bills" (Young 1989, 75). During the Great Depression, League membership shrank to an all-time low of 35,000, and Wells decided to focus on a broadly shared value among women—ridding the government of patronage and thereby improving policy formulation and the performance of democracy (113–14). In subsequent years, the League's energies were directed at issues such as international relations, citizens' rights, the well-being of disadvantaged people, and the conservation of natural resources (162). Thus, in the decades after suffrage, the League went from having a difference orientation focused on maternal concerns and women's rights to a hybrid orientation that implicitly drew on notions of women's civic virtue to advance nongendered causes. The League thus "succeeded in establishing itself in many quarters as the spokesman for the general interest" (Bauer, Pool, and Dexter 1963, 393).

In advocating on behalf of progressive domestic legislation and internationalist trade and foreign policy, League representatives couched their arguments in the language of the nation's interests and responsibilities. In interpreting such interests and responsibilities for Congress, the League implicitly put itself in the position of representing the undifferentiated public interest. Anna Lord Strauss, president of the League from 1944 to 1950, supported full U.S. participation in the United Nations on the grounds that America must participate in international decisions and lead the way or "accept the results of the decisions made without us." She added that the United States should put "all the great force of our physical and spiritual power on the side of right and justice in the society of nations."[20] The League's conception of the U.S. role closely paralleled the League's conception of its own role: to pursue intensive engagement as both a mechanism of achieving full and equal standing and as a responsibility of good citizenship. The good-citizen rationale allowed women to perform caregiving on a national scale, without sentimental appeals to maternal nurturing. In this account, women were looking out for others but were not grounding such concern in explicit claims of gender difference. Rather, the League exemplified the promise of a fulsome citizenship rooted in the public interest.

Other scholars have picked up on aspects of the good-citizen identity. Costain locates its origin among moderate feminist veterans of the suffrage movement who sought to blend into the broader Progressive movement, which meant surrendering women-specific claims. Stone, a political scientist and League vice president, argued in 1947 (81) that the framework was the product of women's (and men's) political maturation. She believed that both genders had reached beyond self-interest to "take responsibility through government for the welfare and interests of others." By midcentury, women were "much less consciously women citizens, more consciously citizens" and were "re-evaluating their personal and family habits to make room for regular civic participation" (86). These degendered female supercitizens answered the clarion call of the League's Maud Wood Park, who had argued in her 1922 presidential address that women "must preserve the right to choose their own path, use their own techniques, and fashion their own political role" as guardians of the public interest (Young 1989, 64).

Tronto (1993, 15) has argued that women's activists historically have been stymied by "the strategic problem of trying to gain power from the margins," which "necessitates the logic of sameness or difference in order to persuade those with power to share it." Forced to choose between these two frameworks, she suggests, women have had "no logical way to escape from the many dimensions of the difference dilemma." The good-citizen rationale constituted a strategic adaptation to this quandary. Rather than choosing sameness or difference, each of which had its accompanying sand traps, groups such as the League combined them in ways that muted the assailable aspects of each.

The Equal-Claimant Identity and Women's Civic Place

I term the third identity the equal claimant. This identity is rooted in women's experience of disadvantage and the expectation of recourse to bring about equal conditions and treatment. Roughly speaking, this identity maps onto the sameness construct. The equal-claimant identity was present in women's advocacy in certain key policy domains, such as (logically) women's rights. However, the testimony shows that over time, these narratives came to dominate women's testimony in policy domains other than women's rights. The claimant identity had two variants: one that promoted women's equality through the identification of women's different needs; and one that promoted women's equality through the lens of women's sameness.

Claims for Equality through Different Needs

Witnesses using difference-based equality claims grounded their testimony in discussions of the ways in which women, by virtue of their physiology and social roles, had particular vulnerabilities or disadvantages. Such traits gave rise to what Fraser (1989) has termed needs claims. In the interest of women's equality, policymakers had a duty to address women's needs born of women's difference. Such rationales became increasingly important beginning in the 1970s in both health and foreign policy.

During the 1970s and 1990s, when national health insurance was on the congressional agenda, feminist groups called attention to women's unique health needs and disparate treatment under the existing system. For example, in 1975 testimony, a representative of the Women's Lobby stated, "No health care legislation should be considered by this Congress which does not address itself to the specific needs of more than one-half of our population: women." She cited various ways in which women's needs were distinctive. Women make more doctor and hospital visits. Women stay home with sick children. Women take more prescription drugs, often with understudied or extreme side effects. Women constitute more health care workers but fewer health care policymakers. Women face discrimination in insurance rates. Women face particular diseases that could be prevented with better care.[21] In 1995, Representative Patricia Schroeder (D-CO), representing the Congressional Caucus for Women's Issues, echoed these concerns, noting that women's health differences affect "every system from cardiovascular, to urological, to psychological" as well as reproductive, and pointing out that "that means research, treatment and insurance must respond appropriately."[22] At the same time, Schroeder made clear that, while rooted in difference, her claim was unabashedly in the egalitarian tradition: "We are here because we are terrified that the health care train is going to leave the station and women are not going to be on it in equal seats. . . . [W]e are full citizens and we want to be treated the same as any other citizen."[23]

In the foreign policy realm, the equality-through-difference claims show up in earnest in the 1990s, by which time women's groups' dominant foreign policy concern had shifted from international organizations to human rights, particularly violations against women. A representative of the Women's Commission for Refugee Women and Children, for example, reported back from an early-1990s trip to the Balkans and declared that "women are the targets of this war." She cited the use of rape as a weapon of war and urged the United States to open its doors to these "traumatized women and children."[24] Echoing those sentiments, a representative of the Women's Rights Project of Human Rights Watch cited an epidemic of violence against women for political objectives and urged that women's rights consequently must be made a more integral part of U.S. foreign policy.[25]

Claims for Equality through Sameness

While difference-based equality arguments recognized women as a special class in need of targeted policies to effect equity, sameness-based claims saw gender distinctions as wrongheaded artifacts of patriarchal systems. Here, the role of public policy was to make a public statement that downplayed differences and to create legal mechanisms to advance women's equal treatment.

In the health care domain, nurses' associations were key representatives of equality claims. Roughly 110 nursing groups cumulatively testified more than 800 times from 1910 to 2000, constituting more than 7 percent of all appearances by women's groups. For the most part, this testimony staked a claim that nurses' perspectives and experiences with patients made them just as worthy as doctors—and arguably more so—to speak to shortcomings in the health care system and to suggest reforms. Thus, nursing organizations drew on their members' professional experiences to advocate equal status in health care debates. At the same time, nurses' organizations testified that government programs unjustly treated nursing services as inferior to services provided by doctors for purposes of reimbursement formulas. Anyone reading nursing organizations' statements to Congress would hear a clear message, emerging in 70–80 percent of the testimony: (Female) nurses were just as qualified as (male) doctors to speak authoritatively about health care policy, and the government must treat nursing services as equally worthy.

Within foreign policy, the equality-as-sameness rationale emerged in the debate over ratification of the United Nations Convention on the Elimination of All Forms of Discrimination against Women (CEDAW).

The debate over CEDAW, which in my sample unfolded on Capitol Hill in 1990 and 1994, pivoted on the same question that had bogged down the Equal Rights Amendment in the 1970s. Liberal feminist groups insisted that CEDAW was necessary to ensure equal treatment; conservative women's groups insisted that equal treatment would harm women by ignoring very real gender differences; and moderate groups sought to thread the needle by arguing that equality could be gained without trampling on difference. A representative of the International Women's Rights Action Watch articulated the equality-as-sameness view: CEDAW would provide "full citizenship to women."[26] Harking back to the good-citizen rationale, she invoked U.S. national interest and leadership on women's rights as a reason to support ratification.[27]

Conversely, a representative of the conservative Concerned Women for America argued that although the group supported antidiscrimination policies and equality under law for women, CEDAW would eliminate "commonsense distinctions between men and women."[28] Thus, even in embracing an equality-as-difference rationale in this particular case, Concerned Women for America accepted the premise that public policy should, within reason, promote gender equality.

The Emergence of the Equal-Claimant Identity

These narratives reflect the confluence of three developments: the expansion of the state as a locus for the making of constituency claims, the movement of women into professional roles, and the development of a second wave feminist consciousness in the 1960s and 1970s, together with a backlash in the 1980s and 1990s. The movement of women into the paid labor force helped to fuel the creation of women's occupational and policy advocacy organizations and encouraged the spread of women's emerging feminist consciousness. These groups brought that consciousness to their critique of federal programs. As the state expanded into areas such as foreign development aid and health care provision, feminist and women's occupational groups staked women's claims to government resources. The conservative backlash created women's groups uncomfortable with what they considered overly expansive interpretations of women's sameness with men. In sum, women's occupational and professional advocacy groups identified grievances and brought claims for redress to Congress.

The shift toward the equal-claimant identity was driven not so much by changes in rhetorical strategies by the same groups over time but rather by changes in the types of groups that testified. Although women's occu-

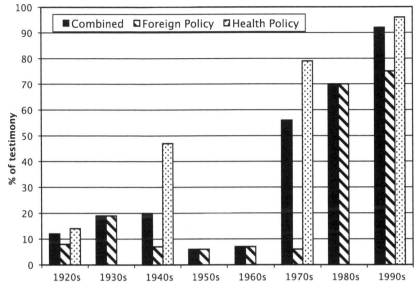

Fig. 5.3. Occupational and feminist group testimony

pational groups—such as those representing nurses, tradeswomen, and lawyers—had testified on foreign policy and health care issues throughout the 20th century, the second wave women's movement brought about a flowering of occupational and feminist advocacy organizations. These groups by and large disregarded claims rooted in a special female ethic of care or good citizenship. Figure 5.3 charts the rise in occupational and feminist advocacy groups in my sample of foreign policy and health testimony.

The trends observed in the foreign policy and health fields generalize to women's testimony across issue domains. More than 600 new second wave feminist groups appeared before Congress from 1966 through 2000. The percentage of women's group testimony given by just the 7 most prominent second wave groups rose from 0 before the 91st Congress (1969–70) to 20 percent in the 94th Congress (1975–76). The story is similar for women's occupational groups. They constituted at most 10–15 percent of women's groups testifying in the decades before the 1960s, but by the 1990s, that number was close to 55 percent. Through these two pathways—the professional feminist and the occupational lobby—women developed new sources of authority.

Does Civic Identity Have Broader Implications for Women's Voice?

Throughout the 20th century, women's groups drew on female identities rooted in family responsibilities, good citizenship, and equality claims. Yet over time, the balance of these civic identities evolved, as did the types of policies that women's groups advocated. Women's identity as biological and social mothers as well as stewards of family legacies dominated the early decades after suffrage and remained important through midcentury. Such relational identities allowed women to forge a civic place in which they were considered expert on everything from children's health to peace to national sovereignty.

Around midcentury, women's groups elaborated an identity of women as good citizens who were both equal to and implicitly superior to men. America faced threats to its national interests, founding values, and global leadership, and women were eager to take their place alongside men in articulating a defense of all three. After all, women were still on a path to fulfilling the promises they had made in exchange for the vote: that they would use their political inclusion as the basis for a deeply engaged, conscientious citizenship advocating government that would serve all people. The good-citizen identity formed the basis for women's civic place as guardians of the public interest.

The postwar progression of women into the paid labor force (particularly educated women, wives, and mothers), together with the feminist movement's attentiveness to gender inequalities, laid the groundwork for a third civic identity—the equal claimant. Groups drawing on this identity used it to critique systematic gender inequities in society and policy and to make the case that the state had a duty to redress those inequities. The women's groups that staked these claims tended to be associations of female professionals and second wave feminist advocacy groups. These groups articulated a vision of women as inherently equal to men. These groups' handling of gender difference was distinct from that of their foremothers. In the traditional formulation, difference was a strength—it gave women a distinctive perspective and source of policy authority. In the modern formulation, difference was a social artifact or even a necessary evil of biology. Rather than serving as a rhetorical springboard, difference served as the basis for claims of redress. Women were different, but they aspired to be equal; the state's role was to enact policies that kept difference from impeding equality. Women had become in a sense a "special interest"—or, rather, an amalgamation of interests with claims against the state for recognition of their equal rights and contributions in the professional sphere.

Women's Civic Place(s): A Summary

This chapter has explored the notion of women's civic place—or "places"—as developed by women's organizations and articulated on Capitol Hill to advance policy goals. Throughout the 19th and 20th centuries, women's organizations interpreted the social and political environment to identify and articulate civic identities for women as a basis for collective participation in important national policy debates. Women's groups linked female identities to public issues—mothers to children's health programs, good citizens to internationalist foreign policy, professionals to equal treatment in government programs. In so doing, they carved out a civic place for themselves.

These notions of civic place evolved with women's lives and political opportunities. Women's place was rooted in family, in nation, and in the workplace, and each place implied different rhetorical claims and policy agendas. Each identity and corresponding civic place was present throughout the 20th century, for their philosophical foundations of women's sameness and difference remained alternately vibrant and unresolved. Yet a clear pattern emerged. Claims to women's civic place as family caregivers were more prominent in the early 20th century than in the late 20th century, civic place as good citizenship peaked in the middle decades, and place as equal claimant came to dominate as second wave feminism birthed occupational and advocacy groups focused on gender discrimination.

Civic identities provide a basis for group claims to authority over policy issues. Thus, one might infer that the availability of civic identities has implications for groups' capacity to insert themselves in policy debates. We might hypothesize that the more civic identities that women's groups have available to them, the larger will be women's voice in national policy debates. According to this hypothesis, women's groups should be most prominent on Capitol Hill—and testifying on the broadest range of issues—when they can credibly and compellingly activate maternal, good-citizen, and equal-claimant identities. Put another way, women's groups should be most prominent when they can deploy difference, sameness, and hybrid understandings of gender roles. Chapter 7 explores this question. In chapter 6, however, I begin to unravel the puzzles presented thus far by systematically examining a host of theoretically grounded and intuitively plausible explanations for the evolution of women's groups' presence, agendas, and voice on Capitol Hill from the late 19th through the 20th centuries.

SIX

What Drove the Changes?
The Not-So-Easy Answers

Women's collective engagement in national policy affairs unfolded over the 20th century in ways that defy much of the conventional wisdom, in part because scholars of women's history have tended to focus their attention on waves of feminism. This focus leads to the easy conflation of rights movements on one hand with women's collective action on the other. While the outside strategies pursued by protest movements generate media attention, much of women's collective action unfolded through less visible inside strategies, such as advocating for and against legislative proposals behind the doors of congressional committee rooms.

A more important question, however, remains unresolved. What drove these trends? Why did women's groups grow in prominence on Capitol Hill through midcentury, when women lacked the political and economic clout they would later achieve, and then mostly decline when women's political resources and status had never been higher? Why did the scope of women's groups' issue interests broaden over the course of decades and then narrow fairly quickly? Why did women's groups largely abandon policy domains such as foreign policy and environmental conservation where they had once been very active?

Providing compelling causal stories about major sociopolitical transformations over long swaths of history poses obvious challenges. History is complex. Many forces operate at once, sometimes in parallel, sometimes in interaction with one another. In the period examined in this study, America witnessed staggering social, technological, and economic transformations, all of which may have affected the constraints and opportunities available to domestic interest groups. The political transformations were no less significant. They included the emergence of a federal welfare and regulatory state, the prosecution of two world wars, the rise and fall of the Soviet bloc, transformative civil rights movements, party realignments, and the reorientation of mass politics around postmaterialist, values-based cleavages. As half of the population—and a well-organized sector of the pressure-group community—women both influenced and were influenced by these transformations. So far, I have focused on women's attempts to influence public policy and by extension American political, social, and economic development. I now turn to exploring how the transformations of the 20th century influenced women, not as individuals but as collective actors seeking to be heard in Washington.

I evaluate explanations for the rise and fall of women's groups' presence on Capitol Hill as well as for the broadening and narrowing of their agendas, patterns that I believe are related. The explanations are drawn from the literature on political engagement at the individual, organizational, and structural levels. I also draw on the insights of scholars who saw this study in its early stages and graciously agreed to engage the puzzle. I unravel the story in two parts. First I examine proximate causes of the observed patterns—social and political forces that directly and immediately shaped the volume and content of women's collective engagement. In the next chapter, I examine a common driver behind these proximate factors—public policy. Behind the social, economic, and political factors that typically explain large-scale change, policy is playing the lead role in this drama. In scholarly parlance, I suggest that policy feedback effects are operating on women's organizations as they interpret women's collective identity and pursue policy agendas. Policy feedback effects have powerfully shaped women's civic place.

This chapter examines three categories of proximate explanations for the expansion and contraction of women's presence on Capitol Hill. Some of these explanations are hard-pressed to explain the trends, while others contribute to the story but call our attention to deeper forces at work. The three categories of proximate explanations are as follows:

1. *Institutional Explanations: Congress.* I examine whether the observed patterns in women's collective engagement can be explained by (a) changes in congressional openness to input from interest groups of all sorts; (b) changes in Congress's role in District of Columbia affairs; (c) partisan differences in receptivity to women's policy advocacy or interest in courting the women's vote; (d) shifts in the alignment between women's organiza-

tional agendas and congressional agendas; or (e) changes in the gender composition of Congress. I find that the observed patterns in women's collective engagement were not driven by changes in Congress.

2. *Organizational Explanations: Interest Groups.* I examine whether (a) in the wake of the explosion of advocacy organizations (Berry 1997), women's groups have simply been crowded out; (b) women's groups have lost patronage support from government and philanthropic funders, undermining their ability to secure resources necessary to be powerful players in Washington; and (c) women's groups have simply shifted strategies away from testifying before Congress and toward other activities. I conclude that developments in the interest group sector are relevant but play only a supporting role in the story.

3. *Individual Explanations: Women.* I examine whether the observed trends are explained by (a) the movement of women into the paid labor force, which may have strengthened women's organizations by creating the possibility of shared narratives or weakened women's organizations by depriving them of volunteer labor (or both); or (b) shifting patterns of gender identification affecting women's willingness to affiliate with sex-segregated organizations, again affecting the vitality of these groups. Each of these factors no doubt influenced women's collective engagement, though, again, these effects are minimal, indirect, or endogenous to the larger process of policy feedback. Women's movement into the paid labor force does not track women's groups' participation in congressional hearings, though it may account for changes in the types of women's groups testifying. Changes in women's willingness to organize separately may indeed be part of the story, but we are left with the prior question of how women come to think about gender as a political identity. To the extent that women's organizations' appeal fluctuates over time, these fluctuations may be an effect of changes in the state's treatment of women. That is, policy feedback effects on women's identities may be driving not just the volume and scope of women's groups' advocacy but also the capacity of these groups to mobilize women as women.

I now turn to these three categories of proximate explanations. Some of these forces indeed have played a role, while other forces—plausible as they may seem—had little or no effect.

Is This a Story about Congress?

Throughout the 20th century, Congress underwent changes in partisan control, institutional arrangements, policy engagements, and constituency demands. Perhaps the patterns of women's groups' engagement on Capitol Hill merely reflect underlying transformations in Congress. The possible effects of four such transformations are evaluated here.

Changes in Congressional Openness to All Interest Groups

This is a book about patterns of women's groups' national legislative advocacy over time. But the data raise a fundamental question: Are the observed patterns unique to women's groups, or do women's groups simply reflect larger developments in the interest group universe? Either way, the patterns are interesting. But to explain them, we must first understand whether this is a women's group phenomenon or a more general one. To my knowledge, there is no dataset similar to mine that encompasses testimony by all witnesses or even all interest groups. Thus, as described in appendix A, I have assembled a dataset that counts and categorizes different types of witnesses in a random sample of hearings at five-Congress intervals from the 45th Congress (1877–79) through the 95th Congress (1997–98). The dataset includes 1,680 hearings and testimony from nearly 20,000 interest groups, corporations, governmental agencies, and private citizens.[1]

The data suggest that patterns of women's groups' participation do partly track larger patterns of interest group participation. Women's group appearances and all interest group appearances rose from the turn of the century through the 1950s in both absolute and hearing-adjusted terms. Both women's groups and all interest groups saw an uptick in testimony in the late 1970s and a drop-off in the late 1990s. However, even after adjusting for congressional willingness to invite witnesses to testify, the distinctive rise-and-fall pattern among women's groups remains. Figure 6.1 shows women's groups' appearances as a share of (1) all witness appearances and (2) all interest group appearances during the period examined.

The figure leads to two conclusions about women's groups' advocacy. First, the broad pattern documented in earlier chapters—a rise in women's group appearances through the late 1940s, a bit of slippage followed by stable prominence through the 1950s, then decline through 2000 except for a brief uptick in the late 1970s—holds even after controlling for the volume of testimony by witnesses of all types. That is, women's groups are not merely mirroring larger dynamics on Capitol Hill; something is distinctive about these organizations. That said, when looking at women's groups' appearances as a share of all interest group appearances, a slightly different pattern emerges. Here, the overall pattern shows general decline over the 20th century, with brief upticks in the late 1940s and the late 1970s, consistent with the broader data. In this view, women's groups have been

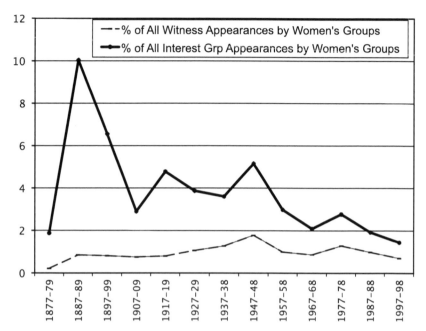

Fig. 6.1. Decline in women's groups' relative presence on Capitol Hill. (Based on a random sample of published hearings: $n = 10$ for 1877, 1887, 1897; $n = 10\%$ of all hearings thereafter.)

losing ground as a share of all interest groups since well before the late 1940s. Regardless of the difference in these two ratios—women's groups as a share of all witnesses or of all interest groups—the basic puzzle remains. Why is women's groups' prominence on Capitol Hill at an all-time low in the 1980s and 1990s, when women themselves had gained the political resources that command attention from lawmakers, such as educational attainment, economic status, and political engagement?

District of Columbia Bills as a Confounding Factor?

The congressional hearings capture women's groups' participation on national issues, with one exception: District of Columbia affairs. Congress plays an important role in the governing the federal city. National lawmakers may overrule policies enacted by the District's council and mayor, and congressional appropriations committees must review and may modify the city's annual budget. The hearings dataset contained roughly 950 appearances by women's groups advocating for D.C.-related issues, including appropriations, self-governance, and social programs.

However, since 1974, D.C. has been granted limited home rule in the form of an elected mayor and city council, raising the possibility that part of the pattern in women's organizational engagement could be attributed to the declining importance of Congress as a locus for women's groups' advocacy on D.C. issues. However, further analysis finds that, when District-related appearances are removed, the same patterns remain. Changes in the relationship between Congress and the District of Columbia are not driving the overall pattern in women's group engagement. And, indeed, the D.C. appearances actually offer insights into a potential concern—that this study would not capture any reorientation of women's groups around subnational issues. If such a reorientation happened, we would expect to see an increase in women's groups' appearances on D.C. issues between the late 1940s–1950s (when women's group appearances peaked) and 1974, when the District received limited home rule and Congress became less relevant. In fact, however, appearances relating to D.C. issues began falling in the early 1960s—mirroring the larger trend—and showed no anomalously large decline after 1974. Thus, the D.C.-affairs data lay to rest two worries. Fluctuations in District-oriented appearances did not drive the pattern in women's organizational engagement, and women's groups did not abandon national advocacy in favor of efforts at the state and local levels.

Partisan Differences in Seeking Women's Input or Vote

Another possibility is that the patterns of women's groups' presence on Capitol Hill reflect differences in the openness of the Republican and Democratic Parties to women's perspective. If they exist, such partisan differences might show up in the sponsorship of bills of interest to women or in attention to women's votes. If the women's vote was an issue, we would expect one of two outcomes. Either women's groups would testify more often in years when the more sympathetic party was in control of Congress, or women's groups would testify more often when the less-sympathetic party was in control yet eager to win women's allegiance. Either way, we should observe a pattern between partisan control of Congress and women's presence on Capitol Hill.

Evaluating partisan differences in sponsoring bills of interest to women is tricky because women's interests—certainly through the 1970s—were broad and diverse. Furthermore, women's groups themselves represented the full spectrum of American politics, from leftist consumer and peace groups to pragmatic-centrist civic organizations to conservative mothers' and patriotic organizations. In addition, some of the issue positions that women's groups championed in the decades after suffrage—such as war relief, internationalist foreign policy, and Prohibition reform—had support on both sides of the aisle. On the narrower issue of women's rights legislation, which consumed a fair amount of women's groups' time in the 1930s and 1940s, little partisan cleavage occurred. Both the Republican and Democratic Parties endorsed the Equal Rights Amendment in the 1940s, for example (Mansbridge 1986). Christina Wolbrecht (2000, 94–95) notes that in the 1950s and early 1960s, "women's rights mapped only weakly on to the general left-right spectrum." In fact, her research shows that little difference generally existed between the parties in the average number of cosponsorships of women's rights bills from the early 1950s until the early 1970s in the House and the late 1980s in the Senate.

These findings cause us to ask whether women were in play as a voting bloc subject to interparty contestation. Perhaps the observed pattern in women's groups' prominence on Capitol Hill is related to the parties' efforts to woo women into a Democratic or Republican coalition or to keep them there. Anne N. Costain (1992, 33) calls attention to this possibility when she notes that women were "objects of interparty competition" during the 1950s. In both the 1952 and 1956 presidential elections, Republican Dwight D. Eisenhower enjoyed a 5–6 percentage point advantage among women, shored up by his pledge shortly before the 1956 run to push for passage of the Equal Rights Amendment. Recognizing the importance of women's bloc, Eisenhower's successor, Democrat John F. Kennedy, sought to reach out to women's organizations, including by creating the President's Commission on the Status of Women shortly after he took office (133).

Yet compelling evidence demonstrates that party contestation over the women's vote was at best a peripheral contributor to the observed patterns in women's legislative advocacy. First, women did not form a coherent voting bloc after gaining the right to vote, as legislators figured out fairly quickly—certainly by the late 1920s. If women's presence at hearings is a product of legislators' seeking to woo their votes, we would expect to see testimony to rise in the early years after suffrage and then to fall once the expected women's bloc failed to materialize. Instead, women's groups continued to rise in prominence throughout the 1930s and 1940s and settled back into a slightly lower yet still quite respectable presence in the 1950s.

The hypothesis that women's testimony is related to the women's vote also does not fit the pattern of the 1980s, when a pronounced gender gap

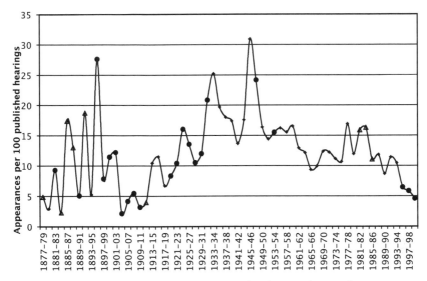

Fig. 6.2. No relationship between party control and women's groups' presence. (Triangles = divided Congress; diamonds = Democratic Congress; circles = Republican Congress.)

favoring Democrats emerged, or the 1990s, when suburban soccer moms became the subject of interparty contestation. In both cases, women emerged as a clearly identifiable voting bloc. Yet women's groups' prominence on Capitol Hill declined steadily during both decades. Those patterns are hard to square with the suggestion that parties use testimony opportunities to woo or reward electoral constituencies.

Perhaps the most compelling argument against the partisanship hypothesis is the visual evidence presented in figure 6.2, which shows the rise and fall of women's testimony with markers showing party control of Congress. A simple visual inspection makes clear the lack of a systematic relationship between the two variables.

If there were a relationship, we would expect to see women's testimony to rise (or fall) in predictable ways when a favored party came to power. In fact, no pattern is discernible. When Democrats lose one or both chambers to Republicans, women's appearances rise 62 percent of the time; when Republicans lose ground to Democrats, women's group appearances rise 60 percent of the time. When the transition is good for Republicans (they either hold both chambers or pick up one), women's groups' appearances rise 57 percent of the time; when the transition is good for Democrats, the comparable figure is 47 percent. If anything, women's groups do better in Republican eras, though across the sweep of history, no meaningful difference really can be found. These findings square with Christine DeGregorio's (1992, 979) observation that the vast majority of committee staff members attempt to assemble a full range of views at hearings and that "the nature of the institution ensures that some balance" of competing viewpoints "is preserved."

Changing Alignment between Congressional and Women's Agendas

Even if partisanship is not the answer, perhaps Congress as a whole is moving away from issues that women once championed and toward issues over which women lack or are unable to credibly claim policy expertise. In this case, the explanation would be rooted in the changing composition of congressional agendas over time. One obvious difficulty with this argument is that Congress has moved into policy domains that women pioneered—social legislation, education policy, health care, and so forth. The maternal public policies that women championed in the Progressive Era are now firmly entrenched in the modern welfare state. Moreover, congressional attention to foreign policy rose during a period, the 1980s and 1990s, when women's Capitol Hill presence declined precipitously (Goss 2009).

In addition to social and foreign policy, the other major policy domain that women's groups have occupied over time is the women's rights domain. One might speculate that with the election of Ronald Reagan in 1980 and the resurgence of conservatism, congressional attention to women's rights declined and with it opportunities for women's groups to testify. However, the opposite appears to be true. Hearings on women's issues rose dramatically through 1992 before falling back (Baumgartner and Mahoney 2005). More feminist bills were introduced in the 98th Congress (1983–84) than in the Congresses during the height of the women's movement (1973–78) (Costain 1988, 159). By at least three measures—number of unique bills sponsored, number of congressional cosponsorships, and number of members sponsoring any women's rights bill—attention to feminist lawmaking soared in the 1980s (Wolbrecht 2000). Even issues such as abortion, over which women's groups were battling in courts and statehouses by the 1980s and 1990s, continued to command congressional attention. Women's groups' testimony on reproductive rights and health was just as common in the 1980s as in the 1970s, and such appearances remained quite frequent (and a larger portion of all testimony) in the 1990s. Thus, even though many people see abortion as the quintessential women's issue, it was not driving the decline in women's testimony in the 1980s and 1990s.

Yet, whether women's groups were able to take advantage of opportunities to testify is an open question on which the evidence is quite mixed. A survey conducted by Kay Lehman Schlozman (1992, 365) in 1985 found that 94 percent of women's groups reported testifying before Congress, and equal numbers said they directly contacted members of Congress. Women's groups' access was aided by the political leverage they gained when a pronounced gender gap in voting patterns emerged in 1980 and continued in 1982 and 1984 (Costain 1992, 103; Costain and Costain 1987, 206). As Costain (1992, 103) notes, "The emergence of women as a distinct political constituency in the 1980s, for virtually the first time since 1920 when women got the right to vote, made it easier for women's groups to obtain a hearing on 'women's issues' in Washington." The director of the Congressional Caucus for Women's Issues reported that the gender gap was "the basic mechanism that powers the whole thing," meaning legislative influence (104). Aiding matters, the Reagan "threat" proved a brief boon for feminist groups' memberships, presumably adding to their leverage (105).

But Costain's (1992, 103) study of women's groups during this time also found that the flagship feminist organization, the National Organization for Women (NOW), "was quite distant from this Washington-centered activity after Reagan's election" and, with the exception of fighting an anti-abortion measure, did not focus "on national politics or on the Congress." My data show that, indeed, testimony by leading feminist groups declined precipitously beginning in 1985, a pattern that more or less tracked that of the leading traditional mass-membership groups and occupational groups. Figure 6.3 shows this pattern.

It is hard to know what to make of the hypothesis that women's groups' declined in prominence because of a mismatch between their policy agendas and those of Congress. Congressional attention to women's issues did not wane until the early 1990s, a decade after the decline in women's group appearances had begun. Furthermore, women's groups historically have testified on a wide range of issues beyond women's rights. Indeed, the high-water mark for women's group testimony came in the feminist doldrums of the 1940s and 1950s, meaning that Congress need not be paying attention to feminist issues for women's groups to be prominent players on Capitol Hill. I believe that a connection exists between women's groups' rights orientation and the volume and scope of their legislative advocacy,

Fig. 6.3. The rise and fall of women's groups, by category

but the explanation is not at root about a mismatch between congressional and organizational policy agendas.

Changes in the Gender Composition of Congress

Female legislators are more likely than their male counterparts to champion the interests of women citizens, including both feminist issues and issues advanced by traditional women's groups (see Swers 2001 for a review). Perhaps, then, as female legislators have grown in number, women's groups have become if not obsolete at least less important in the eyes of male members of Congress. Male legislators who wish to understand women's interests can simply ask their female colleagues or even invite them to testify. Female legislators then become a proxy for women's organizations.

Although this scenario has intuitive appeal, it fails on several counts. First, organizations of female government workers, such as bureaucrats and legislators, are counted in my data as interest groups, meaning that I am accounting at least in part for the lobbying that occurs within government. Second, these intragovernmental lobbies were never as prominent as were the outside women's groups. For example, the Congressional Caucus for Women's Issues testified 34 times over its two decades, fewer than half the 87 appearances made by NOW.[2] Indeed, the caucus was more of a complement to than a substitute for outside feminist groups, with its prominence in hearing rooms very closely tracking that of outside feminist groups. Finally, there is reason to believe that female legislators would be a boost to women's groups' access to Congress rather than a substitute. Studies by Beth Reingold (1992) and Sue Thomas (1994, 1997) have found that women lawmakers "expressed a sense of responsibility to represent the interests of women and they were more likely than men to view women as a distinct part of their constituencies" (Swers 2001, 217). In my interviews, one veteran feminist organization leader in Washington said that a hallmark of the feminist movement's maturity was the development of close, mutually supportive ties to prominent female (and some male) members of Congress, including Senator Barbara Boxer (D-CA) and House Minority Leader Nancy Pelosi (D-CA) (Smeal 2009).

Is This a Story about Changes in Interest Groups?

The period under study encompasses the creation of the pressure group community in Washington in the early 20th century and its "explosion" during the 1970s and beyond (Berry 1997). It also encompasses a period in which institutional patrons, including government agencies and philanthropic foundations, became important sources of start-up and operational funds for interest groups in Washington (Walker 1991). Finally, it encompasses a period in which interest groups expanded their advocacy repertoire beyond traditional strategies, such as legislative lobbying, to alternative means of affecting policy, such as litigation, mass media campaigns, and political action committee contributions. Could these larger changes in the interest group environment be driving the observed pattern in women's groups' engagement on Capitol Hill? Here, I consider explanations revolving around the advocacy explosion, patronage resources, and interest group strategies.

The Advocacy Explosion

Interest groups proliferated in the second half of the 20th century, a phenomenon whose various dimensions have been well documented

(Baumgartner and Leech 1998; Berry 1997, 1999; Walker 1991). Jack L. Walker Jr. (1991, 1) chronicles an interest group "march on Washington," while Mark P. Petracca (1992) reveals that the number of lobbyists more than tripled between 1977 and 1991. The advocacy explosion was centered in two segments of the interest group universe—public affairs and social welfare—that women's groups traditionally dominated. Public affairs groups witnessed a more than 18-fold increase between 1959 and 1995, while social welfare groups enjoyed an 8-fold increase (Baumgartner and Leech 1998).

The proliferation of interest groups in Washington has led scholars to think about how system-level factors, such as the density of the interest group community, affect organization-level outcomes, such as strategies and survival. One key finding is that the denser the pressure group community, the more likely it is that any individual group will withdraw from lobbying (Gray and Lowery 1996). Another key finding is that, given the increasing number of issue advocates seeking to be heard inside the Beltway, interest groups spend a lot of time worrying about how to stand out from the crowd—that is, how to establish a unique, politically valuable identity that will give them access and leverage in policy debates (Heaney 2004, 627). One way they do so is by carving out niches along various dimensions, such as membership cadres and source of support, in which they find themselves in competition with other organizations (Gray and Lowery 1996). A second, arguably more important, type of niche-seeking behavior involves the quest to occupy a particular portion of the policy terrain.

Although interest groups multiply their power by working in coalitions to advocate for common issue interests (Strolovitch 2007, 185), organizations also seek to own issues as a means of establishing their political bona fides. In an influential article, William Browne (1990, 502) argued that an interest group "gains a recognizable identity by defining a highly specific issue niche for itself and fixing its specified political assets (i.e., recognition and other resources) within that niche." Citizens' organizations in particular seek policy niches to establish their identities in Washington (Heaney 2004). My interviews with women's groups underscored that finding. Asked how they set their issue agendas, women's group leaders invariably said they surveyed what issues peer organizations were working on and then selected important issues that seemed neglected. Once groups have become known for their expertise, they are more likely to dig in than to branch out (Strolovitch 2007, 106). In short, while women's groups mobilize through coalitions when issues of common concern top the legislative agenda, in normal times, women's groups focus on a few identified policy niches where they can dominate.

Such niche seeking may stem from the need for external funds. To attract grants from philanthropic foundations, nonprofit organizations often must demonstrate that they are working on issues or approaches that are new and distinct from those of their peer organizations (Fleishman 2009). Meanwhile, as interest groups have moved away from recruiting through social networks and toward direct mail, advocates have had to rely on specific, often alarmist appeals built around narrow issues (Skocpol 1999, 503).

Together, these findings suggest that the decline in women's groups' prominence—and the growing particularism of their issue agendas—may result in part from a larger set of transformations in the Washington pressure group community, especially the proliferation of specialized groups moving into issue niches that women's groups once dominated and the need to define policy interests narrowly to attract money from donors and recognition from political elites. Jennifer Leigh Disney and Joyce Gelb (2000) argue that the ability to find a specialized niche within the women's movement was a critical factor in feminist groups' ability to survive into the 1990s. These larger transformations play a role in what has happened to women's groups but also leave deeper questions unsettled. For example, why might an influx of issue-based citizens' groups necessarily drive women's groups out of long-established niches? Might women's groups have created an opening in which a new generation of public interest advocates could arise? To the extent that women's groups seek policy niches, was it inevitable that they would settle on women's rights and status as opposed to any of the scores of other issues around which women had mobilized?

External Patronage

Money fuels the interest group community in Washington. Walker (1991) and Jeffrey Berry (1997, 1999) have documented how patronage support from wealthy individuals, philanthropic foundations, and even the government created and sustained the advocacy explosion of the 1970s and 1980s. Beyond being necessary to establish groups, patronage support pays for the professional staff required for an organization to be a player in Washington. These realities call our attention to the role of money in the fate of women's organizations. The available evidence suggests that external patronage probably did not drive the volume of women's group testimony but played an important role in shaping women's groups' agendas.

First, I turn to the question of the rise and fall of women's groups' appearances. During the first six decades considered in this study, social movement philanthropy was largely nonexistent. Most nationally active women's groups were funded by members. Thus, the generosity of external patrons cannot explain the rising prominence of women's groups in the first few decades after suffrage. Conversely, external support was important to institutionalizing the second wave feminist movement in the 1970s–90s (Jenkins and Halcli 1999). While government patronage was never a significant source of feminist group funding, foundation patronage flowed generously and helped the women's movement in key ways.

However, as with the pre-second-wave period, the 1980s and 1990s cast doubt on the proposition that the availability of external patronage support drove the overall trends. During those later decades, foundations stepped up their support of women's movement, but the movement's Capitol Hill presence declined. Women's movement organizations received more foundation support than any other movement in 1980 and the third-highest level in 1990 (Jenkins and Halcli 1999; Walker 1991). The Ford Foundation, the largest funder of feminist issues, greatly expanded such support in the 1980s (Goss 2007). While women's groups in the 1980s were more likely than many other types of Washington lobbies to cite insufficient financial resources as a source of ineffectiveness, only 27 percent of women's groups felt this way, fewer than public interest groups (Schlozman 1992, 356). In addition, a survey of five leading feminist groups found that two enjoyed increased inflation-adjusted funding between the mid-1980s and mid-1990s, and all groups surveyed increased their staffs (Disney and Gelb 2000, 55).

Figure 6.4 shows foundation data that I compiled on giving to women's groups and causes at five-year intervals between 1970 and 1990. Spending on feminist causes rose slightly in real terms throughout the 1980s, then ratcheted up in 1990. The number of grants distributed rose at a consistently steep pace. A similar pattern is observed in giving to all types of women's groups, including visiting nursing organizations, female religious orders, and mainline service organizations such as the Young Women's Christian Association and Girl Scouts.

Although my data on foundation patronage end in 1990, a subsequent study covering 1990–2006 found that foundation giving to women and girls rose by 223 percent in inflation-adjusted terms over this period, 50 percentage points higher than the overall increase in giving to all causes (Foundation Center 2009). Thus, the evidence suggests that external patronage did not directly drive either the increase in women's organiza-

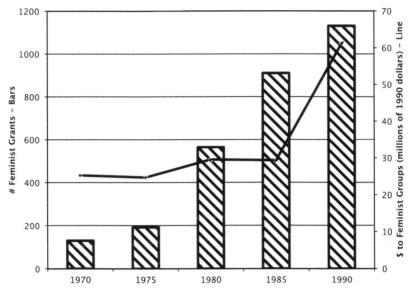

Fig. 6.4. Foundation support for feminist groups. (Data from author's compilations from Foundation Grants Index.)

tions' prominence on Capitol Hill in the first half of the 20th century or the sharp decline after 1981.

However, patrons may have played a role in the other observed trend, the narrowing of women's groups' issue agendas. In this way, the patronage effects may have been subtle and indirect. Anecdotal accounts suggest that in the Reagan and George H. W. Bush years, women's groups competed to differentiate themselves from one another in the quest for foundation funding (Burk and Hartmann 1996, 19). My study of foundation patronage from 1970 through 1990 supports the view that foundations and their feminist grantees worked in tandem to construct an array of new female identities. Foundations made a strategic decision to increase their impact by supporting specialized grant-seeking groups. That decision in turn provided a strong incentive for those groups to establish a policy niche that would enable them to catch the eye of professional funders. Through this interactive process, foundations enabled identity diversification and segmentation, in which women no longer considered themselves members of a heterogeneous community but rather members of one or more female subcommunities: poor women, minority women, lesbians, abused women, traditional women, nontraditional women, mothers, pregnant or potentially pregnant women, victims of gender discrimination, feminist activists, and so forth. Foundations tacitly validated and in many cases overtly encouraged the segmentation of female identities by providing financial support to nonprofit organizations that saw U.S. women not as a unified whole but rather at best as a loose confederation of interests based on occupation, class, race, vulnerability, age, sexual orientation, and other characteristics.

In this way, organized philanthropy did not merely professionalize feminist activism but also helped reorient women's issue priorities and in turn legitimized new gender identities and gender roles. Thus, foundations' major contribution was not simply to affect strategic or organizational forms but also to promote and legitimize certain public ideas and norms over others. As I discuss in the next chapter, philanthropic patrons played an important supporting role in the redefinition of women's issues and interests that public policy had been central to bringing about.

Seeking Alternative Strategies?

This study relies heavily on one measure—congressional testimony—to think about the evolution of women's groups over time. I have argued that testimony is a good lens for viewing the issues that women's groups have chosen to champion or oppose as well as those issues on which political elites consider women's perspectives to be authoritative. The volume of testimony offers a rough proxy for women's groups' relevance to public debates. However, Congress is only one venue in which interest organizations seek to influence public policy at the national level, and legislative advocacy is but one of many strategies through which organizations seek social change. Thus, one might ask whether this study is simply picking up a shift in women's groups' strategies away from legislative advocacy (or hearing testimony more specifically) and toward other methods of effecting change.

Again, this possibility, while intuitively plausible, appears not to be the case. Grossman (2012, 150) found that while women's groups were underrepresented relative to their numbers in congressional testimony from 1995 to 2004, they were even more underrepresented in executive branch proceedings, such as agency rulemaking and presidential directives, and in the use of the federal courts. These findings parallel those in Schlozman's (1992, 367) study, which showed that women's groups were far more likely to target Congress than the executive or judicial branches and that relative to other advocacy groups, women's groups were significantly under-represented in administrative advocacy and litigation. For example, while 72 percent of Washington pressure groups engaged in litigation, only 45 percent of women's groups did so (363). Joyce Gelb and Marian Lief Palley (1996, 211) state that "the women's movement has made limited use of the courts, in part because of the uneven response of the judiciary to questions dealing with sex discrimination."

Thus, there is good reason to doubt that women's groups abandoned Congress for other venues of political influence. As important as the executive and judiciary may be, Congress is the dominant locus of public policymaking. It is structurally permeable to interest group influence and has become more so over time. In addition, Congress's agenda is constantly shifting, providing ample opportunities for pressure groups to seek influence. For these and other reasons, according to my interviews, women's groups still view Congress as a key venue for pressing social, political, and economic change.

Is This a Story about Changes in American Women?

This study concerns women's organizations, not women per se. Nevertheless, because women start, join, staff, and lead women's organizations, it is reasonable to ask whether the fortunes of these organizations are related to changing attitudes, lifestyles, resources, or other characteristics of their individual constituents. Here I consider two hypotheses that are commonly offered in discussions of changes in women's participation (or participation generally; see Putnam 2000). These hypotheses concern the increase in women's labor force participation and changes in women's gender consciousness, meaning the propensity to identify collectively as women with distinct experiences and perspectives.

Women's Labor Force Participation

Women's labor force participation may have both positive and negative effects on women's participation. On the positive side, the workplace provides a locale wherein collective identities can develop. The development of common interests and shared fates may lead women to join professional associations and unions to advance sympathetic public policy or respond to policy threats. Because women dominate many professions (for example, nursing), growing female workforce participation may translate into increased political power for women's occupational organizations (for example, the American Nurses Association). The workplace also can be a site of sex discrimination, helping to solidify women's collective identity as an aggrieved group and propelling them to join organizations advocating on behalf of equal rights. Finally, working can provide women (and men) with the civic skills, resources, and recruitment opportunities that facilitate engagement (Burns, Schlozman, and Verba 2001; Verba, Schlozman, and Brady 1995). Counterbalancing these potentially positive effects of employment on engagement, work diminishes the amount of time available for civic and political participation. As feminist scholars Martha Burk and Heidi Hartmann (1996, 20) have argued, "The very sociological shift that the women's movement helped to create is now working against the organizing and political tactics women's groups pioneered in the seventies. Most women no longer read newspapers, don't have time to go to meetings and wouldn't consider attending a rally or march (for a cause they feel only remotely connected to) in their precious time."

Thus, labor force participation can both encourage and discourage individual political participation. What remains unclear is whether these countervailing forces, on balance, have increased, decreased, or had no effect on the overall volume and scope of women's organizational advocacy on Capitol Hill.

The simplest and roughest way to assess the women-working theory is to examine the trend of female labor force participation against the trend in women's group' prominence on Capitol Hill. Good long-term time series data on female labor force participation are elusive, but separate series pieced together tell a consistent story, which is that women marched steadily into the workplace over the 20th century. This story contrasts with the organizational engagement trend, which shows an overall rise during the first half of the 20th century and a fall thereafter, with scattered peaks and valleys in between. Women's labor force participation and organizational engagement tracked each other upward in the early decades, then diverged in the later decades.

This inconsistent pattern leads to a couple of possible conclusions. One is that labor force participation and organizational engagement are unrelated—the correlation is zero. Another is that they are related but in different directions in different eras (positively in the first half of the 20th century, negatively thereafter). The possibility of different relationships in different eras, along with the muddled theoretical predictions from the participation literature, means that we need to dig deeper into the empirical evidence.

Scholars have found little evidence that female labor-force participation wreaked havoc on women's civic engagement. Nancy Burns, Kay Lehman Schlozman, and Sidney Verba (2001, 321–22) were curious to test the popular assumption that after "housewives who once functioned as the foot soldiers in voluntary endeavors have marched off to work," the "relatively small number of women who remain at home are left with all the responsibility for volunteer efforts." Contrary to the stereotype, their analysis found that employed mothers of school-aged children "are considerably more active in politics, more likely to have gotten involved in community activity, to have given time to charitable activity, and to be affiliated with a PTA or other kid-centered activity" than their counterparts who do not work outside the home (323). In fact, the rate of political engagement among stay-at-home mothers was "alarmingly low" (323). The only place where the stereotype showed up was among married college graduates with children and full-time jobs; these women were slightly less likely to be involved in youth organizations than were their counterparts. These findings echoed the conclusion of Robert Putnam (2000, 196), whose definitive study of civic engagement in America reported that between 1965 and 1985, employed women's organizational engagement increased, while nonemployed women's engagement declined.

However, evidence indicates that female labor force participation affects the types of organizations in which women engage, and this finding is relevant for understanding the broader patterns of women's organizational advocacy on Capitol Hill. The movement of women into the professions certainly has fueled the rise of occupational organizations, which show up in increasing numbers in my dataset. Women's movement into occupations formerly dominated by men also brought them face-to-face with gender discrimination, including wage differentials, sexual harassment, inequitable expectations, and other sorts of demeaning treatment. These experiences no doubt helped fuel the rise of second wave feminist groups (Klein 1984).

Finally, common sense suggests that employment—particularly if combined with full-time parenthood—made it more difficult for women to participate in women's civic organizations, such as the League of Women Voters, that make heavy demands on women's time. Members are expected to research and write detailed studies of issues, assemble in frequent committee and consensus meetings, engage in public education campaigns, and travel to state and national capitals to advocate on behalf of issues. As Theda Skocpol has observed, not only do these activities require a lot of time, but perhaps more important, they also require the coordination of schedules, an added complication for working women with kids.[3] The

League of Women Voters does not collect demographic information on its members, but my eight-year experience in a fairly typical League is instructive. Most of the leaders were nonworking, longtime members in their 60s and 70s. As of this writing, I have seen only one leader who both worked and had children at home. This composition is a radical change from the postwar era, when the typical Leaguer was a married woman in her 40s, presumably with children in the home (Ware 1992, 284–87). The shift in the prototypical League leader reflects many changes, but one of them certainly is the decreasing ability of women to commit concurrently to three especially time- and labor-intensive activities—work, parenting, and the League. Women's capacity to participate in these traditionally labor-intensive organizations has important implications for the larger patterns documented in this study, for the League and similarly structured women's groups relied on active memberships for their political vibrancy. Because they were the most active women's organizations on Capitol Hill during women's groups' most active period, their weakening has the power to depress overall rates of organizational participation.

Thus, full-time work—particularly combined with motherhood—had multiple indirect effects on the patterns of women's organizational presence on Capitol Hill. The experience of work drew women into different kinds of organizations—that is, occupational and feminist groups. And work combined with motherhood complicated women's ability to meet the heavy time and labor demands of traditional women's civic organizations. In the next chapter, I suggest that the pressure of combining parenthood with work is a proximate cause of the observed patterns but that public policy acted in the background to reinforce the reordering of women's civic identities away from other-regarding policy agendas and toward the advancement of women's rights, well-being, and occupational advancement. I suggest that the difficulty of balancing work and family obligations may have affected individual engagement in and hence the vitality of some types of women's groups. But the story is considerably more complex than that.

Gender Consciousness

When women positively identify with one another and have a shared sense of fate, they are said to have gender consciousness (Rinehart 1992, 14). Gender consciousness may play a role in the fortunes of women's organizations and in turn influence the volume of their public engagement and their issue agendas. Gender consciousness may influence women's groups directly by facilitating the recruitment of leaders, members, and donors, on which voluntary organizations rely to fuel their operations. The sense of "we" embodied by gender consciousness also provides a foundation on which political entrepreneurs can build narratives and agendas for collective action. Gender consciousness may affect women's groups indirectly as well. By facilitating organization and constituency building, gender consciousness may help women to be taken seriously in the political sphere. Although gender consciousness is an individual construct, it has the potential to affect organizational fortunes.

What has happened to gender consciousness over time? Might women's feelings of collective identity and shared fate influence the patterns of engagement by women's organizations at the national level? These questions are difficult to answer, particularly over such a long time. But it is possible to cobble together a partial story from clues in membership and polling data.

The definitive study of gender consciousness and politics is Sue Tolleson Rinehart's 1992 volume. Using American National Election Study (ANES) data at four-year intervals from 1972 to 1988, she examines trends in women's self-reported closeness to other women and to feminists. The major finding is that throughout this period, women showed a strong sense of collective identity, with anywhere from 43 to 58 percent of both white and African American women reporting that they felt close to other women—one of the highest degrees of group identification in the survey. Furthermore, for white women, the data show no clear trend—gender closeness was highest in 1976 and 1984 and lowest in 1972 and 1980. Black women's gender identification increased throughout the series, from 47 percent in 1972 to 57 percent in 1988 (Rinehart 1992, 52–53).

Conversely, among college- and graduate-school-educated women—those most likely to be members of and donors to Washington-based women's organizations—gender consciousness increased steadily throughout the period, from roughly 62 percent in 1972 to roughly 93–94 percent in 1988 (Rinehart 1992, 61). Moreover, by the late 1980s, compared to the early 1970s, women with traditional views of gender roles were considerably less likely to identify with other women, while women with egalitarian views were considerably more likely to identify with other women (82). As Costain (1992, 98) notes, "Women were increasingly able to identify structural conditions that limited their opportunities and to see these problems as collective rather than individual."

Although Rinehart's study ends in 1988, other sources allow us to examine related aspects of women's gender identification through the 1990s. For example, the American National Election Study has for decades asked people to score their feelings toward various groups—including women, the women's liberation movement, and the women's movement—on a "thermometer" scale of 1 to 100. By all three measures, gender identification held steady or even warmed during the last three decades of the 20th century, remaining in the 75–83 range from 1976 to 2004. Women's warmth toward the women's liberation movement rose from 1970 (31) to 1984 (59). Women's warmth toward the women's movement (the question wording changed after 1984) then hovered between 64 and 67 between 1986 and 2000.[4]

These findings of more stasis than change parallel the conclusions of Elaine J. Hall and Marnie Salupo Rodriguez (2003) and Leonie Huddy, Francis K. Neely, and Marilyn R. Lafay (2000), who tracked attitudes toward the women's movement through survey questions posed during the last three decades of the 20th century. Surveys taken between the mid-1980s and mid-1990s showed that the majority of women (59–69 percent) thought that the women's movement (or feminists) had had a good effect on the country (Huddy, Neely, and Lafay 2000, 340). Likewise, polls taken between 1985 and 1998 showed that most women (between 53 and 59 percent) thought that the women's movement was generally in touch with the needs of women and of working women (327). Women polled between the mid-1980s and mid-1990s also felt that the women's movement had helped improve the lives of professional women (82–92 percent) and working-class women (74–78 percent) (346).

Yet media accounts in the late 1980s and 1990s routinely declared that feminism was over. The period between 1989 and 2001 featured 160 newspaper articles referring to the death of feminism or the postfeminist era (Hawkesworth 2004, 962–63). Implicit in these articles is the assumption that women's self-identification as feminists was in decline during the waning decades of the 20th century.

The survey data offer mixed support for that view. On the hopeful side for feminist organizations, the ANES "feeling thermometer" finds women's warmth toward feminists holding steady between 1988 and 2004 (between 53 and 59 on a 100-point scale). Likewise, surveys in the 1990s showed no diminution in women's willingness to say they considered themselves feminists except among women aged 30 to 39 (Huddy, Neely, and Lafay 2000, 327).

However, other polls are more in line with the narrative that feminism is either declining as a political identity or resonating with very few women. From the late 1980s to the late 1990s, a series of national polls of women revealed a 7-point decline in feminist self-identification, from

33 percent to 26 percent, and a concomitant increase in the percentage of women who said they were decidedly not feminists (Goss and Heaney 2010; Huddy, Neely, and Lafay 2000). At the same time, Huddy, Neely, and Lafay (2000, 323) report a 6-point increase between 1992 and 1997 in the number of women who think that calling someone a feminist would be an insult (though most people in both surveys considered it a neutral or complimentary term). In polls taken between 1984 and 1996, the percentage of women who felt "particularly close to" feminists "in their ideas and interests and feelings about things" hovered between 9 and 19 percent (328–29)—hardly a groundswell of support for a mass movement. And only 5 percent of women in 1983 reported having ever given money to an organization concerned with the women's rights issue (330).

These findings suggest general support among women for the women's movement—which perhaps invokes a largely successful egalitarian policy agenda—and mixed feelings about feminism as a political identity. An oft-repeated charge holds that this discrepancy between support for feminist policies and wariness of the feminist label results from the attitudes of post-baby-boom women, those whose socialization included both the professional access and opportunity afforded by second wave policy achievements and the political and media backlash against feminism as a framework for collective action (Faludi 1991). The second wave's founding mother, Betty Friedan (1985, 26), bemoaned the "failure to mobilize the young generation who take for granted the rights we won and who do not defend those rights as they are being taken away in front of our eyes" and concluded that the women's movement was in a period of "profound paralysis." Two decades later, a young mother, Kristin Rowe-Finkbeiner (2004), sought to revive the women's movement within the post-second-wave generation by focusing on a policy agenda centered on the needs of working mothers. Her book title frankly acknowledged the state of feminism within her cohort: *The F-Word.*

The evidence for the decline of feminist identity among young women is just as muddled as the evidence for overall trends. For example, Huddy, Neely, and Lafay (2000, 317) found that "young women identify as feminists at about the same rate as women now in their 40s despite extensive media discussion in the late 1980s and early 1990s of younger women's rejection of the movement." And Hall and Rodriguez's analysis of 1998 data suggested that young women (18–29) were more positive toward the women's movement and feminism than were older cohorts. Conversely, Jason Schnittker, Jeremy Freese, and Brian Powell (2003) found an association between generation and feminist identity for women born from the mid-1930s through the mid-1950s but not for either younger or older cohorts. Pia Peltola, Melissa A. Milkie, and Stanley Presser (2004) revealed that women born in the 1960s and 1970s were less likely to think of themselves as feminists than would be predicted based on their background characteristics. Other studies of young cohorts of women found general reluctance to self-identify as feminists even as these women support feminist principles (see, e.g., Aronson 2003; Buschman and Lenart 1996 on women born in the 1970s; Renzetti 1987 on women born in the 1960s).[5]

Perhaps most relevant for this study is the question of whether younger women, regardless of whether they identify with the feminist label or policy project, believe that collective action by women for women is necessary. Here the evidence is scant but consistent with the decline-of-feminism narrative. An analysis of 1992 ANES data found that women who came of age after the second wave were significantly less likely than older cohorts to believe that collective effort was necessary to improve women's position (Peltola, Milkie, and Presser 2004, 139). This finding was echoed in Buschman and Lenart's (1996) study of college women in the mid-1990s. They found that three-quarters of these women fell into either a postfeminist or "precarious feminist" category in which individual ability was seen as more important to a woman's advancement opportunities than was women's collective action. These findings dovetail with my anecdotal evidence. As I have presented these findings to politically liberal undergraduate and graduate women at elite universities, they have commonly expressed the attitude that they see no particular need to join a women's group and had not thought about doing so.

Nevertheless, looking at one dimension of gender consciousness (feminist) during one era (the 1970s–2000s), it is hard to make a clear case that mass attitudes drove the observed trends in women's organizational engagement. During the period when women's organizations showed a rise and then fall in their presence on Capitol Hill, women's gender consciousness was either fluctuating or holding steady. Looking at the critical subgroup of highly educated women, we see a growth in gender consciousness coinciding with a growth in women's organizational presence during the second wave movement, perhaps suggesting a link. Yet educated women's gender consciousness continued to rise throughout the 1980s, when women's organizational engagement was dropping. Even if the findings show that post–Baby Boom women are more reluctant than their foremothers to embrace feminist collective action, it is doubtful that they could be driving the trends in the 1980s and 1990s, when they were just beginning to come of age. Together, these data raise questions about gender consciousness as an explanation for the observed trends in women's organizational activity on Capitol Hill.

The difficulty with using gender consciousness to understand trends in organizational engagement extends beyond muddled survey findings. There are myriad other limitations. For one, studies of gender consciousness (and most of the opinion data on which they are based) arose in the 1980s and 1990s. There are no longitudinal data to assess, for example, gender consciousness during the first half of the 20th century, when women's organizational advocacy expanded significantly. Second, the connection between gender consciousness and political engagement, at least at the individual level, is very weak (Rinehart 1992, 137). Gender-conscious women are no more politically active than are other women, although gender-conscious women are more likely to work on women's issues such as abortion (Burns, Schlozman, and Verba 2001). Perhaps the biggest limitation concerns the dominant interpretation of gender consciousness itself. Most of the longitudinal studies of women's gender consciousness are based on data that tap only one type of collective orientation—toward feminism or the women's movement. With the exception of the ANES's "closeness to women" series, there are no good data that capture other types of collective identities—for example, the maternal and good-citizen frameworks that women's organizations historically used to frame their policy arguments. To draw a causal connection between gender consciousness at the individual level and the vitality of women's advocacy organizations would require an understanding of the full range of ways that women understand their collective place in the political sphere and the changes over time in those ideas' power to inspire women to action.

Conclusion: Making Sense of "Commonsense" Explanations

This chapter has examined a wide range of possible explanations for the observed trends in women's groups' engagement on national policy issues from the late 19th through the 20th centuries. I have examined institutional explanations, centered on changes in congressional tastes and practices; organizational explanations, centered on the larger interest group community; and gender-focused explanations, centered on changes in women's lives and identities.

Some intuitively attractive explanations were ruled out. The trends were not driven by the partisan and gender composition of Congress, a change in the alignment of lawmakers' issue agendas with those of women's groups, or congressional openness to interest group testimony. Nor were the trends driven by a shift among women's groups away from Congress and toward other venues of policy influence or by reductions in patronage support for women's issues. However, as would be expected with any massive political transformation spanning more than a century, a number of factors no doubt played contributing roles. These include the proliferation of specialized pressure groups colonizing issue niches previously dominated by women's multipurpose, mass-membership groups; changes in educated women's labor force participation; and perhaps shifts in women's gender identification. I now turn to the linkages among policy, identity, and women's collective engagement.

SEVEN

How Public Policy Shaped
Women's Civic Place

Throughout American history, sex-segregated organizations have emerged both to capture and to inspire women's yearning for fully incorporated citizenship. The pioneering feminists assembled at the 1848 Seneca Falls convention set the agenda for more than a century to come: "Because women do feel themselves aggrieved, oppressed, and fraudulently deprived of their most sacred rights," they observed in their Declaration of Sentiments, "we insist that they have immediate admission to all the rights and privileges which belong to them as citizens of the United States" ("Declaration of Sentiments" 1848). The first wave suffrage movement delivered an unprecedented victory for organized womanhood—the constitutional right to vote—and the second wave women's rights movement followed with many other successes, including federal protections for pregnant, unmarried, and abused women.

Yet even as women's inclusion expanded over time—and women's leadership roles in major social, economic, and political institutions likewise proliferated—women's organizational presence in national policy debates followed a curious and often counterintuitive road. In the wake of suffrage, women's collective advocacy rose and broadened; in the wake of the women's rights victories of the 1970s and 1980s, it declined and narrowed. This pattern is surprising. Why should women's increasing incorporation give way to expanding participation in one era but contracting participation in another? Changes in women's lived experience and in the larger political context played a part but cannot fully explain the curious trajectory of women's policy advocacy.

To an underappreciated degree, I argue here that gender-specific policies are the dominant, underlying force driving the evolution of women's collective engagement. *Public policy* is an expansive term encompassing a wide array of laws, administrative rules, and court decisions. With such a broad reach, one would be hard-pressed to identify any social or political transformation that policy has not shaped. However, I focus on one primary set of policies, those expanding women's political and economic inclusion—precisely the policies that feminist movements sought to enact and build on. These policies, reinforced by broader political developments identified previously, have driven the core trends that we have observed: the rise and then fall of women's presence on Capitol Hill and the expansion and then narrowing of their policy interests. In both social policy and equal rights policy, women's groups played an important advocacy role. In turn, the product of women's groups' energies shaped their subsequent collective action.

To construct the story of women's collective political development, I extend a line of inquiry alternately termed policy feedbacks or feedback effects. Feedback theory holds that policy design shapes political participation through various mechanisms, well described by Suzanne Mettler and Joe Soss (2004). This study both builds on and tests core premises of feedback theory. For one, feedback studies have typically examined the effects of policy design on mass publics or political elites. This study, by contrast, examines the effect of policy design on interest groups and social movements, which often organize mass publics for collective action.[1] Second, even though the term *feedback* by definition means an over-time process, no systematic, longitudinal studies of such effects have been conducted (at least to my knowledge). I examine feedbacks unfolding over the course of a century. Finally, feedback studies have reached a fairly consistent and commonsense conclusion about the content of policy and the volume of participation—that policies conferring dignity and inclusion promote participation, while demeaning policies depress it (Campbell 2003; Mettler 2005; Soss 2000). Patterns of Capitol Hill engagement by women's groups raise questions about that premise.

My case for a policy feedback model proceeds in two parts. First, I mine the data to identify the proximate drivers of the rise and fall (and widening and then narrowing) of women's organizational advocacy. This part uses longitudinal variation in categories of groups and issues to understand the patterns. Second, I develop a policy feedback explanation for the underlying driver of those observed patterns. The feedback account is consistent with my data and integrates seemingly unrelated empirical observations by scholars of women's political history. Applying feedback theory to a universe as large and diverse as women's organizations—and in a time frame as long as 122 years—poses obvious challenges and risks explanatory overreaching. Thus, this chapter seeks to tell a plausible, inductive story about the rise and fall of women as the nation's public interest lobby on Capitol Hill. Women's groups' presence, numbers, and policy agendas expanded in the first half of the 20th century, then narrowed along these lines as groups assembled around a feminist agenda. Policy feedback theory can account for these developments in a way that alternative explanations cannot.

What Drove the Patterns? Clues from the Data

Women's collective advocacy has undergone important transformations over the past century. I have documented these transformations at scattered points to evaluate various hypotheses or illustrate different arguments. Here, I pull together these seemingly disparate transformations to offer a cohesive account of the immediate drivers of the observed patterns.

The most salient changes in women's collective engagement involve both the types of groups appearing on Capitol Hill and the types of issues (or issue dimensions) on which they testified. First, as chapter 4 documented, a pronounced decline occurred in participation by mass-membership organizations, many of which were founded in the late 19th and early 20th centuries to promote women's participation across a broad range of issues. A sharp relative increase also occurred in participation by women's occupational groups, which were responsible for more than half of all women's group testimony by the 1990s (more than twice the rate observed in the 1960s). In chapter 6, we saw the rise and fall of testimony by prominent organizations of all sorts—traditional voluntaries, occupational groups, and second wave feminist organizations—while less prominent women's organizations proliferated beginning in the 1970s, reflecting a weakening of the stronghold that the large mass-membership groups had developed in the Washington advocacy community.

In addition to illustrating changes in the composition of testifying groups, the data revealed significant changes in the issue domains and dimensions that attracted women's groups' interest. Women's groups' participation in foreign policy dropped far more precipitously than did their participation in domestic policy. Across policy domains, women's groups shifted in their attentiveness to women's rights, status, and well-being. Advocacy on such feminist dimensions followed a U-shaped pattern, with

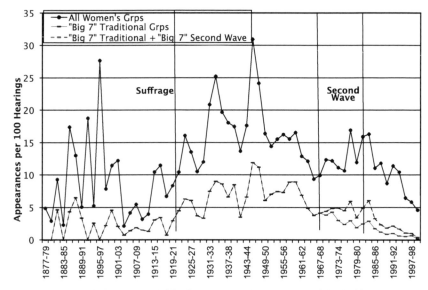

Fig. 7.1. The rise and fall of women's policy advocacy, 1877–2000

attention relatively high through the 1930s and relatively low through the middle decades, then rebounding sharply from the 1970s through the 1990s.

Putting these disparate clues together, we can begin to make sense of how changes in organizational types, policy agendas, and levels of engagement are interrelated. Figure 7.1 shows the entire time series for the volume of women's testimony (adjusted for hearings); the volume of testimony by the "big seven" traditional groups, those that relied on maternal and/or good-citizen understandings of women's civic identity; and the combined volume of testimony by the "big seven" traditional groups and the "big seven" second wave feminist groups.

The years before 1910 show a lot of variation because there were very few appearances and very few hearings, so it is best to focus on the period from 1910 onward. As the graph shows, women's organizational presence on Capitol Hill was highest in the 1940s and 1950s and experienced another local peak in the mid- to late 1970s. Except for the 1970s, the overall trend and the trend for the big seven traditional groups closely track one another. Including the major feminist lobbies brings the lines into closer parallel.

These data suggest two possible, though not mutually exclusive, explanations for the rise-and-fall trajectory. One explanation is that traditional,

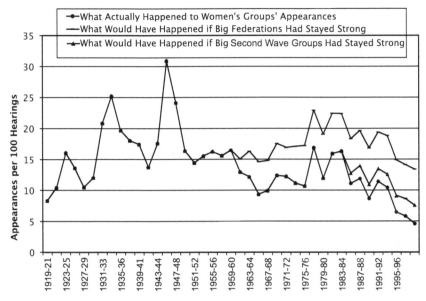

Fig. 7.2. Decline of big federations depressed overall advocacy

multipurpose groups declined after midcentury, bringing women's overall presence with them. The other is that the flagship organizations of the second wave movement (or perhaps the movement itself) helped to stave off some of the decline begun earlier but eventually surrendered to the same downward spiral. A counterfactual analysis is in order: What would have happened to the overall volume of women's organizational participation if these large, flagship organizations had maintained the presence they enjoyed during the peak periods? Figure 7.2 plots the overall volume of women's organizational testimony against two hypothetical scenarios: (1) the big seven traditional groups continued to testify at their 1959–60 rate; and (2) the big seven second wave groups continued to testify at their 1983–84 rate.

The figure shows that if the difference- and good-citizen-oriented groups that grew to dominance by midcentury had been able to maintain their momentum, the general picture of women's organizational presence on Capitol Hill would have looked very different. The upper trend line shows that while women's groups still would have shown some backsliding in the 1980s and 1990s, it would not have been nearly as pronounced. In fact, except for some outlier years in the late 1940s and during the feminist 1970s, the overall trend line would have remained fairly constant at a typical rate of 15–20 appearances per 100 hearings. Conversely, if the big seven feminist groups had maintained their peak presence (middle trend line), the observed post-1970s fall would have looked much the same, indicating that the decline of the most prominent feminist groups contributes little to the story.

In this counterfactual world, a puzzle would remain: Why didn't women's presence post uninterrupted growth after suffrage, when women as citizens acquired greater economic and social status and the number of women's groups testifying grew? The graph provides clues to unraveling the mystery of the up-and-down trajectory of women's groups' congressional presence. An important part of the decline in women's testimony is traceable to the decline of mass-membership, multipurpose women's organizations. These traditional associations had two characteristics that newer groups lacked. First, the traditional associations understood women's civic identity to encompass logics of maternalism (difference), sameness (equality), and a hybrid of the two (the good citizen). This ideational flexibility allowed these groups to interpret women's civic place broadly and to claim expertise on everything from children's welfare to international relations to the Equal Rights Amendment. When women's groups were positioned to call on multiple civic identities as conditions warranted and when those various identities were recognized by political elites as authoritative, women's groups played a more prominent role in politics than when their repertoire of identities was more limited. Likewise, the traditional associations had networks of civically resourceful women in most congressional districts, adding to the prospects that they could gain a hearing.

As upholders of the full range of traditional and progressive American ideals and as representatives for mass memberships that took seriously their civic duty, these organizations formed a powerful voice for women in the decades when they were otherwise marginalized. Yet in chapter 5, I chronicled how the second wave movement delivered a devastating critique of difference identities rooted in women's special qualities on the grounds that promoting difference perpetuated inequality. Likewise, I showed how in two key policy domains, policy authority rooted in maternal and good-citizen logics (associated with women's difference) gave way to authority rooted in equality claims (associated with women's sameness). The modern model of female organizing relied on feminist activists and professional experts with a more focused understanding of what a women's issue should be.

These observations give rise to a large, uncomfortable question. Is it possible that the increase in women's presence in the halls of policymaking

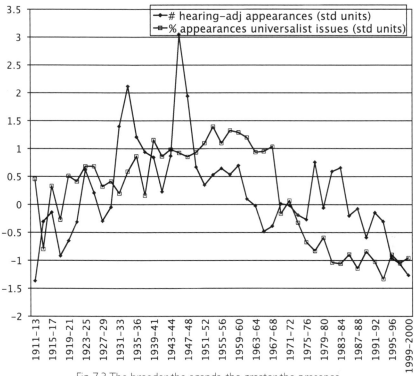

Fig. 7.3. The broader the agenda, the greater the presence

power had something to do with their relative focus on broad, public issues as opposed to feminist issues? Figure 7.3 plots the number of women's group appearances (per 100 hearings) against the share of those appearances in which the organization's testimony was oriented around other-oriented claims (both in standardized units). With the exception of the second half of the 1970 and the early 1980s, when feminism was ascendant on Capitol Hill, the lines are strikingly parallel.

What does the figure tell us? To put it starkly, women's voice is most prominent on Capitol Hill when women are represented by multipurpose mass-membership groups with broad issue agendas. Feminist waves can boost women's participatory opportunities, both by allowing traditional groups to speak to feminist concerns and by creating new groups with new issue agendas. However, congressional attention to feminist goals waxes and wanes, and when women's groups (or members of Congress) define women's issues as solely those affecting gender equality, women's groups' prominence will wax and wane as well. An important caveat is in order here. The figure merely shows an association between the expansiveness of women's organizational agendas and their presence on Capitol Hill. It does not suggest that women lack influence during the periods of greater focus yet smaller presence. It merely suggests that their opportunities for influence are narrower.[2]

To illuminate the argument, let us look at a pivotal decade: the 1960s. In retrospect, the 1960s were a transitional period between the postwar hey-day of women's assertive citizenship and the 1970s, when the second wave agenda provided new energy to many older groups and spawned a feminist advocacy community. The 1960s marked a local trough in the number of women's groups testifying and in their hearing-adjusted appearances. Why? A closer look at the data reveals that appearances by the big seven mass-membership groups dropped dramatically in that decade, pulling the line down with them. The drop was driven largely by two traditionally oriented federations that had not changed with the times—the General Federation of Women's Clubs and the Woman's Christian Temperance Union, whose appearances dropped by 55 percent and 100 percent, respectively, from the 1950s to the 1960s. No large mass-membership, multipurpose groups came to replace them. The 1960s also marked a time of regrouping for the other traditional mass-membership groups, such as the League of Women Voters and the American Association of University Women, multipurpose groups born of feminist ideology that sought to adapt and survive. Finally, the 1960s marked the lull before the feminist storm—a period in which the new "harvest" (Ferree and Martin 1995) of women's occupational and feminist groups had not yet ripened to command the time in congressional hearing rooms that the traditional associations were ceding.

The 1960s constituted a transitional decade not only for women's groups but also for national politics as a whole. New social movements were arising (or, in the case of the black civil rights movement, consolidating) but had not yet institutionalized as an authoritative force for legislative advocacy on Capitol Hill. These new social movements included those for welfare rights, environmentalism, consumer interests, and gay rights. Women's groups had championed many of these issues in earlier decades and would join forces with new social movement organizations—but not until the 1970s, when Congress was paying sustained attention. For example, while the League of Women Voters had been ahead of the curve on environmental and natural resources policy, testifying in the late 1950s and early 1960s, the group did not provide consistently frequent testimony until the environmental move-ment was well under way, during the 1970s and early 1980s.

The 1960s also marked the era in which women's organizations' attention to foreign policy fell both as a share of all congressional hearings in that domain and as a percentage of all women's appearances. At that point, the patterns reflected not so much women's pulling away from foreign policy—in absolute numbers, the appearances were close to the same in both decades—or a change in the composition of the groups testifying but a shift of women's groups' relative efforts toward domestic policy. Women's groups' participation in foreign policy hearings dropped at a faster rate than did congressional committee attention to foreign policy issues. In this way, the 1960s foreshadowed the pattern of women's organizations' nearly abandoning the peace and international cooperation agenda that had been so important to them in the first half of the 20th century (Goss 2009).

What the Data Show: A Summary

In the decades after suffrage, and to some extent before, women's organizations interpreted their civic place broadly. They could draw on a variety of women's identities to legitimize deep engagement in a wide array of issues. Women's organizations used these identities or constructions thereof to mobilize women into politics. In the first half of the 20th century, when women's political status was in transition, these organizations assembled mass memberships, developed elaborate procedures for internal democracy, and made expansive use of the repertoire of women's civic identities. These tactics gave women's groups both flexibility and authority to speak out on the pressing issues of the day. The institutional vehicle for such advocacy was the locally rooted membership organization, which was able to draw on and at times creatively combine understandings of both gender equality and gender difference—the League of Women Voters, for example.

In the 1960s, conceptions of gender difference began to change. It was a time of flux, and women's congressional presence reflected that reality. Old-fashioned women's groups, particularly those that relied on maternalism of both the progressive and conservative/isolationist varieties, were fading. And neither the second wave movement nor other liberal movements that were to make claims against the state for greater regulation of economic and social relations had fully arrived.

The 1970s are easy to interpret. The decade showed an increase in hearing-adjusted appearances, groups, and range of issues embraced. The era represented the first gasp of the second wave groups and some of last gasps of the traditional multipurpose groups, which hitched their wagons to feminism and the other new social movements. With these two types of groups working both together and separately, the period from the early 1970s through the early 1980s saw women make important contributions to public policy. However, in the 1970s, we begin to see women's policy communities fragment. New specialized advocacy organizations and public interest groups start to colonize policy niches once occupied by women, while women's organizations—encouraged by philanthropic foundations—emerge to represent specific identity groups disadvantaged in different policy spheres.

Between the early 1980s and 2000, women's engagement crashed. The trend is most noticeable in the number of appearances (and hearing-adjusted appearances), but it also shows up in declines in the number of women's groups testifying, the range of issues they covered, and their presence in especially important policy debates. On the surface, the period is mystifying, but in some respects it is easily explained. Women's groups' attention to general public issues dropped in the 1980s, but Congress remained interested in feminist concerns. Both second wave groups and traditional membership organizations were called to testify. Thus, while women's groups' appearances declined, they did not plunge. The 1990s, however, represented an unfortunate confluence of forces that drove down women's participation. Congressional hearings on feminist issues dropped, creating fewer opportunities for the narrowly focused second wave groups to testify. Indeed, Kira Sanbonmatsu (2004, 219) has gone so far as to state that political elites, including party leaders, demonstrated an "overall lack of attention to gender equality issues" in the 1990s, a viewpoint that had implications for women's collective engagement. At the same time that feminism was waning on the national agenda, the traditional groups that had survived the feminist era—the League of Women Voters, the American Association of University Women, the Parent-Teacher Association—were losing membership. Moreover, their interpretation of women's civic place, drawing on notions of female superiority rooted in maternal care and exceptional citizenship, had fallen into disrepute amid the egalitarian ethos of the rights-based culture.

Raising a Deeper Set of Questions

A close examination of trends within the data can shed light on the proximate drivers of the overall patterns. The rise and fall of appearances and the widening and narrowing of policy agendas seem to be related to the types of women's groups that were prominent in American life and to the way that they defined "women's issues." But these conclusions raise a deeper question: What drove these organizational and ideational changes? Why should women's organizations and the civic identities they represent have changed over the 20th century? After all, it is not as if women ceased wanting to participate in public life or stopped caring about children's welfare, war and peace, the health of the planet, food and drug safety, consumer prices, and other issues on which they had traditionally been vocal. Public policy—especially laws that deliver particular benefits to females—is a central, underlying force (though not the only force) driving the puzzling patterns in women's organizational engagement. Such patterns have been reinforced by broader changes in the social and policy environments. But women's policies—how the state related to women—had powerful feedback effects on how women related to the state.

Policy, the State, and Women's Organizational Advocacy

From the late 19th century onward, Congress introduced, debated, and passed scores of bills relating explicitly to women's rights, status, or well-being. Such proposals included labor laws, maternal health programs, and universal suffrage in the early decades; Women's Commissions and the Equal Pay Act in the middle decades; and antidiscrimination, women's health, and family leave policies in the latter decades. Women's policies, usually but not always pushed by women's groups, operated on those groups and congressional elites to structure collective participation. The effect of these policies was reinforced and even magnified by the growth of the federal state, which shaped the pressure-group context in which women's groups sought their policy niches.

Consistent with the policy feedback effects identified by Mettler and Soss (2004), I suggest that these women's policies helped to orient women's collective action around certain types of policy claims. Several mechanisms were at work to varying degrees over time. First, women's policies created constituencies of defenders and detractors. Second, in some cases, these policies conferred resources on women's groups or their members. Third, and perhaps most important, these policies helped to define the meaning of women's political citizenship. While influenced by public policy, these outcomes, in turn, helped to define the issues that women's groups sought to influence and that congressional elites saw as rightfully women's concerns. This reorientation of women's groups' policy agendas is reflected in the volume and scope of their congressional testimony.

However, this is not a simple story of policy feedback operating in predictable ways over time. As chapters 2 and 3 showed, advances in women's rights and social protections were followed by very different patterns of engagement. Labor, suffrage, and maternal health measures in the 1910s and 1920s were followed by an expansion in women's engagement. Equality measures of the 1970s, by contrast, were followed by a decline and narrowing of women's presence on Capitol Hill. What accounts for these different trajectories? Why are efforts to extend women's inclusion as citizens followed by more robust participation in one era yet more constrained participation in another era?

The puzzle has two possible answers. One is that feedback effects are not present. Public policy delivered a raft of fundamental political and social rights to women, but their greater incorporation in the polity had no impact on their collective action. This possibility seems remote in light of common sense, the consistent finding that policies structure engagement, and the considerable problems, outlined earlier, with alternative explanations. Another possible answer is that feedback effects are present but are contingent. This alternative hypothesis calls our attention to policy design. As interpreted by organizations operating within shifting sociopolitical contexts, different policies of inclusion can have different effects on participatory citizenship. To make the case for contingent feedback effects, I examine the major public policies associated with the first two women's movement waves: the 19th Amendment's guarantee of national suffrage, the crowning achievement of the first wave; and the cluster of administrative, legislative, and judicial measures that expanded women's equality and bracketed the second wave. I review how women's groups interpreted those policies in a larger political context that was at the same time indirectly shaping women's groups' agendas.

The Legacy of Suffrage: Rights and Responsibility

Women's fight for suffrage began officially in 1848 at Seneca Falls and culminated more than 70 years later, on August 26, 1920, when Tennessee became the last state needed to ratify the 19th Amendment. The amendment reads simply, "The right of citizens of the United States to vote shall not be denied or abridged by the United States or by any State on account of sex." In extending the vote to women, the amendment conferred both a fundamental right of citizenship and a sacred responsibility to participate in democratic self-governance. Yet by 1930, the conventional wisdom was that women had accepted the right without embracing the responsibility. This conclusion, based on women's individual voting patterns, got the story wrong. In fact, women's collective engagement on Capitol Hill grew throughout the 1920s, 1930s, and 1940s, before leveling off in the 1950s.

The 19th Amendment embodied the duality of American citizenship, which encompasses both rights (to ballot access) and responsibilities (to take part in collective decision making). In incorporating rights and responsibilities, the amendment also embodied the parallel constructs in women's political history: the rights derived from doctrines of human equality and the caregiving responsibilities derived from patterns of gender difference. Although only 28 words long, the 19th Amendment provided a framework for a flexible and expansive interpretation of women's citizenship after 1920.

Suffrage could be and was embraced by "sameness" feminists as a launching pad for their efforts to secure the next step in women's political inclusion: an Equal Rights Amendment to the Constitution. The groups embracing the next step in the equality agenda included the National Woman's Party, the National Federation of Business and Professional Women's Clubs, the National Association of Women Lawyers, and the American Medical Women's Association (Rupp and Taylor 1987, 46). The National Woman's Party, founded by Alice Paul in 1916, began as a breakaway organization from the National American Woman Suffrage Association. The party explicitly embraced the term *feminist* and was focused on women's rights (45–53).

Yet the 19th Amendment was also used by "difference" feminists and others who saw it as a new, potent way for women to bring their distinctive sensibilities—as mothers—to bear on issues such as world peace and children's well-being. In this view, the vote was simply a mechanism for the full expression of women's unique voice. Groups espousing this view included the National Consumers League, the Woman's Christian Temperance Union, the General Federation of Women's Clubs, the Young Women's Christian Association, and the Association of Collegiate Alumnae, which became the American Association of University Women in 1921. These organizations and others formed the Women's Joint Congressional Committee, whose policy agenda throughout the 1920s included passage of a child and maternal health bill, a constitutional amendment giving Congress the power to regulate child labor, and two bills regulating food safety (Jan Wilson 2007). The agenda reflected the maternal orientation of women's mass membership groups and their desire for the state to assume and facilitate caregiving roles occupied by wives and mothers. Suffrage had enshrined in the Constitution the notion that women had a legitimate right to contribute to public policy, and the Women's Joint Congressional Committee represented women's groups' efforts to speak with a loud, united voice on traditional female concerns.

Finally, the duality of the 19th Amendment in activating gendered notions of both equality (rights) and difference (responsibility for the public good) created the context in which a third, hybrid identity could emerge, one oriented around women as good citizens. Like the maternal frame, the good-citizen frame invoked images of women as primarily motivated by concern for others' well-being and as above the self-interestedness of partisan politics. Like the equality frame, the good-citizen frame assumed that women could and should participate on the same footing as men. Exponents of the good-citizen frame believed that the explicit invocation of gender difference, except in the context of discrimination, was unhelpful or even counterproductive to women's influence. This interpretation was developed and carried forth most prominently by the League of Women Voters, the top-testifying women's organization in American history. In 1949, the League's president summarized the sex-segregated group's orientation by averring that members "think of themselves as citizens first and as women incidentally" (quoted in Rupp and Taylor 1987, 49). This hybrid identity allowed women to be both equal to men, in their gutsy claims to authority across a broad range of salient issues, and different from men in their public performance of the civic virtues traditionally associated with and assigned to women. The frame took advantage of but did not articulate beliefs about sex difference. It was implicitly but not explicitly gendered.

In sum, regardless of their orientation toward the sameness-difference question, women's groups could claim the 19th Amendment as the moral foundation for their political advocacy. In embracing both rights and responsibilities, the amendment provided an expansive, flexible platform for women's collective action, allowing them to be the same as men, different from them, or some nimble combination of the two. The amendment did not create the equality and difference narratives, which had jockeyed for support during the 70 years of the suffrage movement (Kraditor 1971), but validated both. Thus, whatever their place on the sameness-difference spectrum, women's organizations could use the newly amended Constitution as a clarion call and source of moral authority for their collective action. Suffrage, as a hybrid policy that encompassed both rights and responsibilities, served as a broadly interpretable framework for the expansion of women's organizational advocacy.

Consistent with policy feedback theory, the 19th Amendment helped to forge women's membership in the polity. As Mettler and Soss (2004, 61) suggest, "Public policies define the boundaries of political community . . . and the content and meaning of citizenship." While individual women were free to exercise the vote, it fell to women's groups to tell women what that vote meant. Women's groups took the expanded boundaries of political community that the 19th Amendment afforded and articulated for women their special responsibilities. Furthermore, women's groups linked such narratives of inclusion to women's policy agendas. These policy agendas supplied content to the expression of women's full political citizenship.

As a policy that embodied both rights to equality and responsibilities to participate, the 19th Amendment provided a platform for women's collective engagement across a wide range of issues. Scholars have long noted that policies create policy particularism by mobilizing beneficiary groups to protect public programs. For example, financial benefits provided through Social Security and the G.I. Bill contributed significantly to the high levels of political engagement among American seniors and veterans, respectively (Campbell 2003; Mettler 2005). This study suggests that policy, as interpreted by organizations, also can create the context for policy generalism. Women's groups, relying on maternal identities, were active in a wide range of issues before suffrage, including temperance and peace. In validating women's special contributions with respect to the protection of children and families and providing equal standing at the ballot box, the 19th Amendment encouraged women's groups to expand their policy portfolios. Just as the newly formed League of Women Voters sought to be "an everywoman's organization," so too did women's groups come to perceive every issue as a women's issue.

Policy feedbacks were important drivers of women's expansive embrace of participatory citizenship, but they operated in a fertile context. Women were increasingly educated, affording them resources, skills, and networks to ply their newfound political influence. Working in settlement houses and other charities had enabled women to develop expertise that gave them the credibility to speak out on those social problems that state governments and to some extent the federal government were beginning to consider targets for public policy. The 19th Amendment built on mothers' pensions and other early welfare-state policies that had put the state in the business of performing maternal functions (McDonagh 2010; Skocpol 1992). In associating state roles with women's roles, these policies allowed women to claim not only the obligation to participate in democratic governance but also the expertise to do so (Kraditor 1971).

Finally, the first two decades of the 20th century witnessed a decline in the power of mass-mobilizing political parties and a proliferation of citizens' groups (Tichenor and Harris 2002–3). Women's groups were a core component—perhaps *the* core component—of this new citizens' lobby. Enshrined in the U.S. Constitution, suffrage provided women with the highest possible acknowledgment of their civic worth, turning women's political authority into what Mansbridge (1986, 141) has termed, in a different context, a "social fact." Suffrage validated not only women but also the policy agenda they had championed, one focused on government in the public interest. Newly empowered, women's groups carried this agenda with gusto through the 1960s, when their civic place began evolving.

1960–1980: How Rights Came to Eclipse Responsibility

As a policy, suffrage conferred rights as well as responsibility. It legitimated women's collective claims to equality protections while providing a foundation for participation across an expansive policy terrain. Beginning with the African American civil rights movement of the 1950s and 1960s, American politics underwent a gradual shift in which identity groups increasingly turned to claims for in-group equality as opposed to professions of dutiful citizenship toward "the other" or "the public interest." To be sure, collective engagement was encouraged in this new era. Robust civic participation was obviously central to the great social movements of the 1960s and 1970s, including the women's movement, and was enshrined in government programs, such as the War on Poverty's mandate of "maximum feasible participation" by the economically and politically marginalized. But the purpose of participatory citizenship had shifted.

By the 1960s, rights were in the air. Activist women, having participated in the black civil rights movement and encountered sexism there, were primed for a movement of their own (Evans 1980). Furthermore, women's experience in the labor force was bringing them face-to-face with institutionalized discrimination, raising their expectations of autonomy and connecting them with similarly situated women (Freeman 1975; Klein 1984; Wolbrecht 2000). That said, feminist consciousness did not arise until the mid-1960s, even though women's labor force participation had been increasing steadily throughout the 20th century. Even though workforce participation, with its strains and contradictions, may have softened women to equality rights claims, working women clearly did not spontaneously find one another and mobilize for equality at the grassroots. Rather, public policy, as interpreted by women's organizations, provided the necessary framework for women's collective mobilization. Policy created both an ideational space and a political spur to equal rights advocacy. Naturally, gender policies interacted with larger political forces, but these policies were the primary mechanism shaping women's groups' interpretation of women's civic place in the second half of the 20th century.

Three significant policy developments preceded the second wave women's movement and facilitated its emergence: the President's Commission on the Status of Women, formed in 1961, which quickly spawned two additional federal equal rights committees and 50 state commissions; the Equal Pay Act of 1963, which began the process of incorporating women as full participants in economic life; and Title VII of the 1964 Civil Rights Act, which barred gender discrimination in employment but whose lax enforcement catalyzed the creation of second wave feminism's flagship organization. These three policies created a context for thinking about women's place in the political order. In the first half of the 20th century, most women's groups focused on the civic duty dimension of political citizenship, while some organizations continued to push for an expansion in rights policies, such as equal pay for equal work and a constitutional Equal Rights Amendment (Rupp and Taylor 1987). Beginning in the 1960s and escalating from the 1970s through the 1990s, women's groups saw their mission primarily as redressing inequities.

To some, this statement may seem controversial, so a very brief detour into "feminisms" is in order. Scholars have identified different ideological strains of the second wave feminist movement, including the radical, socialist, cultural, and liberal strains. Ironically, the first three strains rested on assumptions about women's difference—that is, that women had superior insights into the proper social, economic, or political order that necessitated their overturning or separating from that order. The liberal strain was distinctive. It saw difference as a social construction that public policy, with a dose of moral suasion, could remedy. The first three strains never developed significant policy advocacy organizations (and they appeared extremely rarely in my dataset). However, the liberal strain developed professional advocacy organizations, forged close ties with sympathetic feminists in government, and became the face of the women's movement on Capitol Hill. The liberal feminist view was that women's place naturally was and in the real political order ought to be equal to men's. Women were equal citizens by constitutional right and moral law, and government had a duty to guarantee their equal treatment. Where necessary, government had the obligation to correct conditions that impeded such equality—for example, by subsidizing day care so that women would be able to work on the same footing as men. Where policies treated women differently—for example, giving women (but not men) the right to terminate a pregnancy—these policies were legitimate insofar as they contributed to women's flourishing as autonomous, rights-bearing individuals. Liberal feminism emerged as dominant because its understanding of women's place—and its policy agenda—was consonant with the policy context established in 1961, 1963, and 1964. The second wave's interpretation of women's civic place revived mid-19th-century feminism's emphasis on women's group disadvantage and the obligation of the state to redress gender-based oppression.

Scholars have offered several explanations for the triumph of liberal, equal rights feminism over other interpretations. One explanation is that liberal feminism embraced mainstream American values—equality, freedom of contract, and personal autonomy—in a way that radical, socialist, and cultural critiques did not. As Anne N. Costain (1992, 37) has argued, the second wave movement "accepted the course of action rewarded by government institutions." This interpretation forms a sort of metaargument for policy feedbacks, in which the founding documents, such as the Declaration of Independence and the U.S. Constitution, shape the boundaries of politically acceptable arguments.

The question of why liberal (equality) feminism triumphed over more radical, separatist strains is certainly interesting. But an equally intriguing question is why equality feminism eclipsed other difference-oriented frameworks for women's collective action. After all, throughout much of American history, women had organized around the notion that they possessed superior insights into the flaws of the male-dominated political order and that such flaws could be effectively addressed through gender-segregated organizations. As stylistically and politically distinct as the two categories of organizations were, the maternal and good-citizen-oriented women's groups of the first half of the 20th century shared some assumptions about gender difference with the more fringe feminists of latter decades. Thus, how do we account for the decline of women as a public interest lobby founded on women's maternal and civic virtues and their concomitant rise as a set of rights-based pressure groups mobilized around female-specific claims? The answer is that two decades' worth of national policies, enacted by Congress and handed down by the courts, provided political and economic incentives, discursive repertoires, and moral validation for women's groups to pursue equality claims.

Policy and the Redefinition of Women's Civic Identity

In a masterful work on the redefinition of the terms of debate over women's rights, Christina Wolbrecht (2000) describes the process by which women's interests came to be defined as advancing women's rights. Until the early 1960s, there were competing conceptions of what kinds of policies would best advance women's interests. One conception focused on protection, which grew out of a belief that women were inherently different from men in key ways that deserved state recognition and support. The other conception focused on equality—the idea that women were more similar to men than different and that protectionist legislation in fact perpetuated inequities. By the late 1960s, however, the idea of advancing women's interests through protectionist legislation had fallen out of favor, leaving the equality frame as the dominant, consensus understanding (Costain 1988; Wolbrecht 2000).

Several policy developments made possible the redefinition of women as a rights-based constituency and the sidelining of traditional civic republican identities rooted in maternal and civic caretaking. These policies operated through two categories of mechanisms: an identity mechanism, in which women's place and their interpretation thereof was reoriented around liberal concepts of rights, individualism, and autonomy; and a resource mechanism, in which women's groups stressing grievance-based identities and claims against the state received tangible assistance from the state and other patrons.

The Second Wave: Feedback on Women's Equality Identity

Equal appeared in the names of two of the three major women's policy innovations of the early 1960s: The Equal Pay Act of 1963 and the Equal Employment Opportunity Commission (EEOC), which was created to enforce the 1964 Civil Rights Act, including Title VII's prohibitions on gender discrimination. And it was implicit in the third, the President's Commission on the Status of Women, whose authoritative report (which sold 64,000 copies in less than a year) chronicled a pattern of gender inequities permeating all aspects of American society (Davis 1999, 37). While these early 1960s policy innovations were not the product of a women's movement, they laid the groundwork for one. Both the Equal Pay Act and Title VII enshrined gender equality as the central orienting principle of gender relations, directing women—in particular elite women—toward an agenda of dismantling institutionalized inequalities. The President's Commission pointed them to where the problems were and provided authoritative data documenting the scope of those problems. These three policies created both a discursive context and a government apparatus for women to pursue the same rights as men.

One effect of the EEOC and the President's Commission was to catalyze the creation of the National Organization for Women (NOW), thereby establishing a flagship organization for the emerging women's equality movement. NOW began at a meeting of state commissions of women whose members were disgusted at the EEOC's perceived failure to take seriously women's rights claims. NOW quickly went to war with the EEOC over its 1965 ruling that sex-segregated help-wanted ads—in which "women's jobs" were listed separately from "men's jobs" in newspapers—did not violate Title VII. NOW used a combination of protests and a lawsuit to pressure the EEOC, which reversed itself in 1967. NOW also moved quickly to press President Lyndon Baines Johnson to issue an order banning sex discrimination by federal contractors and subcontractors, which he did in May 1967. Finally, NOW pushed the administration to appoint more women to top government positions; the Civil Service Commission responded by asking for lists of qualified women (Davis 1999, 57).

NOW's founding Statement of Purpose outlined the case for women's equality with men, dodging mention of women's purported difference. The statement held that "the time has come for a new movement toward true equality for all women in America, and toward a fully equal partnership of the sexes" and stated that NOW's purpose was "to take action to bring women into full participation in the mainstream of American society now, exercising all the privileges and responsibilities thereof in truly equal partnership with men." The statement harked back to early suffrage rhetoric, which emphasized women's inherent rights: "NOW is dedicated to the proposition that women, first and foremost, are human beings, who, like all other people in our society, must have the chance to develop their fullest human potential" (Carabillo, Meuli, and Csida 1993, 159). With this equality orientation, NOW became an early anchor of the interest group wing of the second wave movement. As founder Betty Friedan noted, "The absolute necessity of a civil rights movement for women had reached such a point of subterranean explosive urgency by 1966, that it only took a few of us to get together to ignite the spark—and it spread like a nuclear chainreaction" (quoted in Hole and Levine 1971, 81).

Within a few years of NOW's creation, a host of feminist advocacy groups sprang up. The Women's Equity Action League, formed in 1968, focused on discrimination in jobs and education and "barraged the courts with charges of sex discrimination" (Klein 1984, 24). Federally Employed Women, also formed in 1968, watched out for discrimination in the civil service. The National Coalition of American Nuns was founded in 1969 to "support civil rights and to pressure for women's equality within the Catholic Church" (24). In 1971, many groups were established, including the Women's Rights Project of the American Civil Liberties Union, the NOW Legal Defense and Education Fund, the National Women's Political Caucus, the Women's Legal Defense Fund, and the Network for Economic Rights as well as women's caucuses in nearly every professional association (Deckard 1983; Rosenberg 1993, 254). In 1972, the Women's Lobby was created, as were Equal Rights Advocates and the Center for Law and Social Policy's Women's Rights Project, which would become the National Women's Law Center in 1981 (Rosenberg 1993, 254).

These organizations relied on a mix of educational, advocacy, and litigation strategies, but they were united in their pursuit of equality claims. Policies that guaranteed equality naturally encouraged women's groups to identify situations where such promises were being breached and to pursue those claims through administrative bodies such as the EEOC and through the courts. The EEOC itself encouraged women's groups to pursue remedies through litigation, as the federal courts, including the Supreme Court, had shown themselves willing to validate group claims for equal rights (Davis 1999; Wolbrecht 2000).

The most famous of these decisions, *Brown v. Board of Education* (1954), had held that race-based educational inequality was unconstitutional. The *Brown* ruling encouraged women's groups to pursue gender-equality actions, and the Court obliged with a series of rulings finding unequal treatment of women and men unconstitutional under the 14th Amendment. Although not as famous as *Brown*, these rulings—including *Reed v. Reed* (1971), *Frontiero v. Richardson* (1973), and *Craig v. Boren* (1976)—moved American public policy away from uncritical acceptance of gender classifications in the law and toward the position that such distinctions must meet important government objectives (Mansbridge 1986). Interestingly, the laws at issue in the *Reed* and *Craig* decisions were not social welfare statutes aimed at protecting women but rather were laws that treated men and women differently—in one case (*Reed*) favoring men and in the other case (*Craig*) favoring women. In its rulings, then, the Court went beyond invalidating laws that protected women from risk; it made a deeper statement about the obsolescence of gender difference broadly understood. These rulings cast authoritative doubt on the principle of women's distinctiveness, which had inspired and framed women's groups' policy advocacy at least since the Progressive Era.

These court rulings, based on a newly expansive interpretation of the 14th Amendment's Equal Protection Clause, reinforced equality policies enacted by executive order and by Congress. By undermining the legal basis for protective legislation, the Court helped to unite women's groups, including unions, around the frame of equal rights and the accompanying legislative agenda (Wolbrecht 2000, 153). As Nancy MacLean (2006, 123, 149) has observed, Title VII provided women—especially minority and self-supporting working women—with "a wedge with which to open up the whole gender system to question," in the process greatly strengthening women's involvement in the labor movement for decades to come. Second wave groups' equality efforts were supported by feminists within the executive branch who created offices on women to legitimize feminist policy demands (Banaszak 2010). Rights had become the dominant, consensus frame around which demographically based identity groups were to mobilize. Within that context, feminists pursued a broad set of targets in the public, nonprofit, and private sectors.

Second wave advocacy groups' attachment to the equality (sameness) identity—and the rejection of women's difference—reached its apotheosis in the struggle for the Equal Rights Amendment (ERA) in the 1970s and early 1980s. The amendment passed the House of Representatives in 1971 and the Senate in 1972—in both cases by overwhelming margins—and was ratified by 30 of the required 38 states by early 1973 (Mansbridge 1986). The pro-ERA charge was led by NOW and a coalition of traditional women's groups under the banner of ERAmerica, but the intellectual godmothers and leading strategists were a cadre of feminist lawyers with a singular commitment to the sameness vision of gender relations. Under Phyllis Schlafly's STOP ERA group, conservative women, many of them homemakers and church volunteers whose civic identity was rooted in traditional female care work—that is, difference identities—fueled a vigorous countermovement to stop what they perceived as egalitarianism run amok.

The amendment as passed by Congress read in part, "Equality of rights under the law shall not be denied or abridged by the United States or by any State on account of sex." As Jane Mansbridge (1986) has chronicled, feminist groups repeatedly rejected attempts to alter the amendment's wording in a way that might leave open the possibility for women to be treated differently from men in cases where public sentiment clearly favored doing so, such as the military draft. For example, women's groups rejected an alternative version introduced by Senator Birch Bayh (D-IN) that read, "Neither the United States nor any State shall, on account of sex, deny to any person within its jurisdiction the equal protection of the laws," on the grounds that such a "flexible" standard (in Bayh's words) would leave room for unequal treatment. Their concerns were reinforced by experience with other members of Congress, such as Sam Ervin (D-NC), who proposed wording changes in an effort to strip the amendment of its practical meaning.

During the heat of the political battle for ratification, when Schlafly's forces had halted the amendment's momentum in the states, feminist organizations held firm in their commitment to a pure egalitarian interpretation of the ERA and its effects. A major point of contention, seized by the anti-ERA forces, was whether the amendment would require the military to draft women into combat. Mansbridge (1986) suggests that the Supreme Court's ruling in *Rostker v. Goldberg* (1973) allowed courts interpreting the War Powers Clause to defer to military judgment on manpower questions, meaning that the Courts were unlikely to interpret the ERA as requiring women in combat. The Court essentially solved a political problem for the feminist ERA advocates by removing one of the major public concerns about the ERA's potential effects. The proponents could have cited the Court's ruling to reassure wavering legislators and members of the public that the ERA would not require women to be drafted into combat. However, as Mansbridge (1986, 67) writes, the "organizations campaigning for the ERA had come to insist more and more strongly that the Amendment would do exactly this"—put women in harm's way. Feminists embraced a purist egalitarian vision both because they believed in it and because they feared that a watered-down amendment would not sufficiently protect women. Nevertheless, their refusal to budge meant that many legislators could not support the ERA, leading to its demise in 1982 (164).

Feminist policy victories of the early 1960s created a context for the egalitarian identity to dominate second wave advocacy strategies. To be sure, policy was not solely responsible for such interpretations. The civil rights movement had created a model for pursuing rights claims—and had given many women direct experience with discrimination. The influx of elite, educated women into the labor force likewise put them face-to-face with frustrating and degrading inequities. But three policy innovations—the Equal Pay Act, Title VII and the EEOC, and the President's Commission—created an opportunity structure in which women's groups could credibly voice and institutionally pursue equality claims. With the courts reinforcing these claims and raising doubts about policies that treated groups of people differently, the triumph of the equality identity was complete. As the director of the Congressional Caucus for Women's Issues said in 1981, "We . . . tell members of Congress how women would be affected by a piece of legislation. We are a constituency just like blacks and Jews" (Costain 1988, 167).

Second Wave Feminism: Policy Feedback on Women's Group Resources

In addition to working through the identity mechanism, policy feedback encouraged egalitarian feminism by conferring benefits on and enlarging the capacities of feminist groups. Most directly, the President's Commission on the Status of Women provided resources, networks, legitimacy, and a political opportunity for the emergence of the second wave movement (Costain 1992; Davis 1999; Klein 1984). After the commission had completed its work, it persuaded President John F. Kennedy to create the Citizens' Advisory Council on the Status of Women (made up in part of commission members). He also established the Interdepartmental Committee on the Status of Women, a cabinet-level body composed of administration officials (Davis 1999, 38). The two national status-of-women entities, both of which were directed by feminist Catherine East, began holding national conferences of state commissions in 1964. These meetings brought together hundreds of feminist leaders from around the country to share information and grievances with one another and with sympathetic government officials, including feminists within the executive and legislative branches. Attendance nearly quintupled from the first to the second meeting, which cabinet members and President Johnson attended (Carabillo, Meuli, and Csida 1993, 12). These conferences galvanized women, who were "mingling in workshops and expanding their knowledge beyond the boundaries of their individual states," providing "a forum for an expression of women's rising expectations for correcting injustices" (12).

Furthermore, at the urging of the Federation of Business and Professional Women, commissions were set up in every state and many counties, providing a platform for sharing information, networking, and conducting policy advocacy at the subnational level (Carabillo, Meuli, and Csida 1993, 4–6; Davis 1999, 38). State commissions, working with a newly energized base of women's organizations, were successful in lobbying for policy changes. Between 1963 and 1965, state legislatures enacted a slew of laws to remove barriers to women's employment, jury service, and property rights. Thus, the President's Commission defined the problems and spun off organizations at the national and state levels that fed the broader movement and its lobbying groups. At the 1966 meeting of state commissions, grievances reached a boiling point, and NOW and the second wave movement were born.

How the Equality Orientation Affected Women's Collective Engagement

A core assumption of democratic theory and practice is that more civic inclusion leads to more civic participation. After suffrage, that assumption indeed held true. Women's organizations that had existed before suffrage grew in size and ambition, and new organizations were created to provide opportunities for the deep exercise of participatory citizenship. The women's lobby (or lobbies) grew in prominence on Capitol Hill and represented women's interests and perspectives on an ever-widening range of domestic and international policy issues. Suffrage as a public policy was good for women's democratic engagement. Yet the policy victories of the 1960s and 1970s seem to have left a different pattern in their wake. To be sure, women's groups' presence on Capitol Hill rose in the late 1970s, when Congress was attentive to feminist claims, but that presence subsequently fell. Unlike suffrage, the policy triumphs of the 1960s and 1970s seem not to have bumped women's collective engagement to new and enduring heights. Why would two sets of policies, both so important to women's inclusion and status, have left such different patterns of democratic participation in their wake?

The equality frame might be expected to increase rather than decrease the volume and scope of women's collective action. After all, it allowed constituencies of women to see themselves as relatively disadvantaged and provided a rhetorical framework and opportunity structure to mobilize for redress. Thus, as the women's movement diversified, we might predict fewer appearances for any given organization but a growth in groups overall and a concomitant increase in the volume of women's voices on Capitol Hill. Such was the case for a short period in the late 1970s and early 1980s, but not over the long term. Why? I offer four answers that illuminate the complex interactions between policy as a set of ideas and incentive structures and organizational participation as an adaptive response to those ideas and incentives.

First, though both suffrage and the equal rights policies of the 1960s and 1970s were about inclusion, they were about fundamentally different kinds of inclusion. Suffrage was about political inclusion, the right to take part in democratic decision making. The landmark Equal Pay Act and Title VII of the 1964 Civil Rights Act—along with later successes such as Title IX of the Education Amendments (1972), the Women's Educational Equity Act (1974), the Equal Credit Opportunity Act (1974), and the Pregnancy Discrimination Act (1978)—were about economic inclusion, the right to reap the full rewards of one's effort and talent. Both types of inclusion are important, but only the first—political inclusion—conveys an expectation of responsibility to participate in matters of public concern. Economic inclusion provides incentives to participate, but around a much narrower set of questions bearing on access and treatment in market relationships. Suffrage, as a policy encompassing both rights claims and expectations of civic duty, provided a platform for a more expansive policy agenda.

A second way in which the demise of difference and the triumph of sameness affected policy agendas lies in the types of groups that were oriented around each. The types of groups that embraced difference identities—both in the maternal and good-citizen incarnations—were mass-membership, multipurpose organizations rather than single-issue groups. Groups such as the Woman's Christian Temperance Union (motto: "Do everything") and the League of Women Voters ("An everywoman's organization") created a space where women with different policy interests could find a home. Theda Skocpol (1992, 1999, 2003) has emphasized that these mass-membership federations possessed structural advantages from which they drew strength—their local-state-national organization paralleled that of the U.S. policymaking system. But their broad policy agendas also paralleled the government's agenda, meaning that they did not need to wait for Congress to address a narrow set of issues. They were poised to speak out on virtually anything that was on the congressional agenda. The League of Women Voters, for example, has carefully studied and debated policy positions on more than 40 issues—from international trade to pay equity to gun control—at the national level and hundreds more at the various state and local levels. The downward trajectory of women's engagement at congressional hearings would not have been nearly as steep had these multipurpose groups maintained their strength.

While the traditional federations' policy agendas were broad and adaptable to ever-changing congressional agendas, feminist groups had narrower, more rigid agendas. They could not jump into every public debate, nor did they want to do so. Rather, the job of feminist groups was to identify an issue of inequality and persuade Congress to pay attention to it (e.g., by holding hearings). Their other option was to wait until Congress's issue-attention cycle turned to questions of gender. Neither of these strategies could guarantee women's rights advocacy groups a steady or loud voice before Congress. Yet, as I discussed in chapter 5, second wave feminism had undermined the moral basis for the difference identities as encouraging women's unequal status. The groups deploying frameworks of women's care and good citizenship were faltering, depriving women of the most versatile rationales in their persuasive arsenal.

The equality agenda, both as an aspiration and as a body of legislative, judicial, and administrative policy, related in one additional way to women's organizations' prominence on Capitol Hill. This agenda encouraged women's groups to form around narrow constituencies based on a particular situation of discrimination and to advocate public policies that would address that particular situation. Mary Fainsod Katzenstein (2003, 214–15) argues that equal opportunity policy narrowed agendas by encouraging women in whatever situation to compare themselves to similarly situated men and to mobilize around those inequities. In this way, policy gave rise to what she calls "the localization of feminist activism" rooted in professions such as journalism and the military and in social institutions such as charities and churches. The equality framework fed the diversification of feminism by pointing to the distinctive experiences and concerns of subgroups of equality-minded women. Thus, women's groups proliferated around new political identities, such as lesbians, black women, Latinas, displaced homemakers, female prisoners, prostitutes, female immigrants, poor women, battered women, divorced women, and so forth (Davis 1999; Goss 2007). The availability of philanthropic foundation support for the women's movement encouraged this fragmentation and the making of more particularistic claims (Goss 2007).

A third consequence of the raft of gender equality policies was their shifting of the locus of the inequity problem. The feminist victories of the 1960s and 1970s provided policy answers to many of the major grievances of feminist women. Although national policies did not eliminate gender inequality, they did limit what could feasibly be accomplished through further action by Congress. Once legally sanctioned inequality was eliminated, women were left to defend against threats to the antidiscrimination laws (rare, because equality came to be accepted as a mainstream value) and to seek protectionist policies that fit within the bounds of what feminists were comfortable supporting (such as policies to protect women from violence and provide family and medical leave). In the 1980s, for example, women's groups were key in defending affirmative action (MacLean 2006). However, by the 1990s, a growing chorus of feminist leaders had come to believe that the second wave's unfinished business was not legislative in nature. Rather, the unfinished business lay in the private sphere of marriage and child rearing, in society's failure to embrace diversity in all of its complex and intersecting forms, and in women's need for sexual expression. Such priorities do not easily lend themselves to congressional hearings or lawmaking.

Fourth, equality feminism's policy victories created the conditions under which gender-based organizing became problematic. These triumphs made women much better off in education, employment, credit markets, and government programs. These advances helped to undermine women's disadvantage, around which women's organizations had mobilized their members. With policies that prohibited systematic discrimination and improved women's lot, it was hard for women to see themselves as a distinct class. Women had full access, so what was the problem? Such effects at the individual level may have trickled up to the organizational level, as women, especially younger women, became less likely to see the need for gender-separatist organizations as sources of women's power. As they gained political and economic status, women had individual opportunities to influence policy other than as members of women's groups. Women could and did serve as appointed and elected officials, as lobbyists for nongendered groups, and as leaders of prominent social and economic institutions. Through these examples, women saw that power need not be collective if it can be individual. Women could still identify as women if they wanted to, but they no longer felt the imperative to work collectively to resolve problems. In a 1989 survey, Nancy Burns, Kay Lehman Schlozman, and Sidney Verba (2001, 76) found that only 17 percent of women reported that their most important organizational involvement was an all-women's group. While I have no comparable data for the 1950s and 1960s, it seems virtually certain that the number would have been far higher in those earlier decades.

Summing Up: Feminist Feedback

The President and Congress clearly facilitated the emergence of the second wave movement. Policies put in place in the 1960s had profound feedback effects on women's collective action. These policies offered tangible antidiscrimination protections that women's groups rallied to defend and expand and offered resources (networks, conferences, money) to support women's organizing.

But the feedback effects of these early policies were not limited to supplying benefits and resources to facilitate mobilization. These policies also helped to redefine women's relationship with the state in the decades going forward. Mettler and Soss (2004, 61) have suggested that policies "may influence the ways individuals understand their rights and responsibilities as members of a political community." Early 1960s feminist policies defined women as an economically disadvantaged constituency relative to men. These policies conferred rights claims on women and placed the responsibility for adjudicating those claims on the state. As feminism evolved, women's organizations focused on needs-based policies, such as pregnancy leave and breast cancer research, that sought the advancement of women's equality through the recognition of women's difference.

The claims were aimed at enlarging women's participation as individuals for their own sake—to permit the full flourishing of female minds and talents. If women's economic inclusion had spillover effects on their civic engagement, that was all to the good. But equality was not an instrumental proposition. The point of second wave feminism was to give women what was rightfully theirs—an unfettered opportunity to develop and thrive on the same terms as men, without any expectation of responsibility toward the commonweal. The creation of women as an aggrieved group seeking redress for historic inequities would have profound effects on the development of the women's movement and the trajectory of women's policy agendas for decades to come.

Second wave feminism harked back to the feminism of 1848 as embodied in the Declaration of Rights and Sentiments, which emphasized the natural right to equality. But the second wave rhetoric and policy agenda represented a sharp break from the feminism of the early 20th century, which delivered universal suffrage. Suffrage, as a public policy, had incorporated women as full political citizens and facilitated their contributions as such to the commonweal. Like the Equal Pay Act, Title VII, and the women's commissions, suffrage was an equal rights policy. But unlike those later policies, suffrage was by design a policy to facilitate democratic participation and contributions to the commonweal. The early 1960s policies incorporated women into economic life and facilitated their participation as individuals. The distinctions between suffrage and the latter gender policies would prove critical to understanding the transformation in women's collective presence, identities, and agendas in national policy debates over the 20th century.

EIGHT

Women, Citizenship, and Public Policy in the 21st Century

From the 1870s, when this study begins, through 2000, when it ends, the United States underwent profound changes in its economic, political, and social organization. War, the elimination of discriminatory laws, economic need, and changing beliefs facilitated the movement of married women and mothers into the full-time paid labor force. The interest group universe that women had played a central role in building was fundamentally reconfigured, with broad, mass-membership federations losing clout to professional lobbies with niche agendas, including feminist agendas. With advocacy by women's groups, the national welfare and regulatory state was invented and then expanded to encompass a broad array of policies—income support and pensions, worker protections, health care research—that affected women's lives in profound and intimate ways. In key respects, women embody the evolving relationship between Americans and the state.

The case of American women also raises important questions about what these changes have wrought. On the positive side, the dismantling of discriminatory laws and antiquated belief systems has helped to free women to pursue their dreams and deploy their talents to their highest and best ends, both for the benefit of the woman herself and for the benefit of others. Liberty and the pursuit of happiness, values that Americans hold dear, have become more fully available to women. To be sure, women's lives are still limited by informal job segregation, lack of affordable child care, wage differentials, domestic abuse, racism, and barriers to reproductive health services, among other issues. But the large-scale, deeply entrenched systems of gender oppression—denial of fundamental privileges of citizenship, abysmal working conditions, laws that kept women out of jobs and in abusive marriages—are less pervasive than they once were. Women's advocacy on behalf of women's interests clearly has helped to transform many women's lives for the better.

But in achieving these gains, what, if anything, have women lost? This book has documented the decline over the second half of the 20th century in women's collective presence in national legislative debates and a concomitant narrowing of their advocacy efforts. Particularly after the 1960s, women's groups collectively shifted from advocacy in the public interest to advocacy on behalf of women's particular rights and needs—what one might call women's "special interests." I have suggested that the focusing of women's agendas on feminist policies contributed to the decline in their presence on Capitol Hill and hence to the diminishment of their public voice.

Before investigating this unsettling claim, a brief digression on the term *special interests* is in order. The term carries negative connotations, particularly for women. As Nancy F. Cott (1989, 822) has observed, scholars "often identify women's social reform efforts on behalf of other classes of persons—slaves, the poor, or children—as humane or beneficial, while seeing women's reform efforts on behalf of women (merely half the human race) as narrow or selfish." To my mind, there is nothing wrong and everything right with women's or any group's assembling to petition government for equitable treatment under law and for resources to help that group's constituency to live healthy, happy, and fulfilled lives. The feminist movements have delivered those goods for American women, for the benefit of both women and men. Indeed, as Nancy MacLean (2011) points out, most women probably would prefer to live under the rights regime, where they participate less through women's groups, than under prior regimes, where they participated more often but with fewer legal protections. Selfless altruism is vital to any society, but no single group need be expected to shoulder its burdens in the public square.

That said, the transformation of women's organizations' agendas and their sharply declining prominence on Capitol Hill in the last two decades of the 20th century raise important questions about women's representation and voice, both on their own behalf and on behalf of other disadvantaged or underrepresented groups. One set of questions revolves around the apparent decline: If women's groups are becoming less important aggregators of women's interests and perspectives, can we conclude that women as a group (or aggregation of groups) are losing their influence in national policy debates? Put another way, do women's organizations provide some political good to women that other avenues of individual or collective engagement might not provide to the same degree? Or are women's interests and perspectives—to the extent that they are distinct from men's—adequately represented through nongendered organizations or other means? A second set of questions revolves around women's groups' increasing focus on feminist issues. Does the reorientation of women's groups' policy agendas make them better or worse advocates for women as a collective? Is women's perspective missing from some issues because of the narrowing of women's groups' collective focus? Does women's transformation into a set of special interests contribute to the much-bemoaned polarization of our politics?

At root, these questions ask how concerned we should be about the fate of women's organizations. Answering that question requires exploring the continuing relevance of at least two assumptions underlying the rationale for women's separate organizational sphere. The first assumption is that women have distinctive policy commitments and that women's groups have a comparative advantage in representing those distinctive commitments. The second assumption is that regardless of any gender gap in policy positions, women's groups are particularly effective at providing civic goods to women—for example, opportunities for leadership. If these assumptions hold, then we have reason to be concerned about the declining presence of women's organizations in the national policymaking process. I consider these assumptions in turn.

Do Women's Policy Commitments Differ from Men's?

Although men and women tend to agree more than they disagree on most public issues, studies have found consistent evidence over many decades that the sexes diverge in limited but important ways.[1] One way to think about gender differences is in the direction of preferences on policy questions. For example, polls have consistently found that women are slightly more supportive than are men of government social programs and government regulations to mitigate economic hardship, sickness, addiction, environmental contamination, disability, and other causes of human suffering. In a comprehensive review of nearly 200 survey questions, Robert Y. Shapiro and Harpeet Mahajan (1986) found an average gender difference on "compassion issues" of about 3 percentage points. Women also are considerably more supportive than are men of regulations to curb potentially unhealthy or unsafe practices. Thus, women are more likely than men to oppose nuclear power and to support a 55-mph speed limit, fines for people who do not wear seat belts, jail terms for drunk drivers, and bans on cigarette advertising and sales (Shapiro and Mahajan 1986). In a review of more than a dozen polls taken in the 1990s, Theda Skocpol and I found consistent gender gaps of 5–21 percentage points on issues such as support for universal health care, regulation of nicotine in cigarettes, and stricter workplace safety laws.

The gender gap in preferences is more pronounced on questions of violence and domestic security, with women tending to be more pacifistic than men. Reviewing nearly 300 poll questions between 1936 and 1982, Tom W. Smith (1984) found that in 87 percent of cases, women were less inclined than men to favor the violent or forceful option, while men were more pacifistic than women in just 5 percent of cases. Shapiro and Mahajan (1986) found an average gender gap of 9 percentage points on domestic force issues (e.g., gun availability and capital punishment) and 6 percentage points on international force issues (such as defense spending), with women more opposed in both cases. My analysis of gun control surveys found an average gender gap of 13 percentage points (Goss and Skocpol 2006).

These findings on preference gaps are important and interesting, but a caveat is in order. Although a gender gap appears in nearly all welfare and violence/security questions, men and women as a group do not fundamentally disagree on most of these issues. That is, where most women support a particular proposal, most men do so as well. In fact, what may matter more is an intensity gap between the two genders. Intensity matters because it predicts political participation far better than attitudes do. If we show that women not only think differently from men about certain clusters of issues but also care more about them, we would have greater a priori reason to believe that women's organizations play a distinctive role for women.

Although little research exists on the intensity with which women and men approach different issues or the priority that the different genders place on different concerns, some evidence indicates that such differences exist. For example, women tend to be more likely than men to rate social welfare issues as being very important or the most important to them (Goss and Skocpol 2006). Such findings are more pronounced on issues of gun control, which surveys suggest has grown in salience more for women than for men, and on guns in the home, to which women were more strongly opposed than were men (Goss and Skocpol 2006). During the 1960s, 1970s, and early 1980s, surveys found that women became less likely to answer "don't know" on policy preference questions, providing suggestive evidence that part of the gender gap may result from women's shifting from ignorance or ambivalence to positions in favor of government intervention to protect the citizenry.

While men's and women's attitudes and intensity vary systematically across a broad range of social welfare, social regulation, and foreign policy questions, their participation regarding these issues is much less likely to differ significantly. For example, Nancy Burns, Kay Lehman Schlozman, and Sidney Verba (2001, 120) find that on only one social welfare issue—education—did women participate significantly more than men.[2] Perhaps more strikingly, although women were more likely than men to favor gun control and to feel strongly about the issue, a 1996 survey found that women participated less often in advancing firearms regulation (Goss 2006, 131).

The gender gap in gun control participation virtually disappeared after the school shootings of the late 1990s. In those years, gun control advocates were increasingly reframing the issue as a mothers' issue: More regulation would protect children (Goss 2006). In 2000, women tested this frame by attaching it to a mass mobilization, the Million Mom March on Washington. Not only was the mothers' march the largest demonstration for gun control in American history, but it also signaled that women saw the issue differently from men. The march's founder and principal organizer, Donna Dees-Thomases, a suburban mother and part-time publicist, saw the gender gap up close when male-dominated gun control interest groups quickly dismissed her idea, while her fellow suburban mothers immediately and intuitively saw its potential (Dees-Thomases 2004). My panel survey of Million Mom March participants found that those who viewed gun control through a maternal frame, as a child-protection issue—as opposed to alternative framings centering on crime control or excessive gun availability— were significantly more likely to stay involved in gun control advocacy and more deeply involved in the months after the march (Goss 2006, 138). In short, changing ideas about what an issue is about can change who participates and for how long.

Even after the feminist movement had made great strides in advancing women's equality and promulgating a message of women's sameness, a gap persisted in men's and women's policy preferences and in the depth of concern about different issues. Some evidence suggests that bringing a traditionally female perspective can encourage women's involvement in issue advocacy in the feminist (or postfeminist) era. However, these findings do not necessarily mean that women's organizations are needed. Perhaps women could operate just as effectively as members or leaders of mixed-gender organizations. Or perhaps women's interests and perspectives could be amply represented by the growing numbers of women in positions of political leadership. The postfeminist argument would be that in a largely egalitarian world, women no longer need to find strength in numbers. They can act as individuals (or at best cadres within mixed-gender settings) to represent women's interests.

Do Women's Groups Hold an Advantage for Women?

Women's groups were especially important when women were excluded from or marginalized in centers of political power. Such centers included mixed-gender interest groups, political parties, the executive branch, and Congress. Particularly since the second wave, however, women have moved in force into these venues, leaving us with a question: Has women's advancement rendered women's groups less relevant, even obsolete, as voices for women's issues and interests?

Women's Leadership in Political Institutions

In truth, while the core political institutions—parties, the Congress, the courts, and the executive branch—have incorporated women, their inclusion has been fitful and uneven. On the positive side, both the Democratic and Republican Parties have rules encouraging or requiring equal representation by women as convention delegates and on party committees. As of 2011, the top leadership of both parties was evenly divided between men and women. Women have served on the Supreme Court since 1981, and as of 2012, they occupied three of the nine positions. In the executive branch, women now routinely serve in important cabinet positions, such as Secretary of State. That said, in the period under study, women were seldom leaders. Just three women served as chair of the Republican or Democratic National Committees, only two served on the Supreme Court, and, of course, none served as president or vice president.

    The question of whether women's political leadership matters has been most closely studied in legislative arenas. These findings help us to assess whether individual female leaders might constitute a good substitute for women's organizations in representing women's interests. Encouragingly, numerous studies have found that female elected officials are effective and attentive to women's policy concerns (Berkman and O'Connor 1993; Boles

2001; Carroll 2001; Dolan and Ford 1995; Kelly, Saint-Germain, and Horn 1991; Reingold 1992; Saint-Germain 1989; Swers 2002; Thomas 1994). Female lawmakers also have been found to possess distinctive leadership styles that may lead to more democratic processes of deliberation in public arenas (Kathlene 1994; Rosenthal 1997, 1998; but see Donahue 1997).

However important these findings may be, there are many reasons to doubt that women in Congress are somehow compensating for the decline and narrowing of women's interest groups. The first cause for concern is sheer numbers: A decade after the period under study ended, women still constituted just 17 percent of the House and of the Senate (and just 34 percent of senior congressional staff members) (Bell 2011).Only one woman—House Minority Leader Nancy Pelosi (D-CA)—served in the top leadership of either chamber. These findings are relevant insofar as studies suggest that elected women best represent female interests when these leaders have reached a critical mass (e.g., see Berkman and O'Connor 1993; Saint-Germain 1989; Thomas 1994).

Second, women's organizations act for women as a collective in a way that individual females in powerful positions often do not have the capacity to do. Even when women do fill positions of elective or administrative leadership, they must be attuned to other interests in and around their positions—voting constituencies, party bosses, the president, congressional committees, cabinet secretaries, and so forth. Simply put, female leaders cannot serve as single-minded champions of women's concerns—and indeed, when their numbers are sparse, women legislators may hesitate to champion women's interests at all (Thomas 1994; Welch 1985). Women's groups allow women leaders to represent gendered interests without these countervailing pressures.

There is a final reason to doubt the suggestion that individual female leaders constitute a substitute for women's organizations. Studies suggest that a main reason female elites do such a good job representing their gender is that women's groups help them to do so (Keiser 1997). Female legislators "are likely to owe their elections in part to the activities of" women's groups, which provide money and volunteers to campaigns (Gelb and Palley 1996, xxiv). Having dense ties to such organizations, female legislators are attuned to women's needs and perspectives. Moreover, participation in women's groups provides "affirmation and sustenance for women legislators," allowing them to resist pressures to conform to male norms (Carroll 2006, 375). Indeed, one study found that having a vibrant, autonomous women's movement, particularly in combination with an active women's bureau, is a strong predictor of female-friendly policies. The same study found that the number of female elected officials made little difference (Weldon 2002).

Thus, the conclusion that female legislators take the place of women's organizations appears to miss the point entirely. Female legislators effectively represent women precisely because women's organizations nurture these lawmakers' careers and encourage legislative efforts on behalf of women's issues. It is perhaps worrisome, then, that the number of state senators and representatives who belong to traditional women's membership groups dropped by roughly 10 percent from 1988 to 2001 (Carroll 2006, 366).

Women's Role in Mixed-Gender Interest Groups

If women in positions of political leadership cannot substitute for women's organizations, perhaps mixed-gender interest groups can do so. After all, women can participate freely in these organizations as volunteers, donors, staff members, executives, and directors. Thus, to put the question bluntly, if the Natural Resources Defense Council had a female president (which, as of this writing, it did), why should we be concerned that the League of Women Voters is no longer a major player in environmental debates?

It is difficult to assess how well mixed-gender organizations incorporate women's perspectives and represent women's interests. As a first approach, one might ask how many women lead mixed-gender political organizations in Washington. Although women are prevalent in the nonprofit sector, they are surprisingly underrepresented in the advocacy community's leadership ranks. Schlozman (1992, 347) found that just 36 percent of Washington lobbies listed women as representatives, and just 23 percent of all Washington representatives were women. A more recent study found that women were also underrepresented on staff positions of public interest groups (Shaiko 1996). Even more strikingly, a 1995 study of more than 1,100 professional, industry, business, trade, and educational associations found that women constituted just 15 percent of executive directors and 19 percent of board members (Shaiko 1997). With men occupying 80 percent or more of elite policy positions, it is hard to argue that women exercise their collective voice through female leaders of nongendered entities.

Nevertheless, in presenting earlier versions of this study, I often heard the argument that women dominate in two advocacy domains: the antiwar movement and the environment movement. Even though these movements were not called "women's movements," I was told, they really were women's movements because women formed the core leadership and volunteer cadres and thus women's perspectives and preferences prevailed. As plausible as these propositions sound, they appear not to hold water.

The foremost scholars of the antiwar movement of the 2000s, Michael Heaney and Fabio Rojas, have identified just one female-dominated group, Code Pink. Furthermore, in surveys at 2007 antiwar demonstrations, they found that women hardly dominated the movement's rank and file, constituting just 52 percent of demonstrators, roughly equal to women's percentage of the total U.S. population (2009). Heaney (2009) reports that both men and women have been important leaders of the movement, in roughly equal numbers. Thus, the modern peace movement is no more a women's movement than a men's movement. Both genders contribute equally.

The environmental movement provides even less support for the proposition that women are leading or otherwise dominating formally mixed-gender social movement organizations. Table 8.1 shows the gender breakdown of board and staff leadership of five leading environmental groups.[3] The groups are listed in order of their total revenues from private sources. Women occupied roughly one-fourth of board positions and fewer than four in ten senior staff positions. In only one category at one organization did women occupy even a bare majority of key positions.

These data, collected 7 and 11 years after the end of the period studied in this book, cast doubt on the argument that women are still mobilizing as women but doing so under the guise of mixed-gender organizations. Based on numbers alone, it is hard to make that case.

Women's groups have been perhaps the most important route to women's political engagement. In addition to aggregating women's preferences and articulating women's perspectives, these organizations have served as training grounds in which women have developed civic skills and networks.

TABLE 8.1. Women's Role in Environmental Movement Leadership, 2011

	Total Revenue ($ millions)	Women on Board (%)	Women on Executive Staff (%)
Nature Conservancy	856.2	18	11
Trust for Public Land	157.6	14	50
World Wildlife Fund	151.6	31	44
Environmental Defense	125.4	38	57
Natural Resources Defense Council	99.2	32	33
Average	**284.0**	**27**	**39**

Source: Chronicle of Philanthropy (revenues); gender statistics compiled from organizations' Web sites.

The benefits were particularly noteworthy when women were excluded from or marginalized in mainstream political institutions, but these groups continued to be important to women's leadership at least through the 20th century. Burns, Schlozman, and Verba (2001, 230) found that female members of women's organizations are significantly more likely than women in mixed-gender groups to serve on the organization's board; to exercise voice in the organization; to feel a sense of control over policy; and to hone skills such as letter writing, meeting planning, and speechmaking. Female members of women's groups are also more likely to be recruited into individual political acts, such as voting. Conversely, gender integration in civic life has not brought women parity with men in terms of political engagement. Years after the peak of the second wave feminist movement, women remained less interested in politics, less knowledgeable about public affairs, and lower in political efficacy than men. These findings hold even after accounting for educational attainment, civic skills, children, occupational status, religious attendance, and income (Verba, Burns, and Schlozman 1997). Mixed-gender groups did not finish the unfinished business of women's groups.

Polling data tell us that historic differences in men's and women's policy commitments outlasted second wave feminism—that gender continued to matter. Yet those women's groups that have traditionally specialized in representing women's distinct perspectives, preferences, and priorities on nonfeminist issues have faded away. Amid the advocacy boom, new organizations and movements arose to occupy the issue niches in which women's groups traditionally played a central role, such as foreign policy and environmental protection. Yet data from even the most recent years suggest that women did not come to dominate those groups' and movements' leadership positions. Nor did they close the gender gap in political participation. Given these findings, one would be hard-pressed to believe that mixed-gender groups are filling the wide array of important roles that women's groups traditionally filled in women's civic lives. Rather, women's groups may still have a relevant place in women's political socialization and mobilization.

Are Women's Groups Aligned with Women's Interests?

A traditional, graying women's civic group expressed interest in a promising nationwide effort to recruit new members. Rather than immediately endorsing the idea, one longtime member sent around an e-mail—shared with me—questioning why younger women would want to join her organization. She reported that her daughters and daughters-in-law, all in their 30s, were busy with husbands, young children, and careers. These young women's civic interests were covered by nongendered groups; if these women wanted to advocate for women's interests, they would join NOW. The e-mail ended with a show of no-confidence in the group's membership-recruitment effort.[4]

The member's perspective was illuminating on many levels. She had absorbed the message that by 2011, feminist groups were the only groups that represented women's distinctive perspectives or interests. Ironically, this longtime, 70-something member of a traditional good-citizen women's organization had embraced, without recognizing it, the conventional wisdom that a women's issue was obviously a feminist issue.

Generally speaking, her view reflects what the hearings data tell us. By the 1990s, when women's groups weighed in at congressional hearings, they usually did so as advocates for women's rights, status, or well-being. As interest groups were developing specialty niches, so were women's groups. Perhaps not surprisingly, their niche was a feminist niche. One might easily argue that specialization was a necessary and productive adaptation to the larger context, which rewarded expertise. In a crowded, professional, and focused interest group universe, women's groups did what they had to do and should have done, given that few mixed-gender groups were going to stand up for women as vigorously as women themselves would.

Scholars know a fair amount about the issues that feminist groups have championed but have paid far less attention to the range of policy priorities that women's groups have dropped and why the abandonment might be of concern to women and to supporters of American pluralism generally. What issues have been "organized off" women's organizational agendas? Are there issues about which women have particular concerns that their groups are not adequately representing in the halls of power?

As a first approach to these questions, let us consider three surveys of women taken over the course of 35 years. In 1973, when the second wave movement was in its eighth year, a Princeton undergraduate asked delegates to the first National Women's Political Caucus convention what they considered to be women's issues. A majority of both Democratic and Republican delegates listed both feminist and general concerns: welfare, child care, inflation and unemployment, wage scales, hunger, pollution, defense spending, racism, consumer protection, drugs, abortion, crime, busing, criminal justice, and population control (Leff 1973, 44). The top issues were clearly feminist issues (abortion, child care), but other issues, such as inflation, wages, racism, and consumer protection, also commanded strong (and bipartisan) agreement.

Nearly two decades later, a 1989 survey of women nationwide found that their interests remained widely distributed. Asked to name the issues on which they participated, women cited education and children (29 percent), abortion (14 percent), taxes (12 percent), basic human needs (10 percent), and crime and drugs (9 percent). Setting aside the abortion issue, so-called feminist issues animated only 1 percent of respondents (Burns, Schlozman, and Verba 2001, 120). This set of findings continued to hold into the mid-2000s, when a study of highly educated, mostly liberal stay-at-home mothers found that their organizational activity was centered on their children's needs and interests (Mehr 2008). Thus, except for abortion (then subject to high-profile court battles and intensive mobilization), women's participation was concentrated in traditional, nonparticularistic concerns.

Thus, studies conducted over nearly 40 years reach similar conclusions: Women are interested in both feminist and traditional maternal and good-citizen issues. Even after women's advocates had prioritized sameness policies and cast withering doubt on assumptions of gender difference, rank-and-file women across the political spectrum continued to pursue a wide range of policy interests. Yet women's organizations may no longer be appealing places for women to come together and address their concerns. By the 1980s and escalating in the 1990s, women's groups were increasingly gravitating or being pulled toward a narrow definition of women's issues—one that did not reflect the broad array of interests that animated rank-and-file women. By the mid-1990s, second wave feminist leaders Martha Burk and Heidi Hartmann (1996, 20) went so far as to argue that leaders of the women's movement "must make ourselves relevant to women's lives—we must make the priorities of women the focus of the women's movement." They noted that polls found that women cared most about economic issues, health care, and violence, yet "the women's movement is primarily identified with abortion." Their call to revive women's collective action resonated in part because the major women's groups that might have spoken to women's collective identity, whether maternal, civic, or egalitarian-feminist, were fading in prominence.

For women whose interests were more universalistic, nongendered groups provided an outlet for participation. However, if the analysis of the leadership of antiwar and environmental groups is any indication, women's perspectives were unlikely to be dominant or even meaningful in articulating most organizational agendas and discourse. For women whose interests are more aligned with the feminist agenda, their perspective (relative to other perspectives) was articulated on Capitol Hill through the 1990s. However, this perspective faded in prominence throughout the 1980s and 1990s. And, as general-purpose and feminist groups lost ground, no newly ascendant women's groups arose to take their place at the congressional witness table. These trends were of concern, for women continued to be affected by problems such as pay inequity, breast and ovarian cancer, threats to reproductive health services, domestic violence and sexual assault, eating disorders, and family poverty. Furthermore, women were also concerned about nonfeminist issues such as children's education, peace, and social welfare programs.

Is a Third Wave Reviving Women's Collective Activism?

During the early 1990s, a third wave of feminism seemed to be arising from the ashes of the 1980s backlash. Its standard-bearers were writers such as Naomi Wolf and Rebecca Walker, both daughters of second wave feminists. The third wave produced a number of anthologies (e.g., Findlen 2001), an underground music scene (Riot Grrrls), several magazines (including *Bust* and *Bitch*), a "manifesta" (Baumgardner and Richards 2000), and at least one organization, the Third Wave Foundation, created by Walker in 1992 (Henry 2004). The bubbling up of a new feminist consciousness directs us to consider whether the third wave would prove to be the new way of women's engagement. Would younger women develop a novel collective female identity and vibrant institutions to advance women's policy agendas into the 21st century?

From the start, third wave feminism was amorphous and hard to characterize; indeed, acknowledgments of the third wave's elusiveness are a staple of its writings. Astrid Henry (2004) detects at least three connotations of the term *third wave*: a generational connotation, referring to its principal theorists' location in Generation X (born 1961–81); a historical connotation, signifying women's connection to broader geopolitical trends, such as global capitalism, postcolonialism, and environmental threats; and an ideological connotation, referring to the third wave's dialogue with the second wave's structural critiques. Third wave writings capture all three dimensions. At the risk of oversimplification, several concerns run through third wave writings and activism: an appreciation for the multidimensionality of human identity and the intersectional nature of women's oppression; a desire to throw off the perceived orthodoxy, even stridency, of the second wave; and a celebration of women's sexual freedom and pleasure.

Third wave feminist groups had not testified before Congress as of 2000, perhaps because the movement had not institutionalized. However, this absence more likely reflects the fact that third wave feminism was, in the words of one of its early theorists, "an ideology without a movement" (E. Ann Kaplan quoted in Henry 2004, 35). With its focus on interlocking identities, individual expression, and sexual empowerment, third wave feminism by the early 21st century had failed to develop a vibrant organizational base or a coherent policy agenda. "The essence of third wave philosophy, though hard to pin down, is that real social change is achieved indirectly through cultural action, or simply carried out through pop-culture twists and transformations, instead of through an overtly political, electoral, and legislative agenda" (Rowe-Finkbeiner 2004, 88). Indeed, the sexual empowerment strand of third wave feminism drew criticism for being, in the words of one media critic, "silly," "wed to the culture of celebrity and self-obsession," and "divorced from matters of public purpose" (Bellafante 1998). Some young feminist writers object to that characterization (Jervis 2004) and have attempted to articulate a policy agenda (Baumgardner and Richards 2000), while others have noted that second wave feminism also concerned itself with sexual liberation and often appeared in the moment to lack cohesion (Strolovitch 2011). Nevertheless, critics make a compelling case that third wave feminism has failed to develop into an effective framework for women's public action. In the absence of such a framework, the third wave's absence from congressional hearing rooms is not surprising. As Kristin Rowe-Finkbeiner (2004, 89) notes, "The lack of a cohesive movement is *the* crisis of the third wave."

Hybrid Organizations: A New Mode of Women's Organizing?

"Woman movements" circa 2011 are beset by confusion and contradictions. Traditional groups such as the League of Women Voters are aging and lack the presence in women's lives and on Capitol Hill that they once enjoyed. Second wave organizations continue to work on feminist issues, such as paycheck fairness and reproductive rights, but struggle to attract younger women to the cause. The third wave never really developed into a force for women's collective policy advocacy. Whereas the second wave's mantra was "the personal is political" (Hanisch 1969), by the early 21st century, the personal had once again become personal, with younger women in particular lacking a sense of shared experience, civic identity, and policy agendas. In short, women seem to be without a civic place.

Or are they? One of the more interesting developments of the 21st century has been the emergence of what Michael Heaney and I have called "hybrid women's organizations." Two such organizations—the antiwar group Code Pink and the gun control group the Million Mom March—provide evidence that demand exists for organizations that can mobilize women as women around a shared set of perspectives and agendas. Both organizations sampled and combined aspects of maternal (difference) and egalitarian (sameness) frameworks to articulate a particular women's voice against violence (Goss and Heaney 2010). A third organization, MomsRising, founded in 2006, is another hybrid organization whose policy agenda blends second wave feminist concerns, such as maternity leave and equal pay for female workers, with issues once championed by traditional women's groups, such as children's health and welfare. The group's rhetoric is maternal, but much of its agenda centers on facilitating women's occupational advancement. These three groups represent attempts to revive female collective action with novel frameworks that will resonate in a post-separatist, postessentialist, postfeminist world.

By the early 21st century, women's groups were beginning to view the different frameworks of women's collective identity—maternalism, egalitarianism, good citizenship, and even third wave expression—as different facets of women's nature or experience. These frameworks had become a rich tool kit of symbols (Swidler 1986) from which to sample as political and organizational conditions warranted. The presence of so many organizing rationales potentially provides a "wide path" to collective action (Arneil 2010). For women to reclaim the broad public vision that animated their work in earlier decades would be particularly important now, when American democracy lacks organizational mechanisms for bringing together people across class boundaries for public purposes (Skocpol 2011).

Many of the findings in this book are sobering, even unsettling. However, if one conclusion emerges from the history of women's collective action, it is that women's organizations have proved remarkably adept at surmounting low expectations and systematic challenges. Long before females were politically enfranchised, women's groups found a way to be heard in the all-male bastion that was Capitol Hill. After suffrage, when many women failed to show up to vote and when the political establishment sought to undermine women's political inclusion, women's organizations expanded their policy engagement in ways that history has failed to appreciate. In the 1960s and 1970s, women's groups contributed mightily to the dismantling of deeply entrenched economic and social practices that obstructed women's advancement. And in the early 2000s, a few female leaders found innovative ways to reinvigorate women's historic role as defenders and promoters of the public good while refusing to surrender women's status as equal-rights-bearing citizens.

For the most part, this study ends in the year 2000. If history is any guide, what has happened and will happen to women's groups in the 21st century will depend powerfully on both the policy context and the ways that women's leaders interpret and respond to it.

Congressional Hearings Data
and Other Sources

The study utilizes four original datasets of congressional hearing testimony: (1) the *Women's Group Appearances* dataset; (2) the *Landmark* dataset; the (3) *Witnesses* dataset; and (4) the *Transcripts* dataset. I assembled and cross-checked each of these datasets by hand from book-length indexes of hearings, transcripts located on microfiche, and the online Lexis-Nexis congressional hearings database.

The *Women's Group Appearances* dataset contains all appearances by women's organizations before congressional committees and subcommittees from 1833 (when systematic recordkeeping began) through 2000. The appearances were culled by hand from a review of all volumes of the Congressional Information Service's *CIS Index* through 2000. This dataset was cross-checked against hearings data recently put online by Lexis-Nexis. The hearings dataset contains more than 10,400 appearances (the first in 1878) by more than 2,100 groups.

To code the content of these hearings, I relied on the Policy Agendas Project, a National Science Foundation–financed project spearheaded by Bryan Jones, Frank Baumgartner, and their colleagues. They have assembled all postwar hearings and assigned each to one of 21 policy domains and one of 228 subdomains. For the postwar hearings, I assigned the codes that Policy Agendas had assigned. For earlier hearings, I used their decision rules to assign the codes. I also coded each women's group appearance according to whether the witness was testifying on women's rights, status, or well-being. In some cases, the content was obvious (a feminist group testifying at a hearing on the Equal Rights Amendment), but in most cases the content had to be visually inspected by reading the hearing transcript. Finally, I coded the testifying groups by various measures of organization type. This dataset provides the opportunity to chart long-term trends in the volume, agendas, and identities of women's groups doing policy advocacy on Capitol Hill.

The *Landmark* dataset examines women's groups' participation in hearings that informed a subset of 709 particularly important laws (Stathis 2003).[1] This dataset, which covers the period 1912–2000, is intended to provide a check on the larger findings. If women's collective voice is waxing and waning on all nationally prominent issues, is it also doing so on those issues that matter most?

The *Witnesses* dataset provides a second validity check on the *Appearances* dataset. The *Witnesses* dataset consists of a random sample of hearings (*n* = 1,680) at 5-Congress (roughly 10-year) intervals from the late 1870s through the late 1990s. Each hearing was coded for the number and type of witnesses appearing. Witnesses fell into four categories: private citizens, government officials or agencies, corporations, and interest groups. These counts allowed me to calculate whether patterns in women's groups' appearances were unique to women or simply reflected larger trends in congressional openness to interest groups or external voices in general.

Finally, the *Transcripts* dataset consists of a carefully constructed sample of women's group testimony over the 20th century in two policy domains: foreign policy and government provision of health care. The dataset includes 368 pieces of witness testimony from 87 hearings or series of hearings. The transcripts allow for a textual analysis of the shifting rhetorical strategies that women's groups used to establish their political and policy authority. (For more information about how the *Transcripts* dataset was compiled, see appendix B.)

In terms of understanding organizational change, congressional hearing testimony satisfies three key criteria: availability, reliability, and validity. With respect to availability, thanks to the Congressional Information Service and Lexis-Nexis, I have a complete record of who has appeared before Congress. With respect to reliability, testimony has been performed in a similar fashion for many decades—in person, before House and Senate committee members—and recorded by authoritative sources within the Congress. Most important, testimony has external validity, offering a very good if not perfect measure of women's democratic voice.

Because this book relies heavily on congressional hearings, it is useful to describe what is known about this forum—why groups testify, who gets invited, and what testimony really means. The question of why groups testify is neatly summarized by Jeffrey Berry (1997, 164): "The most visible part of an interest group's effort to influence pending legislation takes place at congressional hearings. . . . Interest group leaders like to testify because it bestows status on them and their organizations, because it shows members that their group is playing an important part in the legislative process, and because it helps to legitimize further participation." The more perplexing question is why certain groups testify while others do not.

The few studies that have examined this question have found that interest groups are invited to testify when they are already well known to members of Congress and their staffs. Hearing appearances and even hearings themselves often emerge from ongoing relationships between organizations and members of Congress and committee staff members. In interviews with congressional staff members, Kevin M. Leyden (1995, 432) found that "the groups that get invited both spend considerable effort establishing ties with committee staffers or members, and convince staffers or members that the information (or opinion) they wish to convey is relevant or important to the proceedings." Leyden reports that staff members learn who would make good witnesses through repeated interactions with lobbyists long before a hearing is called.

Is being invited the same as being influential? Not exactly, but there is some reason to believe that they are connected. Compared to nontestifiers, groups that appear on the Hill are more likely to have endowments that signal political influence: lobbyists or other political experts on staff (Grossman 2012; Kasniunas 2009; Leyden 1995); large institutional memberships (Leyden 1995); large individual memberships (Grossman 2012; Kasniunas 2009); high media visibility (Kasniunas 2009); and a long lifespan (Grossman 2012). Although testimony may not be directly influential, Grossman (2012, 91) cites a former Hill staff member as saying that "two of the things that cause you to be invited to testify [also] cause influence: the committee staff have respect for [the organization]. That helps your case, you have credibility. [Second,] they are aware of your work. If your name does not come to mind for a hearing, it is not likely to come to mind when they are considering legislation." Grossman (2012, 91) also reports that in personal interviews with congressional staff members in 2006, "no one could name a single advocacy organization that regularly worked with them but did not show up commonly in testimony before their committee. Based on their judgments, the most prominent and involved advocacy organizations in testimony were also the most involved in policymaking behind the scenes." My interviews with women's organizations in Washington underscored these observations.

The shortcomings in using hearings data as a proxy for organizational prominence and agendas are straightforward. Hearing data will not capture issues on which organizations are focusing but legislators are not, nor will the data capture the institution building that organizations undertake outside the halls of Congress—for example, in the case of women's organizations, efforts to build playgrounds and settlement houses in the early 20th century (Anne Firor Scott 1991). Second, the congressional hearing data primarily capture women's engagement with national policy proposals. With the exception of participation regarding District of Columbia bills, the hearing data do not capture women's groups' engagement in state or local policymaking. Third, hearings may underrepresent organizations speaking for disadvantaged subpopulations. Fourth, congressional testimony is not a direct measure of interest group influence, though it may be an imperfect proxy for it. Finally, hearing appearances represent just one kind of political engagement, precluding broader claims about trends in other forms of participation, such as voting or running for office. I am attentive to these shortcomings in the conclusions I draw from the hearings data. Those caveats aside, all the evidence suggests that congressional testimony provides a systematic, long-term, reliable, and valid measure of who counts on which issues. Testimony constitutes an important barometer of women's participation, voice, and perhaps influence.

Other Data

In addition to the four hearings datasets, I use two other sources of information. The first is three censuses, covering 1963 and 1993, of national women's organizations. (I thank Debra Minkoff for supplying data from one of the 1963 directories.) These censuses were coded to capture 28 key features of the organizations, such as their founding date and the key interests they represented.[2] These organizational data help to ensure that the testifying groups were representative of the larger women's group universe in the ways that matter. The second dataset consists of interviews that I conducted with 11 women who have occupied leadership roles in women's organizations from the 1970s to the present. This sample includes a significant percentage of the most prominent women's group leaders in Washington. The interview data provide a reality check on inferences drawn from the quantitative data, help to resolve puzzles presented by the findings, and illuminate how change unfolded on the ground.

How the Foreign and Health Policy Testimony Was Selected

The policy domains of international affairs and foreign aid and health were selected for close examination because these issues drew concerted attention from women's groups throughout the 20th century. They were also different types of issues (one international, one domestic), lending some confidence to the robustness of the conclusions. I coded 368 pieces of witness testimony, which were selected using the following process.

First, for each appearance by a women's group, I assigned the relevant policy issue code from the Policy Agendas Project's codebook of congressional hearing topics. The codebook contains 21 major topics (e.g., "International Affairs and Foreign Aid," "Health") and 228 subtopics within those categories (e.g., "International Organizations," "Comprehensive Health Reform"). I then narrowed the universe of women's groups' appearances on international and health-related hearings ($n = 1,596$) to a smaller sample of appearances on those subtopics that dominated women's groups' attention in each decade (for example, international organizations within the foreign policy field or comprehensive health reform within the health policy field). Then, within each policy subcategory, I used microfiche archives and the Lexis-Nexis congressional online database to pull hearings on the major legislative proposals in each decade (for example, the revision of the United Nations Charter dominated the "International Organizations" subtopic in the 1950s). Table B.1 summarizes these major legislative proposals.

After compiling the sample of testimony, two adjustments were made.

The first concerns foreign aid bills in the 1960s. Because foreign aid hearings were numerous and the same handful of women's groups gave substantively similar (repetitive) testimony year in and year out, I analyzed only foreign aid *authorization* bills for odd years. I selected testimony on authorization bills because it was more substantive than appropriation bill testimony. The second adjustment was in the health category, which includes a wide range of issues prominent in different years. Because I was interested in long-term shifts in the types of groups testifying and the types of claims made, I have focused on one health issue that appeared on Congress's agenda throughout the 20th century: national health care. Thus, the transcript analysis does not consider testimony on other health-related issues that dominated certain decades—alcohol issues, long-term care, or the nursing shortage (bracketed in table B.1).

TABLE B.1. Women's Groups Dominant/Modal Issues (years)

Decade	International Affairs	Health
1920s	World Court (1924)	Maternity and infant health care (1920, 1921)
1930s	World Court, nationality (1932, 1934)	[Prohibition modification/repeal (1930, 1932)][b]
1940s	U.N. Charter ratification (1945) and postwar reconstruction aid (1946–49)	National health insurance (1946, 1947, 1949)
1950s	UN Charter revision (1950, 1954, 1955)	[Regulation of alcohol advertising (1950, 1952, 1954, 1956, 1958)][b]
1960s[a]	Foreign aid authorization (1961, 1963, 1965, 1967, 1969)	[Issues surrounding elders' long-term care/facilities (1961, 1963–65, 1969)][b]
1970s	U.S. contribution to UNICEF, UN (1970, 1971, 1973, 1975, 1977, 1979)	National health insurance (1974, 1975, 1976)
1980s	Women in foreign economic development (1984, 1987)	[Nursing shortage (1988, 1989)][b]
1990s	Discrimination/human rights abuses against women, others (1990, 1992, 1993, 1994, 1996)	National health insurance (1993, 1994)

[a] Hearings analyzed at two-year intervals because of frequent repetition of testimony.
[b] Not included in analysis because of lack of comparability to health insurance issues.

Notes

1. The seven groups were as follows: the General Federation of Women's Clubs, 8,000,000 members (U.S. Senate, Committee on Foreign Relations 1948, 866); the American Association of University Women, 98,000 members (U.S. Senate, Committee on Foreign Relations 1948, 863); the League of Women Voters, 83,000 members in 550 local leagues (League of Women Voters 2009; U.S. Senate, Committee on Foreign Relations 1948, 659); the National Council of Jewish Women, 70,000 women in 202 sections (U.S. Senate, Committee on Foreign Relations 1948, 954); the Women's Action Committee for Lasting Peace, 20,000 members (U.S. Senate, Committee on Foreign Relations 1948, 86); the Women's International League for Peace and Freedom, membership not disclosed; and the National Women's Trade Union League, membership not disclosed.

2. Testimony of Mrs. Donald R. Burgess, Maryland State Division, AAUW, in U.S. Senate, Committee on Foreign Relations 1948, 864–65.

3. Testimony of Mrs. Joseph Willen, National Council of Jewish Women, in U.S. Senate, Committee on Foreign Relations 1948, 954.

4. Testimony of Kathryn Stone, League of Women Voters of the United States, in U.S. Senate, Committee on Foreign Relations 1948, 659.

5. This book focuses primarily on formal organizations of women; I deal with individual women only insofar as they engage as leaders or members through these institutions, and I discuss movements only insofar as they are aggregations of women's groups. The following counted as women's groups: organizations whose name includes a word or suffix connoting female membership (i.e., League of *Women* Voters, Alpha Kappa Alpha *Sorority*, American National *Cowbelles*; American Legion *Auxiliary*); unions and professional associations representing overwhelmingly female employment categories (nurses, secretaries, garment workers, etc.); voluntary associations whose priorities represented disproportionately female con-

cerns and whose leaders were women (i.e., playground associations in the Progressive Era; breast cancer organizations in the late 20th century); and citizens' groups working for abortion rights and family planning. In this study, the terms *women's groups, women's associations, women's organizations,* and *women's collective engagement* are used interchangeably.

6. I thank Nancy MacLean for raising this very important point.

7. Strolovitch (2007, 115) finds that inattention to intersectionally disadvantaged subpopulations is a problem that extends beyond women's groups to social justice groups generally. Indeed, by some measures, women's groups are not as neglectful as other social justice organizations.

CHAPTER 2

1. Statement of Mrs. Milton P. Higgins, National Congress of Mothers and Parent-Teacher Associations, in U.S. House, Committee on Interstate and Foreign Commerce 1920, 55.

2. Statement of Mrs. Margaret Dye Ellis, National Woman's Christian Temperance Union, in U.S. House, Committee on Insular Affairs 1900, 68.

3. Statement of Miss M. Lillian Williamson, General Federation of Women's Clubs, in U.S. House, Committee on Education 1921, 26.

4. Statement of Nannie H. Burroughs, National Association of Colored Women, in U.S. House, Committee on Rules, 18.

5. One might reasonably ask whether women's organizational activities increased after suffrage or whether it was simply the case that congressional recognition of women's organizations increased. The data do not allow us definitively to answer that question, but circumstantial evidence (including organizational censuses) suggests that the upward trend was driven by women themselves. Supporting that conclusion is the fact that there was no sudden jump in women's appearances after 1920, which we might have expected if Congress had suddenly become solicitous of newly enfranchised women's views. I thank Nancy MacLean for raising this important question.

CHAPTER 3

1. I thank Matt Grossman for providing an excellent comparative study and for calculating these ratios for me.

2. I thank Phil Cook for calling my attention to this question.

CHAPTER 4

1. The seven traditional groups are the League of Women Voters and affiliates (990 appearances); the General Federation of Women's Clubs and affiliates (524); the National Congress of Mothers/PTA and affiliates (508); the American Association of University Women and affiliates (303); the National Council of Jewish Women and affiliates (264); the Woman's Christian Temperance Union and affiliates (220); and the Young Women's Christian Association and affiliates (166).

2. According to the Policy Agendas Project, Congress held 16,344 hearings in the 1990s, compared to 11,526 in the 1950s.

3. I thank Robert Putnam for making these data available.

4. The occupational groups tended to have two tiers—state and national—while the traditional women's voluntaries tended to have a third, local, tier. In terms of political authority, this distinction may be more relevant to hearings in the House, where members are attentive to local units in their geographic districts, than to hearings in the Senate, where statewide organizations span senators' geographic territory.

5. Testimony of Jane Galvin Lewis, National Council of Negro Women, in U.S. Senate, Committee on Labor and Public Welfare, Subcommittee on Employment 1971, 361.

6. I coded 368 pieces of witness testimony. In health reform, I selected all hearings during four periods when national health provision was under active discussion: the 1920s, late 1940s, late 1970s, and early 1990s. In foreign policy, I selected all hearings on the subdomain that most occupied women's groups in each decade (e.g., international organizations in the 1920s–50s and 1970s; foreign aid in the 1960s; human rights in the 1990s). These policy case studies allow for a fine-grained, qualitative analysis of the uses of organizational characteristics to convey authority claims.

7. Testimony of Mrs. Glen Levin Swiggett, National Council of Women, in U.S. Senate, Committee on Foreign Relations, Subcommittee on Permanent Court of International Justice 1924, 142; testimony of Mrs. J. L. Blair Buck, General Federation of Women's Clubs, in U.S. Senate, Committee on Foreign Relations 1948, 866; Testimony of Mrs. Raymond Pelissier, American Association of University Women, in U.S. House, Committee on Foreign Affairs 1963, 1665; testimony of Mrs. Warren E. Cox, National Congress of Parents and Teachers, in U.S. House, Committee on Foreign Affairs 1963, 1495; testimony of Mrs. David Bradley, League of Women Voters, in U.S. House, Committee on Foreign Affairs 1969, 1627.

8. U.S. House, Committee on Foreign Affairs 1965, 575. Although men may have been PTA members in a formal sense, the organization was run by female volunteers and staff members at the local, state, and national levels.

9. The question of how open these groups were to dissenting voices is important but is beyond the scope of this study. The key point is that they portrayed themselves as embodying American democracy at its best. I thank Nancy MacLean for raising the question of their functioning reality.

10. Testimony of Mrs. J. L. Blair Buck, General Federation of Women's Clubs, in U.S. Senate 1950, 674.

11. U.S. Senate, Committee on Education and Labor 1946, 344–48.

12. In line with Douglas Arnold's (1990) account of congressional reasoning, legislators were seeking information on the likelihood that "inattentive publics" might be mobilized.

13. U.S. House, Committee on Foreign Affairs 1949, 468.

14. Ibid.

15. U.S. House, Committee on Foreign Affairs 1961, 569–81.

16. U.S. House, Committee on Foreign Affairs 1963, 1334.

17. U.S. House, Committee on Foreign Affairs 1961, 574.

18. U.S. House, Committee on Foreign Affairs 1967, 1123.

19. Testimony of Ruth Clusen, League of Women Voters of the United States, in U.S. Senate, Committee on Foreign Relations 1977, 14.

20. Only one League of Women Voters affiliate appeared in the 1990s: the Mid-Ulster League, which testified in 1998 on a bill involving land classifications in international treaties.

CHAPTER 5

1. Historians have rightly observed that civic republican theory at times romanticizes unequal relations among people. I employ the term because it continues to resonate as the conventional signifier of America's communitarian rather than individualistic tradition. I thank Nancy MacLean for pointing me to the critique of the term. In a fascinating history, Leonard and Tronto (2007) argue that the gendered division between the liberal (male) and civic republican (female) citizen was in a sense "invented" not long after the nation's founding. The division arose when masculinity was redefined to center on self-interest and private economic gain—that is, individualism. Such a conception was anathema to the traditional view of manly citizenship as being oriented around civic responsibility. Under the gendered partitioning of citizenship roles, women were to be the standard-bearers for the participatory, community-oriented, other-regarding citizenship that civic republicans celebrate, while men were freed to represent the individualistic, rights-centered conception of classical liberals.

2. McDonagh here is challenging Kraditor's (1971) argument that difference ("expediency") rationales largely replaced equality rationales in the lead-up to ratification.

3. Testimony of Maud Wood Park, National League of Women Voters, in U.S. Senate, Committee on Education and Labor 1921, 15; see also the testimony of Florence Kelley, National Consumers League, especially 136–37.

4. Testimony of Mrs. Milton P. Higgins, National Congress of Mothers and Parent-Teacher Associations, in U.S. House, Committee on Interstate and Foreign Commerce 1920, 55.

5. Testimony of Mrs. Martin Hutchins, American Association of University Women, in U.S. Senate, Committee on Foreign Relations, Subcommittee on Permanent Court of International Justice 1924, 147.

6. Testimony of Mrs. L. Benge, Mothers of Sons Forum, in U.S. Senate, Committee on Foreign Relations 1945, 570.

7. Testimony of Agnes Waters, National Blue Star Mothers, in U.S. Senate, Committee on Foreign Relations 1945, 351.

8. Testimony of Jane L. Hayford, World Organization of Mothers of All Nations, in U.S. Senate, Committee on Foreign Relations 1950, 561.

9. Dorothy Thompson, "The Progress of a Journal Editorial," *Ladies Home Journal*, February 1950, reprinted in U.S. Senate, Committee on Foreign Relations 1950, 561.

10. Testimony of Mary Stewart, Women's National Republican Executive

Committee, in U.S. Senate, Committee on Public Health and National Quarantine 1920, 42.

11. Testimony of Mrs. Albert T. Leatherbee, Massachusetts Antisuffrage Association, in U.S. House, Committee on Interstate and Foreign Commerce 1921, 68.

12. Testimony of Mrs. Larue Brown, National League of Women Voters, in U.S. Senate, Committee on Education and Labor 1921, 147.

13. Testimony of Mrs. Clark Bailey, Kentucky Society, Daughters of the American Revolution, in U.S. Senate, Committee on Foreign Relations 1954, Part 5, 516.

14. Testimony of Mrs. Howard M. Smith, Minnesota Daughters of the American Revolution, in U.S. Senate, Committee on Foreign Relations 1954, Part 7, 62.

15. In her study of women's groups' rhetoric, Wendy Sharer (2004, 18) likewise noted that "claims about gender difference and women's moral nature would be used by various women's groups to justify their entry into domains of political control in the post-suffrage era."

16. Testimony of Mrs. Harry C. Long, United Church Women of Ohio, in U.S. Senate, Committee on Foreign Relations 1954, Part 2, 116.

17. Statement of Representative Pete Jarman (D-AL), in U.S. Senate, Committee on Foreign Relations 1948, 1058.

18. Testimony of Mrs. Margaret Hopkins Worrell, Ladies of the Grand Army of the Republic, in U.S. Senate, Committee on Foreign Relations 1950, 716.

19. Testimony of Mrs. Niels Jacobson, National Council of Jewish Women, in U.S. Senate, Committee on Foreign Relations 1955, 935.

20. Testimony of Anna Lord Strauss, National League of Women Voters, in U.S. Senate, Committee on Foreign Relations, 1945, 419.

21. Testimony of Carol Burris, Women's Lobby, in U.S. House, Committee on Ways and Means 1974, 3066.

22. Testimony of Patricia Schroeder, Congressional Caucus for Women's Issues, in U.S. House, Committee on Energy and Commerce 1994, 16.

23. Ibid., 13–14.

24. Testimony of Catherine O'Neill, Women's Commission for Refugee Women and Children, in Commission on Security and Cooperation in Europe 1993, 10–14.

25. Testimony of Dorothy Q. Thomas, Women's Rights Project, Human Rights Watch, in U.S. House, Committee on Foreign Affairs 1993–1994, 17, 19.

26. Testimony of Arvonne S. Fraser, International Women's Rights Action Watch, in U.S. House, Committee on Foreign Affairs 1990, 12.

27. Testimony of Arvonne S. Fraser, International Women's Rights Action Watch, in U.S. Senate, Committee on Foreign Relations 1990, 71–79.

28. Testimony of Ellen Smith, Concerned Women for America, in U.S. Senate, Committee on Foreign Relations 1990, 82.

CHAPTER 6

1. A total of 19,732 witnesses appeared. Some of these witnesses may be counted more than once if they appeared at more than one hearing in the dataset.

2. Congress stripped funding from the caucus after the Republican takeover of the House in 1995, but it continued to testify.

3. I thank Theda Skocpol for this observation, which she has offered in multiple conversations.

4. Author's analysis of ANES data, available at www.electionstudies.org.

5. These studies are suggestive, yet their lack of generational-cohort or longitudinal data limits our ability to gauge whether the claiming of feminist identity is actually in decline.

CHAPTER 7

1. I thank Eileen McDonagh for this observation.

2. I thank Dara Strolovitch for calling my attention to the need for clarification on this point.

CHAPTER 8

1. Parts of this section are excerpted from Goss and Skocpol 2006.

2. Perhaps not surprisingly, on a key women's rights issue, abortion, women were twice as likely as men to report participation.

3. These five groups were drawn from the *Chronicle of Philanthropy*'s annual rankings of nonprofit organizations that raise the most money from private sources. The *Chronicle* considers environmental and animal charities in the same category. For this analysis, I isolated the top five groups (as of March 18, 2011) that advocate environmental protection only (i.e., I have excluded groups that have hunting or animal welfare as a major or the sole component of their agenda). See http://philanthropy.com/premium/stats/philanthropy400/index.php?category=Environmental%2Band%2BAnimal%2BWelfare&year=2010&Name_Type=All+the+organizations&search=+Go+ (accessed May 17, 2012).

4. This anecdote is based on my experience as an active member of the organization.

APPENDIX A

1. Determining which hearings informed a particular bill required judgment calls in some cases. I tended to be expansive in my coding. If the hearing topic addressed particular components of the legislation, I considered it to be a hearing on that piece of legislation. I coded hearings in both the present and prior Congress on the theory that legislation often takes more than one Congress to pass.

2. The data were taken from three directories: National Council of Women 1963; *Encyclopedia of Associations* 1963; and Barrett 1993. The data from the *Encyclopedia of Associations* was compiled by Minkoff (1995) and was used to supplement the National Council of Women data for 1963. These directories provide a reasonably complete inventory of significant women's groups that were active at each point in time.

Bibliography

Alonso, Harriet Hyman. *Peace as a Women's Issue: A History of the U.S. Movement for World Peace and Women's Rights.* Syracuse: Syracuse University Press, 1993.

Amenta, Edwin, Neal Caren, Sheera Joy Olasky, and James E. Stobaugh. "All the Movements Fit to Print: Who, What, When, Where, and Why SMO Families Appeared in the *New York Times* in the Twentieth Century." *American Sociological Review* 74, no. 4 (2009): 636–56.

Andersen, Kristi. *After Suffrage: Women in Partisan and Electoral Politics before the New Deal.* Chicago: University of Chicago Press, 1996.

Arneil, Barbara. "Gender, Diversity, and Organizational Change: The Boy Scouts vs. Girl Scouts of America." *Perspectives on Politics* 8, no. 1 (2010): 53–68.

Arnold, R. Douglas. *The Logic of Congressional Action.* New Haven: Yale University Press, 1990.

Aronson, Pamela. "Feminists or 'Postfeminists'?: Young Women's Attitudes toward Feminism and Gender Relations." *Gender and Society* 17, no. 6 (2003): 903–22.

Ashby, LeRoy. *Saving the Waifs: Reformers and Dependent Children, 1890–1917.* Philadelphia: Temple University Press, 1984.

Baker, Paula. "The Domestication of Politics: Women and American Political Society, 1780–1920." *American Historical Review* 89, no. 3 (1984): 620–47.

Banaszak, Lee Ann, ed. *The U.S. Women's Movement in Global Perspective.* Lanham, MD: Rowman and Littlefield, 2006.

Banaszak, Lee Ann. *The Women's Movement Inside and Outside the State.* New York: Cambridge University Press, 2010.

Barakso, Maryann. *Governing NOW: Grassroots Activism in the National Organization for Women.* Ithaca: Cornell University Press, 2004.

Barrett, Jacqueline K., ed. *Encyclopedia of Women's Associations Worldwide.* Detroit: Gale, 1993.

Bauer, Raymond A., Ithiel de Sola Pool, and Lewis Anthony Dexter. *American Business and Public Policy: The Politics of Foreign Trade.* New York: Atherton, 1963.

Baumgardner, Jennifer, and Amy Richards. *Manifesta: Young Women, Feminism, and the Future.* New York: Macmillan, 2000.

Baumgartner, Frank R., Jeffrey M. Berry, Marie Hojnacki, David C. Kimball, and Beth L. Leech. *Lobbying and Policy Change: Who Wins, Who Loses, and Why.* Chicago: University of Chicago Press, 2009.

Baumgartner, Frank R., and Beth L. Leech. *Basic Interests: The Importance of Groups in Politics and Political Science.* Princeton: Princeton University Press, 1998.

Baumgartner, Frank R., and Christine Mahoney. "Social Movements, the Rise of New Issues, and the Public Agenda." In *Routing the Opposition: Social Movements, Public Policy, and Democracy,* edited by David S. Meyer, Valerie Jenness, and Helen Ingram, 65–86. Minneapolis: University of Minnesota Press, 2005.

Beckwith, Karen. "The Comparative Politics of Women's Movements." *Perspectives on Politics* 3, no. 3 (2005): 583–96.

Bell, Peter. "Hill People." *National Journal,* June 20, 2011. http://www.nationaljournal.com/hill-people-who-are-they-and-where-did-they-come-from--20110616. Accessed May 17, 2012.

Bellafante, Ginia. "Feminism: It's All about Me!" *Time,* June 29, 2008. http://www.time.com/time/magazine/article/0,9171,988616,00.html. Accessed July 23, 2011.

Berkman, Michael B., and Robert E. O'Connor. "Do Women Legislators Matter? Female Legislators and State Abortion Policy." *American Politics Quarterly* 21, no. 1 (1993): 102–24.

Berry, Jeffrey M. *The Interest Group Society.* 3rd ed. New York: Longman, 1997.

Berry, Jeffrey M. *The New Liberalism: The Rising Power of Citizen Groups.* Washington, DC: Brookings Institution Press, 1999.

Berry, Jeffrey M., and David F. Arons. *A Voice for Nonprofits.* Washington, DC: Brookings Institution Press, 2003.

Bevacqua, Maria. "Reconsidering Violence against Women: Coalition Politics in the Antirape Movement." In *Feminist Coalitions: Historical Perspectives on Second-Wave Feminism in the United States,* edited by Stephanie Gilmore, 163–77. Urbana: University of Illinois Press, 2008.

Boles, Janet K. "Local Elected Women and Policy-Making: Movement Delegates or Feminist Trustees?" In *The Impact of Women in Public Office,* edited by Susan J. Carroll, 68–86. Bloomington: Indiana University Press, 2001.

Bordin, Ruth. *Woman and Temperance: The Quest for Power and Liberty, 1873–1900.* Philadelphia: Temple University Press, 1981.

Brennan, Mary. *Wives, Mothers, and the Red Menace.* Boulder: University Press of Colorado, 2008.

Browne, William P. "Organized Interests and Their Issue Niches: A Search for Pluralism in a Policy Domain." *Journal of Politics* 52, no. 2 (1990): 477–509.

Burk, Martha, and Heidi Hartmann. "Beyond the Gender Gap." *The Nation,* June 10, 1996, 18–21.

Burns, Nancy, Kay Lehman Schlozman, and Sidney Verba. *The Private Roots of Public Action: Gender, Equality, and Political Participation.* Cambridge: Harvard University Press, 2001.

Burns, Nancy, Kay Lehman Schlozman, and Sidney Verba. "The Public Consequences of Private Inequality: Family Life and Citizen Participation." *American Political Science Review* 19, no. 2 (1997): 373–89.

Buschman, Joan K., and Silvo Lenart. "'I Am Not a Feminist, but . . .': College Women, Feminism, and Negative Experiences." *Political Psychology* 17, no. 1 (1996): 59–75.

Campbell, Andrea Louise. *How Policies Make Citizens: Senior Political Activism and the American Welfare State.* Princeton: Princeton University Press, 2003.

Carabillo, Toni, Judith Meuli, and June Bundy Csida. *Feminist Chronicles.* Los Angeles: Women's Graphics, 1993.

Carden, Maren Lockwood. *Feminism in the Mid-1970s.* New York: Ford Foundation, 1977.

Carroll, Susan J. "Are Women Legislators Accountable to Women?" In *Gender and Social Capital,* edited by Brenda O'Neill and Elisabeth Gidengill, 357–78. Oxford: Routledge, 2006.

Carroll, Susan J. "Representing Women: Women State Legislators as Agents of Policy-Related Change." In *The Impact of Women in Public Office,* edited by Susan J. Carroll, 3–21. Bloomington: Indiana University Press, 2001.

Chafe, William H. *The American Woman: Her Changing Social, Economic, and Political Roles, 1920–1970.* London: Oxford University Press, 1972.

Clemens, Elisabeth S. *The People's Lobby.* Chicago: University of Chicago Press, 1997.

Cobble, Dorothy Sue. *The Other Women's Movement.* Princeton: Princeton University Press, 2004.

Commission on Security and Cooperation in Europe. *Implementation of the Helsinki Accords: War Crimes and the Humanitarian Crisis in the Former Yugoslavia.* 103rd Cong., 1st sess., January 25, 1993.

Costain, Anne N. *Inviting Women's Rebellion: A Political Process Interpretation of the Women's Movement.* Baltimore: Johns Hopkins University Press, 1992.

Costain, Anne N. "Representing Women: The Transition from Social Movement to Interest Group." *Western Political Quarterly* 34, no. 1 (1981): 100–113.

Costain, Anne N. "Women's Claims as a Special Interest." In *The Politics of the Gender Gap,* edited by Carol M. Mueller, 150–72. Newbury Park, CA: Sage, 1988.

Costain, Anne N., and W. Douglas Costain. "Strategy and Tactics of the Women's Movement in the United States: The Role of Political Parties." In *The Women's Movements of the United States and Western Europe,* edited by Mary Fainsod Katzenstein and Carol McClurg Miller, 196–214. Philadelphia: Temple University Press, 1987.

Cott, Nancy F. "Across the Great Divide: Women in Politics before and after 1920." In *Women, Politics, and Change,* edited by Louise A. Tilly and Patricia Gurin, 153–76. New York: Sage, 1992.

Cott, Nancy F. *The Grounding of Modern Feminism.* New Haven: Yale University Press, 1987.

Cott, Nancy F. "What's in a Name? The Limits of 'Social Feminism'; or, Expanding the Vocabulary of Women's History." *Journal of American History* 76, no. 3 (1989): 809–29.

Davis, Flora. *Moving the Mountain: The Women's Movement in America since 1960.* Urbana: University of Illinois Press, 1999.

Deckard, Barbara S. *The Women's Movement.* 3rd ed. New York: Harper, 1983.

"Declaration of Sentiments." In *History of Woman Suffrage,* vol. 1, edited by Elizabeth

Cady Stanton, Susan B. Anthony, and Matilda Joslyn Gage, 70–71. Rochester: Fowler and Wells, 1889.

Dees-Thomases, Donna. *Looking for a Few Good Moms*. New York: Rodale, 2004.

DeGregorio, Christine. "Leadership Approaches in Congressional Committee Hearings." *Western Political Quarterly* 45, no. 4 (1992): 971–83.

Dicker, Rory. *A History of U.S. Feminisms*. Berkeley, CA: Seal, 2008.

Dietz, Mary. "Citizenship with a Feminist Face: The Problem with Maternal Thinking." *Political Theory* 13, no. 1 (1985): 19–37.

DiQuinzio, Patrice. "Love and Reason in the Public Sphere: Maternalist Civic Engagement and the Dilemma of Difference." In *Women and Children First*, edited by Sharon M. Meagher and Patrice DiQuinzio, 227–46. Albany: State University of New York Press, 2005.

Disney, Jennifer Leigh, and Joyce Gelb. "Feminist Organizational 'Success': The State of U.S. Women's Movement Organizations in the 1990s." *Women and Politics* 21, no. 4 (2000): 39–76.

Dolan, Kathleen, and Lynne E. Ford. "Women in the State Legislatures: Feminist Identity and Legislative Behaviors." *American Politics Quarterly* 23, no. 1 (1995): 96–108.

Donahue, Jesse. "It Doesn't Matter: Some Cautionary Findings about Sex and Representation from School Committee Conversations." *Policy Studies Journal* 45, no. 4 (1997): 630–47.

Echols, Alice. *Daring to Be Bad: Radical Feminism in America, 1967–1975*. Minneapolis: University of Minnesota Press, 1989.

Elshtain, Jean Bethke. *Public Man, Private Woman*. Oxford: Robertson, 1981.

Encyclopedia of Associations. Vol. 1, *National Organizations*. Detroit: Gale, 1963.

Estepa, Andrea. "Taking the White Gloves Off: Women Strike for Peace and 'the Movement,' 1967–73." In *Feminist Coalitions: Historical Perspectives on Second-Wave Feminism in the United States*, edited by Stephanie Gilmore, 84–112. Urbana: University of Illinois Press, 2008.

Evans, Sara. *Personal Politics: The Roots of Women's Liberation in the Civil Rights Movement and the New Left*. New York: Vintage, 1980.

Faludi, Susan. *Backlash: The Undeclared War against American Women*. New York: Crown, 1991.

Ferree, Myra Marx, and Beth B. Hess. *Controversy and Coalition: The New Feminist Movement across Four Decades of Change*. 3rd ed. New York: Routledge, 2000.

Ferree, Myra Marx, and Patricia Yancey Martin, eds. *Feminist Organizations: Harvest of the New Women's Movement*. Philadelphia: Temple University Press, 1995.

Findlen, Barbara, ed. *Listen Up: Voices from the Next Feminist Generation*. New York: Seal Press, 2001.

Fiorina, Morris P., Paul E. Peterson, D. Stephen Voss, and Bertram M. Johnson. *America's New Democracy*. New York: Penguin, 2007.

Fleishman, Joel L. *The Foundation: A Great American Secret*. New York: PublicAffairs, 2009.

Flexner, Eleanor. *Century of Struggle: The Woman's Rights Movement in the United States*. Cambridge: Harvard University Press, 1959.

Foundation Center. "Philanthropic Giving by and for Women on the Rise, Study Finds." 2009. http://foundationcenter.org/media/news/20090623.html. Accessed April 6, 2011.

Fraser, Nancy. "Equality, Difference, and Democracy: Recent Feminist Debates in the United States." In *Feminism and the New Democracy*, edited by Jodi Dean, 98–109. London: Sage, 1997.

Fraser, Nancy. "Talking about Needs: Interpretive Contests as Political Conflicts in Welfare-State Societies." *Ethics* 99, no. 2 (1989): 291–313.

Freeman, Jo. *The Politics of Women's Liberation*. New York: McKay, 1975.

Friedan, Betty. *The Feminine Mystique*. New York: Norton, 1963.

Friedan, Betty. "How to Get the Women's Movement Moving Again." *New York Times*, November 3, 1985. http://www.nytimes.com/books/99/05/09/specials /friedan-moving.htmlNYT. Accessed April 6, 2011.

Gelb, Joyce, and Marian Lief Palley. *Women and Public Policies: Reassessing Gender Politics*. Charlottesville: University of Virginia Press, 1996.

Gilligan, Carol. *In a Different Voice*. Cambridge: Harvard University Press, 1982.

Gittell, Marilyn, and Nancy Naples. "Activist Women: Conflicting Ideologies." *Social Policy* 13, no. 1 (1982): 25–27.

Goldin, Claudia. "The Quiet Revolution That Transformed Women's Employment, Education, and Family." *American Economic Review* 96, no. 2 (2006): 1–21.

Goss, Kristin A. *Disarmed: The Missing Movement for Gun Control in America*. Princeton: Princeton University Press, 2006.

Goss, Kristin A. "Foundations of Feminism: How Philanthropic Patrons Shaped Gender Politics." *Social Science Quarterly* 88, no. 5 (2007): 1174–91.

Goss, Kristin A. "Never Surrender? How Women's Groups Abandoned Their Policy Niche in U.S. Foreign Policy Debates, 1916–2000." *Politics and Gender* 5, no. 4 (2009): 1–37.

Goss, Kristin A., and Michael T. Heaney. "Organizing Women as Women: Hybridity and Grassroots Collective Action in the 21st Century." *Perspectives on Politics* 8, no. 1 (2010): 27–52.

Goss, Kristin A., and Theda Skocpol. "Changing Agendas: The Impact of Feminism on Public Policy." In *Gender and Social Capital*, edited by Brenda O'Neill and Elisabeth Gidengill, 323–56. Oxford: Routledge, 2006.

Gray, Virginia, and David Lowery. "A Niche Theory of Interest Representation." *Journal of Politics* 58, no. 1 (1996): 91–111.

Grossman, Matt. *The Not-So-Special Interests: Interest Groups, Public Representation, and American Governance*. Stanford, CA: Stanford University Press, 2012.

Gusfield, Joseph R. *The Culture of Public Problems: Drinking-Driving and the Symbolic Order*. Chicago: University of Chicago Press, 1981.

Gutmann, Amy, and Dennis Thompson. *Why Deliberative Democracy?* Princeton: Princeton University Press, 2004.

Hall, Elaine J., and Marnie Salupo Rodriguez. "The Myth of Postfeminism." *Gender and Society* 17, no. 6 (2003): 878–902.

Hall, Richard L., and Alan V. Deardorff. "Lobbying as Legislative Subsidy." *American Political Science Review* 100, no. 1 (2006): 69–84.

Hall, Richard L., and Frank Wayman. "Buying Time: Moneyed Interests and the Mobilization of Bias in Congressional Committees." *American Political Science Review* 84, no. 3 (1990): 797–820.

Hanisch, Carol. "The Personal Is Political." 1969. http://www.carolhanisch.org /CHwritings/PIP.html. Accessed October 11, 2011.

Hartmann, Susan M. *The Other Feminists: Activists in the Liberal Establishment*. New Haven: Yale University Press, 1998.

Harvey, Anna L. *Votes without Leverage: Women in American Electoral Politics, 1920–1970*. Cambridge: Cambridge University Press, 1998.

Hawkesworth, Mary. "The Semiotics of Premature Burial: Feminism in a Post-feminist Age." *Signs* 29, no. 4 (2004): 961–85.

Heaney, Michael T. "Outside the Issue Niche: The Multidimensionality of Interest Group Identity." *American Politics Research* 32, no. 6 (2004): 611–51.

Heaney, Michael T. Personal correspondence, July 6, 2009.

Heaney, Michael T., and Fabio Rojas. *2007 Survey of Antiwar Demonstrators*. Ann Arbor: University of Michigan, 2009.

Height, Dorothy. *Open Wide the Freedom Gates*. New York: PublicAffairs, 2003.

Heitshusen, Valerie. "Interest Group Lobbying and U.S. House Decentralization: Linking Informational Focus to Committee Hearing Appearances." *Political Research Quarterly* 53, no. 1 (2000): 151–76.

Henry, Astrid. *Not My Mother's Sister: Generational Conflict and Third Wave Feminism*. Bloomington: Indiana University Press, 2004.

Hewitt, Nancy A. "Beyond the Search for Sisterhood: American Women's History in the 1990s." In *Unequal Sisters: A Multicultural Reader in U.S. Women's History*, 3rd ed., edited by Vicki L. Ruiz and Ellen Carol DuBois, 1–19. New York: Routledge, 2000.

Hewitt, Nancy A., ed. *No Permanent Waves: Recasting Histories of U.S. Feminism*. New Brunswick: Rutgers University Press, 2010.

Hole, Judith, and Ellen Levine. *Rebirth of Feminism*. New York: Quadrangle, 1971.

Huddy, Leonie, Francis K. Neely, and Marilyn R. Lafay. "Trends: Support for the Women's Movement." *Public Opinion Quarterly* 64, no. 3 (2000): 309–50.

Jablonsky, Thomas J. *The Home, Heaven, and Mother Party*. Brooklyn, NY: Carlson, 1994.

Jeansonne, Glen. *Women of the Far Right: The Mothers' Movement and World War II*. Chicago: University of Chicago Press, 1997.

Jeffreys-Jones, Rhodri. *Changing Differences: Women and the Shaping of American Foreign Policy, 1917–1994*. New Brunswick: Rutgers University Press, 1995.

Jenkins, J. Craig, and Abigail Halcli. "Grassrooting the System? The Development and Impact of Social Movement Philanthropy, 1953–1990." In *Philanthropic Foundations: New Scholarship, New Possibilities*, edited by Ellen Condliffe Lagemann, 229–56. Bloomington: Indiana University Press, 1999.

Jervis, Lisa. "The End of Feminism's Third Wave." *Ms.*, Winter 2004. http://www.msmagazine.com/winter2004/thirdwave.asp. Accessed October 13, 2011.

Kaledin, Eugenia. *Mothers and More: American Women in the 1950s*. Boston: Twayne, 1984.

Kaminer, Wendy. *Women Volunteering: The Pleasure, Pain, and Politics of Unpaid Work from 1830 to the Present*. Garden City, NY: Anchor, 1984.

Kasniunas, Nina Therese. "Impact of Interest Group Testimony on Lawmaking in Congress." Ph.D. diss. Loyola University, Chicago, 2009.

Kathlene, Lyn. "Power and Influence in State Legislative Policymaking: The Interaction of Gender and Position in Committee Hearing Debates." *American Political Science Review* 88, no. 3 (1994): 560–76.

Katzenstein, Mary Fainsod. *Faithful and Fearless: Moving Feminist Protest inside the Church and Military.* Princeton: Princeton University Press, 1998.

Katzenstein, Mary Fainsod. "'Redividing Citizens'—Divided Feminisms: The Reconfigured U.S. State and Women's Citizenship." In *Women's Movements Facing the Reconfigured State,* edited by Lee Ann Banaszak, Karen Beckwith, and Dieter Rucht, 203–18. Cambridge: Cambridge University Press, 2003.

Keiser, Lael. "The Influence of Women's Political Power on Bureaucratic Output: The Case of Child Support Enforcement." *British Journal of Political Science* 27, no. 1 (1997): 136–48.

Kelly, Rita Mae, Michelle A. Saint-Germain, and Jody D. Horn. "Female Public Officials: A Different Voice?" *Annals of the American Academy of Political and Social Science* 515 (1991): 77–87.

Kerber, Linda K. *No Constitutional Right to Be Ladies.* New York: Hill and Wang, 1998.

Kerber, Linda K. "The Republican Mother: Women and the Enlightenment—An American Perspective." *American Quarterly* 28, no. 2 (1976): 187–205.

Keyssar, Alexander. *The Right to Vote: The Contested History of Democracy in the United States.* New York: Basic Books, 2000.

Kirkpatrick, Jeane J. *Political Woman.* New York: Basic Books, 1974.

Klein, Ethel. *Gender Politics.* Cambridge: Harvard University Press, 1984.

Kleppner, Paul. "Were Women to Blame? Female Suffrage and Voter Turnout." *Journal of Interdisciplinary History* 12, no. 4 (1982): 621–43.

Knoke, David. 1992. "The Mobilization of Members in Women's Associations." In *Women, Politics, and Change,* edited by Louise Tilly and Patricia Gurin, 383–412. New York: Russell Sage Foundation, 1992.

Koven, Seth. "Civic Maternalism and the Welfare State: The Case of Mrs. Humphry Ward." Paper presented at the Seventh Berkshire Conference on the History of Women, 1988.

Kraditor, Aileen. *The Ideas of the Woman Suffrage Movement, 1890–1920.* Garden City, NY: Doubleday, 1971.

League of Women Voters of the United States (LWVUS). Membership figures supplied to author. 2009.

The League of Women Voters in Perspective. Washington, DC: League of Women Voters, 1994.

Leff, Deborah. "Political Woman: Perceptions of the Women's Political Movement." Honors thesis, Princeton University, 1973.

Lemons, J. Stanley. *The Woman Citizen: Social Feminism in the 1920s.* 2nd ed. Charlottesville: University of Virginia Press, 1973.

Leonard, Stephen T., and Joan C. Tronto. "The Genders of Citizenship." *American Political Science Review* 101, no. 1 (2007): 33–46.

Levine, Susan. *Degrees of Equality: The American Association of University Women and the Challenge of Twentieth-Century Feminism.* Philadelphia: Temple University Press, 1995.

Leyden, Kevin M. "Interest Group Resources and Testimony at Congressional Hearings." *Legislative Studies Quarterly* 20, no. 3 (1995): 431–39.

Lindsay, James M. *Congress and the Politics of U.S. Foreign Policy.* Baltimore: Johns Hopkins University Press, 1994.

Lister, Ruth. *Citizenship: Feminist Perspectives.* 2nd ed. New York: New York University Press, 2003.

Luker, Kristin. *Abortion and the Politics of Motherhood.* Berkeley: University of California Press, 1984.

Lynn, Susan. "Gender and Progressive Politics." In *Not June Cleaver: Women and Gender in Postwar America, 1945–1960,* edited by Joanne Meyerowitz, 103–27. Philadelphia: Temple University Press, 1994.

Macedo, Stephen J., et al. *Democracy at Risk: How Political Choices Undermine Citizen Participation and What We Can Do about It.* Washington, DC: Brookings Institution Press, 2005.

MacLean, Nancy. *Freedom Is Not Enough: The Opening of the American Workplace.* Cambridge: Harvard University Press, 2006.

MacLean, Nancy. Personal correspondence, July 8, 2011.

Mansbridge, Jane J. *Why We Lost the ERA.* Chicago: University of Chicago Press, 1986.

Marshall, Susan E. *Splintered Sisterhood: Gender and Class in the Campaign against Woman Suffrage.* Madison: University of Wisconsin Press, 1997.

Marshall, T. H., and Tom Bottomore. *Citizenship and Social Class.* London: Pluto, 1992.

Mathews-Gardner, A. Lanethea. "The Political Development of Female Civic Engagement in Postwar America." *Politics and Gender* 1, no. 4 (2005): 547–75.

McDonagh, Eileen. "It Takes a State: A Policy Feedback Model of Women's Political Representation." *Perspectives on Politics* 8, no. 1 (2010): 69–91.

McDonagh, Eileen. *The Motherless State: Women's Political Leadership and American Democracy.* Chicago: University of Chicago Press, 2009.

McDonagh, Eileen. Personal correspondence, July 6, 2011.

McDonagh, Eileen. "Political Citizenship and Democratization: The Gender Paradox." *American Political Science Review* 96, no. 3 (2002): 535–52.

Mehr, Donna C. "Civic Lives of Affluent At-Home Mothers: The Civic Implications of Intensive Mothering." Master's thesis, Duke University, 2008.

Mettler, Suzanne. "Bringing the State Back into Civic Engagement: Policy Feedback Effects of the G.I. Bill for World War II Veterans." *American Political Science Review* 96, no. 2 (2002): 351–65.

Mettler, Suzanne. *Dividing Citizens: Gender and Federalism in New Deal Public Policy.* Ithaca: Cornell University Press, 1998.

Mettler, Suzanne. *Soldiers to Citizens: The G.I. Bill and the Making of the Greatest Generation.* New York: Oxford University Press, 2005.

Mettler, Suzanne, and Joe Soss. "The Consequences of Public Policy for Democratic Citizenship: Bridging Policy Studies and Mass Politics." *Perspectives on Politics* 2, no. 1 (2004): 55–73.

Meyer, David S., and Nancy Whittier. "Social Movement Spillover." *Social Problems* 41, no. 2 (1994): 277–98.

Meyerowitz, Joanne, ed. *Not June Cleaver: Women and Gender in Postwar America, 1945–1960.* Philadelphia: Temple University Press, 1994.

Michel, Sonya. *Children's Interests/Mothers' Rights: The Shaping of America's Child Care Policy.* New Haven: Yale University Press, 1999.

Minkoff, Debra C. "Organizational Mobilizations, Institutional Access, and Institutional Change." In *Women Transforming Politics: An Alternative Reader,* edited by Cathy J. Cohen, Kathleen B. Jones, and Joan C. Tronto, 477–96. New York: New York University Press, 1997.

Minkoff, Debra C. *Organizing for Equality: The Evolution of Women's and Racial-Ethnic Organizations in America, 1955–1985.* New Brunswick: Rutgers University Press, 1995.

Minow, Martha. *Making All the Difference: Immigration, Exclusion, and American Law.* Ithaca: Cornell University Press, 1990.

Muncy, Robyn. *Creating a Female Dominion in American Reform, 1890–1935.* New York: Oxford University Press, 1991.

National Council of Women. *International Directory of Women's Organizations.* Washington, DC: National Council of Women, 1963.

Offen, Karen. "Defining Feminism: A Comparative Historical Approach." *Signs* 14, no. 1 (1988): 119–57.

Olson, Mancur. *The Logic of Collective Action.* Cambridge: Harvard University Press. 1965.

O'Neill, William L. *Everyone Was Brave: A History of Feminism in America.* New York: Quadrangle/*New York Times,* 1971.

Orloff, Ann Shola. "Gender and Social Rights of Citizenship: The Comparative Analysis of Gender Relations and Welfare States." *American Sociological Review* 58, no. 3 (1993): 303–28.

Orren, Karen. *Belated Feudalism: Labor, the Law, and Liberal Development in the United States.* Cambridge: Cambridge University Press, 1992.

Peltola, Pia, Melissa A. Milkie, and Stanley Presser. "The 'Feminist' Mystique: Feminist Identity in Three Generations of Women." *Gender and Society* 18, no. 1 (2004): 122–44.

Petracca, Mark P. "The Rediscovery of Interest Group Politics." In *The Politics of Interests,* edited by Mark P. Petracca, 3–31. Boulder, CO: Westview, 1992.

Pierson, Paul. *Dismantling the Welfare State.* Cambridge: Cambridge University Press, 1995.

Pierson, Paul. "When Effect Becomes Cause: Policy Feedback and Political Change." *World Politics* 45, no. 4 (1993): 595–628.

Putnam, Robert D. *Bowling Alone: The Collapse and Revival of American Community.* New York: Simon and Schuster, 2000.

Quindlen, Anna. "Public and Private: And Now, Babe Feminism." *New York Times,* January 19, 1994, A21.

Reingold, Beth. "Concepts of Representation among Female and Male State Legislators." *Legislative Studies Quarterly* 17, no. 4 (1992): 509–37.

Renzetti, Claire M. "New Wave or Second Stage? Attitudes of College Women toward Feminism." *Sex Roles* 16, nos. 5–6 (1987): 265–77.

Rinehart, Sue Tolleson. *Gender Consciousness and Politics.* New York: Routledge, 1992.

Rosenberg, Gerald N. *The Hollow Hope: Can Courts Bring about Social Change?* Chicago: University of Chicago Press, 1993.

Rosenthal, Cindy Simon. "A View of Their Own: Women's Committee Leadership Styles and State Legislatures." *Policy Studies Journal* 25, no. 4 (1997): 585–600.

Rosenthal, Cindy Simon. *When Women Lead: Integrative Leadership in State Legislatures.* New York: Oxford University Press, 1998.

Rothschild-Whitt, Joyce. "The Collectivist Organization: An Alternative to Rational-Bureaucratic Models." *American Sociological Review* 44, no. 4 (1979): 509–27.

Rowe-Finkbeiner, Kristin. *The F Word: Feminism in Jeopardy.* Emeryville, CA: Seal, 2004.

Ruddick, Sara. *Maternal Thinking: Towards a Politics of Peace.* London: Women's Press, 1989.

Rupp, Leila J., and Verta Taylor. *Survival in the Doldrums: The American Women's Rights Movement, 1945 to the 1960s.* New York: Oxford University Press, 1987.

Ryan, Barbara. *Feminism and the Women's Movement: Dynamics of Change in Social Movement Ideology and Activism.* New York: Routledge, 1992.

Sainsbury, Diane. *Gender, Equality, and Welfare States.* Cambridge: Cambridge University Press, 1996.

Saint-Germain, Michelle A. "Does Their Difference Make a Difference? The Impact of Women in the Arizona Legislature." *Social Science Quarterly* 70, no. 4 (1989): 956–68.

Sanbonmatsu, Kira. *Democrats/Republicans and the Politics of Women's Place.* Ann Arbor: University of Michigan Press, 2004.

Sapiro, Virginia. "Feminism: A Generation Later." *Annals of the American Academy of Political and Social Science* 515 (1991): 10–22.

Sapiro, Virginia. *The Political Integration of Women: Roles, Socialization, and Politics.* Urbana: University of Illinois Press, 1984.

Sarvasy, Wendy. "Beyond the Difference versus Equality Policy Debate: Postsuffrage Feminism, Citizenship, and the Quest for a Feminist Welfare State." *Signs* 17, no. 2 (1992): 329–62.

Schlesinger, Arthur M. "Biography of a Nation of Joiners." *American Historical Review* 50, no. 1 (1944): 1–25.

Schlozman, Kay Lehman. "Representing Women in Washington: Sisterhood and Pressure Politics." In *Women, Politics, and Change,* edited by Louise Tilly and Patricia Gurin, 339–82. New York: Russell Sage Foundation, 1992.

Schnittker, Jason, Jeremy Freese, and Brian Powell. "Who Are Feminists and What Do They Believe? The Role of Generations." *American Sociological Review* 68, no. 4 (2003): 607–22.

Schreiber, Ronnee. *Righting Feminism: Conservative Women and American Politics.* New York: Oxford University Press, 2008.

Scott, Anne Firor. *Natural Allies.* Urbana: University of Illinois Press, 1991.

Scott, Joan W. "Deconstructing Equality-versus-Difference; or, The Uses of Poststructuralist Theory for Feminism." *Feminist Studies* 14, no. 1 (1988): 32–50.

Shaiko, Ronald G. "Female Participation in Association Governance and Political Representation: Women as Executive Directors, Board Members, Lobbyists, and Political Action Committee Directors." *Nonprofit Management and Leadership* 8, no. 2 (1997): 121–39.

Shaiko, Ronald G. "Female Participation in Public Interest Nonprofit Governance: Yet Another Glass Ceiling?" *Nonprofit and Voluntary Sector Quarterly* 25, no. 3 (1996): 302–20.

Shapiro, Robert Y., and Harpeet Mahajan. "Gender Differences in Policy Preferences: A Summary of Trends from the 1960s to the 1980s." *Public Opinion Quarterly* 50, no. 1 (1986): 42–61.

Sharer, Wendy B. *Vote and Voice: Women's Organizations and Political Literacy, 1915–1930.* Carbondale: Southern Illinois University Press, 2004.

Sklar, Kathryn Kish. "The Historical Foundations of Women's Power in the Creation of the American Welfare State, 1830–1930." In *Mothers of a New World: Maternalist Politics and the Origins of Welfare States*, edited by Seth Koven and Sonya Michel, 43–93. New York: Routledge, 1993.

Skocpol, Theda. "Advocates without Members: The Recent Transformation of American Civic Life." In *Civic Engagement in American Democracy*, edited by Theda Skocpol and Morris P. Fiorina, 461–509. Washington, DC: Brookings Institution Press, 1999; New York: Sage, 1999.

Skocpol, Theda. *Diminished Democracy: From Membership to Management in American Civic Life.* Norman: University of Oklahoma Press, 2003.

Skocpol, Theda. Personal correspondence, June 14, 2011.

Skocpol, Theda. *Protecting Soldiers and Mothers.* Cambridge: Belknap Press of Harvard University Press, 1992.

Smeal, Eleanor. Personal interview, Arlington, VA, July 8, 2009.

Smith, James P., and Michael P. Ward. "Time Series Growth in the Female Labor Force." *Journal of Labor Economics* 3, no. 1 (1985): S59–S90.

Smith, Marie. "President Kennedy Signs Equal Pay Bill into Law." *Washington Post*, June 12, 1963, D1.

Smith, Rogers M. *Civic Ideals: Conflicting Visions of Citizenship in U.S. History.* New Haven: Yale University Press, 1997.

Smith, Tom W. "The Polls: Gender and Attitudes toward Violence." *Public Opinion Quarterly* 48, no. 1 (1984): 384–96.

Somma, Mark, and Sue Tolleson Rinehart. "Tracking the Elusive Green Women: Sex, Environmentalism, and Feminism in the United States and Europe." *Political Research Quarterly* 50, no. 1 (1997): 153–69.

Soss, Joe. "Lessons of Welfare: Policy Design, Political Learning, and Political Action." *American Political Science Review* 93, no. 2 (1999): 363–80.

Soss, Joe. *Unwanted Claims: The Politics of Participation in the U.S. Welfare System.* Ann Arbor: University of Michigan Press, 2000.

Staggenborg, Suzanne, and Verta Taylor. "Whatever Happened to the Women's Movement?" *Mobilization* 10, no. 1 (2005): 37–52.

Stathis, Stephen W. *Landmark Legislation.* Washington, DC: CQ Press, 2003.

Stone, Kathryn H. *25 Years of a Great Idea.* Washington, DC: National League of Women Voters, 1946.

Stone, Kathryn H. "Women as Citizens." *Annals of the American Academy of Political and Social Science* 251 (1947): 79–86.

Strolovitch, Dara Z. *Affirmative Advocacy: Race, Class, and Gender in Interest Group Politics.* Chicago: University of Chicago Press, 2007.

Strolovitch, Dara Z. "Do Interest Groups Represent the Disadvantaged? Advocacy at the Intersections of Race, Class, and Gender." *Journal of Politics* 68, no. 4 (2006): 894–910.

Strolovitch, Dara Z. Personal communication, July 22, 2011.

Stuhler, Barbara. *For the Public Record: A Documentary History of the League of Women Voters.* Washington, DC: League of Women Voters 2003.

Swerdlow, Amy. *Women Strike for Peace.* Chicago: University of Chicago Press, 1993.

Swers, Michele L. *The Difference Women Make.* Chicago: University of Chicago Press, 2002.

Swers, Michele. "Understanding the Policy Impact of Electing Women: Evidence from Research on Congress and State Legislatures." *PS: Political Science and Politics* 34 no. 2 (2001): 217–20.

Swidler, Ann. "Culture in Action: Symbols and Strategies." *American Sociological Review* 51, no. 2 (1986): 273–86.

Taylor, Ula Y. "Black Feminisms and Human Agency." In *No Permanent Waves: Recasting Histories of U.S. Feminism,* edited by Nancy A. Hewitt, 61–76. New Brunswick: Rutgers University Press, 2010.

Thomas, Sue. *How Women Legislate.* New York: Oxford University Press, 1994.

Thomas, Sue. "Why Gender Matters: The Perceptions of Women Officeholders." *Women and Politics* 17, no. 1 (1997): 27–53.

Thompson, Becky. "Multiracial Feminism: Recasting the Chronology of Second Wave Feminism." In *No Permanent Waves: Recasting Histories of U.S. Feminism,* edited by Nancy A. Hewitt, 39–60. New Brunswick: Rutgers University Press, 2010.

Tichenor, Daniel J., and Richard A. Harris. "Organized Interests and American Political Development." *Political Science Quarterly* 117, no. 4 (2002–3): 587–612.

Tierney, John T. "Interest Group Involvement in Foreign and Defense Policy." In *Congress Resurgent: Foreign and Defense Policy on Capitol Hill,* edited by Randall B. Ripley and James M. Lindsay, 89–111. Ann Arbor: University of Michigan Press, 1993.

Tocqueville, Alexis de. *Democracy in America.* New York: Knopf, 1994.

Tronto, Joan C. *Moral Boundaries: A Political Argument for an Ethic of Care.* New York: Routledge, 1993.

Truman, David. *The Governmental Process: Political Interests and Public Opinion.* New York: Knopf, 1951.

U.S. House. Committee on Education. *Federal Aid for Home Economics.* 66th Cong., 3rd sess., February 4, 1921.

U.S. House. Committee on Energy and Commerce. *Health Care Reform.* Part 8. 103rd Cong., 2nd sess., 1994.

U.S. House. Committee on Foreign Affairs. *Extension of European Recovery Program.* Part 1. 81st Cong., 1st sess., February 8–11, 15–18, 1949.

U.S. House. Committee on Foreign Affairs. *Foreign Assistance Act of 1963.* 88th Cong., 1st sess., June 3–5, 6, 7, 10, 1963.

U.S. House. Committee on Foreign Affairs. *Foreign Assistance Act of 1965.* 89th Cong., 1st sess., March 9, 1965.

U.S. House. Committee on Foreign Affairs. *Foreign Assistance Act of 1967.* 90th Cong., 1st sess., May 8–11, 1967.

U.S. House. Committee on Foreign Affairs. *Foreign Assistance Act of 1969.* Part 7. 91st Cong., 1st sess., July 29–31, 1969.

U.S. House. Committee on Foreign Affairs. *Human Rights Abuses against Women.* 103rd Cong., 1st sess., September 28, 29, October 20, 1993, March 22, 1994.

U.S. House. Committee on Foreign Affairs. *The International Development and Security Act.* 87th Cong., 1st sess., June 19–23, 1961.

U.S. House. Committee on Foreign Affairs. *International Human Rights Abuses against Women.* 101st Cong., 2nd sess., March 21, July 26, 1990.

U.S. House. Committee on Insular Affairs. *Committee Reports, Hearings, and Acts of Congress Corresponding Thereto.* 56th Cong., 1st sess., January–February 1900.

U.S. House. Committee on Interstate and Foreign Commerce. *Public Protection of Maternity and Infancy.* 66th Cong., 3rd sess., December 20–23, 28, 29, 1920.

U.S. House. Committee on Interstate and Foreign Commerce. *Public Protection of Maternity and Infancy.* 67th Cong., 1st sess., July 12–16, 18–23, 1921.

U.S. House. Committee on Rules. *Riot at East St. Louis, Illinois.* 65th Cong., 1st sess., August 3, 1917.

U.S. House. Committee on Ways and Means. *National Health Insurance.* Vol. 7. 93rd Cong., 2nd sess., June 28, 1974.

U.S. Senate. Committee on Education and Labor. *National Health Program.* Part 1. 79th Cong., 2nd sess., April 2–5, 9–11, 16, 1946.

U.S. Senate. Committee on Education and Labor. *Protection of Maternity.* 67th Cong., 1st sess., April 25, 28, May 5, 1921.

U.S. Senate. Committee on Foreign Relations. *Charter of the United Nations.* 79th Cong., 1st sess., July 9–13, 1945.

U.S. Senate. Committee on Foreign Relations. *Convention on the Elimination of All Forms of Discrimination against Women.* 101st Cong., 2nd sess., August 2, 1990.

U.S. Senate. Committee on Foreign Relations. *European Recovery Program.* Part 2. 80th Cong., 2nd sess., January 16, 19–24, 26–28, 1948.

U.S. Senate. Committee on Foreign Relations. *Public Attitudes toward the U.N.* 95th Cong., 1st sess., July 27, 1977.

U.S. Senate. Committee on Foreign Relations. *Review of the United Nations Charter.* 83rd Cong., 2nd sess., February 12, June 17, July 10, 1954.

U.S. Senate. Committee on Foreign Relations. *Review of the United Nations Charter.* 84th Cong., 1st sess., March 17, 1955.

U.S. Senate. Committee on Foreign Relations. *Revision of the United Nations Charter.* 81st Cong., 2nd sess., February 2, 3, 6, 8, 9, 13, 15 ,17, 20, 1950.

U.S. Senate. Committee on Foreign Relations. Subcommittee on Permanent Court of International Justice. *Permanent Court of International Justice.* 68th Cong., 1st sess., April 30, May 1, 1924.

U.S. Senate. Committee on Labor and Public Welfare. Subcommittee on Employment, Manpower, and Poverty. *Comprehensive Child Development Act of 1971.* Part 1. 92nd Cong., 1st sess., May 13, 20, 1971.

U.S. Senate. Committee on Public Health and National Quarantine. *Protection of Maternity and Infancy.* 66th Cong., 2nd sess., May 12, 1920.

Uslaner, Eric M. "All Politics Are Global." In *Interest Group Politics*, 4th ed., edited by Allan J. Cigler and Burdett Loomis, 369–91. Washington, DC: CQ Press, 1995.

Verba, Sidney, Nancy Burns, and Kay Lehman Schlozman. "Knowing and Caring about Politics: Gender and Political Engagement." *Journal of Politics* 59, no. 4 (1997): 1051–72.

Verba, Sidney, Kay Lehman Schlozman, and Henry E. Brady. *Voice and Equality:*

Civic Voluntarism in American Politics. Cambridge: Harvard University Press, 1995.

Walker, Jack L., Jr. *Mobilizing Interest Groups in America: Patrons, Professions, and Social Movements.* Ann Arbor: University of Michigan Press, 1991.

Ware, Susan. "American Women in the 1950s: Nonpartisan Politics and Women's Politicization." In *Women, Politics, and Change,* edited by Louise A. Tilly and Patricia Gurin, 281–99. New York: Russell Sage Foundation, 1992.

Welch, Susan. "Are Women More Liberal Than Men in the U.S. Congress?" *Legislative Studies Quarterly* 10, no. 1 (1985): 125–34.

Weldon, S. Laurel. "Beyond Bodies: Institutional Sources of Representation for Women in Democratic Policymaking." *Journal of Politics* 64, no. 4 (2002): 1153–74.

Wells, Marguerite M. *A Portrait of the League of Women Voters.* 1938; Washington, DC: League of Women Voters, 1962.

Welter, Barbara. "The Cult of True Womanhood." *American Quarterly* 18, no. 2 (1966): 151–74.

Wilson, James Q. *Political Organizations.* Princeton: Princeton University Press, 1995.

Wilson, Jan Doolittle. *The Women's Joint Congressional Committee and the Politics of Maternalism, 1920–30.* Urbana: University of Illinois Press, 2007.

Wolbrecht, Christina. *The Politics of Women's Rights.* Princeton: Princeton University Press, 2000.

Wright, John R. *Interest Groups and Congress.* Boston: Allyn and Bacon, 1996.

Young, Louise M. *In the Public Interest: The League of Women Voters, 1920–1970.* New York: Greenwood, 1989.

Zald, Mayer N. "The Trajectory of Social Movements in America." *Research in Social Movements, Conflicts, and Change* 10 (1988): 19–41.

Index

Page numbers in italics refer to figures and tables.